Language, Learning, and Disability in the Education of Young Bilingual Children

CAL SERIES ON LANGUAGE EDUCATION
Series Editors: **Terrence G. Wiley, M. Beatriz Arias** and
Joy Kreeft Peyton, *Center for Applied Linguistics, Washington, DC, USA.*

Current and aspiring education professionals need accessible, high-quality, research-based resources on language learning, instruction, and assessment. This series provides such resources, serving to inform teachers' classroom practice, enhance teacher education, and build the background knowledge of undergraduate and graduate students in applied linguistics and other language-related fields.

The books in this series explore a broad range of issues in applied linguistics and language education and are written in a style that is accessible to a broad audience, including those who are new to the field. Each book addresses a topic of relevance to those who are studying or working in the fields of language learning, language instruction, and language assessment, whether in English as a second language or other world languages. Topic areas include approaches to language instruction and assessment; approaches to content instruction and assessment for language learners; professional development for educators working with language learners; principles of second language acquisition for educators; and connections between language policy and educational practice.

All books in this series are externally peer-reviewed.

Full details of all the books in this series and of all our other publications can be found on http://www.multilingual-matters.com, or by writing to Multilingual Matters, St Nicholas House, 31-34 High Street, Bristol BS1 2AW, UK.

CAL SERIES ON LANGUAGE EDUCATION: 4

Language, Learning, and Disability in the Education of Young Bilingual Children

Edited by
Dina C. Castro and Alfredo J. Artiles

MULTILINGUAL MATTERS
Bristol • Blue Ridge Summit

DOI https://doi.org/10.21832/CASTRO1845
Names: Castro, Dina Carmela, editor. | Artiles, Alfredo J., editor.
Title: Language, Learning, and Disability in the Education of Young
   Bilingual Children/Edited by Dina C. Castro and Alfredo J. Artiles.
Description: Bristol, UK; Blue Ridge Summit, PA: Multilingual Matters,
   2021. | Series: CAL Series on Language Education: 4 | Includes
   bibliographical references and index. | Summary: "Using an
   interdisciplinary perspective to discuss the intersection of language
   development and learning processes, this book summarizes current
   knowledge and represents the most critical issues regarding early
   childhood research, policy, and practice related to young bilingual
   children with disabilities" – Provided by publisher.
Identifiers: LCCN 2020052578 (print) | LCCN 2020052579 (ebook) |
   ISBN 9781800411838 (paperback) | ISBN 9781800411845 (hardback) |
   ISBN 9781800411852 (pdf) | ISBN 9781800411869 (epub) |
   ISBN 9781800411876 (kindle edition)
Subjects: LCSH: Children with disabilities – Education (Early childhood) |
   Children with disabilities – Language. | Bilingualism in children. |
   Education, Bilingual.
Classification: LCC LC4019.3 .L36 2021 (print) | LCC LC4019.3 (ebook) |
   DDC 371.9 – dc23
LC record available at https://lccn.loc.gov/2020052578
LC ebook record available at https://lccn.loc.gov/2020052579

Library of Congress Cataloging in Publication Data
A catalog record for this book is available from the Library of Congress.

British Library Cataloguing in Publication Data
A catalogue entry for this book is available from the British Library.

ISBN-13: 978-1-80041-184-5 (hbk)
ISBN-13: 978-1-80041-183-8 (pbk)

Multilingual Matters
UK: St Nicholas House, 31-34 High Street, Bristol BS1 2AW, UK.
USA: NBN, Blue Ridge Summit, PA, USA.

Website: www.multilingual-matters.com
Twitter: Multi_Ling_Mat
Facebook: https://www.facebook.com/multilingualmatters
Blog: www.channelviewpublications.wordpress.com

Copyright © 2021 Dina C. Castro, Alfredo J. Artiles and the authors of individual chapters.

All rights reserved. No part of this work may be reproduced in any form or by any means without permission in writing from the publisher.

The policy of Multilingual Matters/Channel View Publications is to use papers that are natural, renewable and recyclable products, made from wood grown in sustainable forests. In the manufacturing process of our books, and to further support our policy, preference is given to printers that have FSC and PEFC Chain of Custody certification. The FSC and/or PEFC logos will appear on those books where full certification has been granted to the printer concerned.

Typeset by Riverside Publishing Solutions.
Printed and bound in the UK by the CPI Books Group Ltd.
Printed and bound in the US by NBN.

Contents

	Contributors	vii
1	At the Intersection of Language, Learning, and Disability in the Education of Young Bilingual Children *Dina C. Castro and Alfredo J. Artiles*	1
2	A Sociocultural, Integrative, and Interdisciplinary Perspective on the Development and Education of Young Bilingual Children with Disabilities *Dina C. Castro, Cristina Gillanders, Nydia Prishker, and Rodolfo Rodriguez*	6
3	How Bilingualism Affects Children's Language Development *Carol Scheffner Hammer and Maria Cristina Limlingan*	27
4	Dual Language Learners in Early Intervention Programs: Issues of Eligibility, Access, and Service Provision *Lillian Durán*	46
5	Dual Language Learners with Disabilities in Inclusive Early Elementary School Classrooms *Sarah L. Alvarado, Sarah M. Salinas, and Alfredo J. Artiles*	64
6	Language Learning and Language Disability: Equity Issues in the Assessment of Young Bilingual Learners *Maria Adelaida Restrepo and Anny P. Castilla-Earls*	90
7	Learning from Sociocultural Contexts: Partnering with Families of Young Bilingual Children with Disabilities *Cristina Gillanders and Sylvia Y. Sánchez*	112
8	Preparing Teachers of Young Bilingual Children with Disabilities *Norma A. López-Reyna, Cindy L. Collado, Mary Bay, and Wu-Ying Hsieh*	137

9 Language, Learning, and Disability in an Era
   of Accountability   163
   Marlene Zepeda and Michael J. Orosco

10 Young Bilingual Children with Disabilities: Challenges
   and Opportunities for Future Education Policies
   and Research   182
   Alba A. Ortiz

   Index   214

Contributors

Sarah L. Alvarado obtained her PhD from Arizona State University. Before beginning her doctoral program, Sarah was a bilingual teacher in inclusive settings in Arizona for 16 years. During this time, she taught multiple language program structures, including two-way immersion. Her classroom experiences led to an interest in understanding how practitioners and researchers decipher between learning struggles and second-language factors, especially when making special education identification decisions or planning learning for emergent bilinguals. Her research centers on understanding and improving special education processes and practices for emergent bilinguals with and at risk for disabilities.

Alfredo J. Artiles, PhD, is Professor of Education at Stanford University. He examines paradoxes of educational equity stemming from disability intersections with sociocultural differences (race, language, social class) and from the implementation of inclusive education across contexts and scales. Artiles' programmatic work has theoretical and methodological implications that demand a situated unit of analysis. He has documented the color blind nature of special education research, and his work documents the affordances of a cultural-historical and spatial research approach. He is Series Editor for the book series, Disability, Culture, and Equity. Artiles is an AERA Fellow and an elected member of the National Academy of Education.

Mary Bay, PhD, is Associate Professor Emerita of Special Education at the University of Illinois, Chicago (UIC). Her professional expertise and research focused on reforming programs that prepare individuals to teach. As Executive Director of the Council on Teacher Education, she was liaison between the state agency and UIC and oversaw the redesign of programs to meet state standards and student services for those pursuing the required licensure. Bay directed numerous grants and foundation awards that focused on the redesign of preparation programs and was an Associate Director of a national-level center that provided assistance to faculty at minority-serving institutions who were reforming their programs.

Anny Castilla-Earls, PhD, is an Associate Professor in the Department of Communication Disorders and Sciences at the University of Houston. Dr Castilla-Earls' primary research interests are language development, assessment, and disorders in monolingual and bilingual children. Her current research explores approaches to differentiate typically developing bilingual children from bilingual children with language disorders by examining differences between monolingual and bilingual development and studying the effect of language exposure shifts on bilingual development. Dr Castilla-Earls' current research is funded by the National Institute of Deafness and Other Communication Disorders.

Dina C. Castro, MPH, PhD, is Professor and Velma E. Schmidt Endowed Chair in Early Childhood Education at the University of North Texas. Her research focuses on equity in the early care and education of children from immigrant/transnational and indigenous communities, at the intersection of language, culture, race/ethnicity, and social class. She examines how early education policies, curricula, and teacher preparation are addressing the unique characteristics and experiences of young bilingual children. Her previous research includes efficacy studies of professional development interventions and the development of measures to assess the quality of early education programs serving bilingual children. Castro served as PI and Director of the Center for Early Care and Education Research – Dual Language Learners, a federally funded national research center. Her research has been funded by the US National Institutes of Health, the Institute of Education Sciences, the Administration for Children and Families and the Office for Special Education Programs.

Cindy Collado, PhD, is Assistant Professor of Special Education at California State University, Sacramento. She is coordinator of the Early Childhood Special Education (ECSE) teaching credential with master's program. She conducts research and trains preservice and current teachers on anti-biased evidence-based practices in ECSE, inclusive education, assessment, and engagement of families raising children with disabilities. Her work is grounded in her experiences as an ECSE teacher, co-teaching in inclusive preschool programs in Chicago and coordinating the University of Illinois at Chicago Educational Assessment Clinic. She serves on various state leadership teams, advocating for the inclusion, mental health, and rights of young diverse children with disabilities.

Lillian Durán has a PhD in Educational Psychology from the University of Minnesota and is currently an Associate Professor in the Department of Special Education and Clinical Sciences at the University of Oregon. Her research focuses on improving instructional and assessment practices with preschool-aged dual language learners. She is a co-author of the Spanish Individual Growth and Development Indicators, an early language and literacy general outcome measure for preschool screening and progress monitoring. Dr Durán frequently delivers presentations nationally on the topic of recommended practices in assessment and intervention with young dual language learners with and without identified disabilities.

Cristina Gillanders, PhD, is an Associate Professor at the School of Education & Human Development at the University of Colorado, Denver. She has been involved in early childhood education as a bilingual teacher, director of an early childhood program, professor, and researcher. Her research focuses on young Latino bilingual emergent literacy, early childhood teaching practices for dual language learners, and minority parents' beliefs and practices related to young children's learning and development. She served as a Co-PI in the Nuestros Niños Program: Promoting School Readiness for English Language Learners (funded by the National Institute for Child Health and Human Development).

Wu-Ying Hsieh, PhD, is Associate Professor in the Department of Special Education at the University of Northern Iowa (UNI), where she is currently the Program Coordinator of Early Childhood Special Education. Her passion in teacher education has motivated her to secure multiple grants to support preservice teachers to enhance assessment knowledge and skills through collaboration with in-service teachers, as well as to examine early childhood teachers' perceptions of early math teaching and learning. She has conducted research in inclusive education, coaching early childhood teachers in using literacy strategies, and early math teaching and learning in different cultural contexts.

Maria Cristina Limlingan, PhD, Tufts University, is a Research Scientist at Cultivate Learning at the University of Washington and has more than twelve years of applied experience in early childhood education research related to supporting the implementation of culturally and linguistically sustaining teaching and family engagement. Her research interests focus on improving the quality of educational experiences for linguistically and ethnically diverse young children in the United States and in low- and middle-income countries. She currently leads the efforts of the Washington Research-Practice Partnership for a multi-year, cross-sectoral study focusing on improving the quality of state-funded pre-K programs.

Norma A. López-Reyna, PhD, is Associate Professor and Chair of Special Education at the University of Illinois, Chicago. Her expertise and research are in assessment, learning disorders among English learners, family engagement, and bilingual special education teacher preparation.

She has directed many personnel preparation and research grants, including at the Monarch Center, a national center that provided program improvement and grant proposal services to hundreds of faculty at Minority Serving Institutions. She directs the UIC Educational Assessment Clinic, which serves local community children and prepares future teachers. As a parent of an adult with disabilities, her work is grounded in personal as well as professional experiences.

Michael J. Orosco, PhD, is an Associate Professor in the Department of Educational Psychology at the University of Kansas. He was a bilingual special education teacher in Colorado for five years before earning a PhD in Education from the University of Colorado at Boulder. His interdisciplinary research includes developing a theoretical model of learning disabilities for English learners that includes the socio-cognitive mechanisms that moderate mathematical and reading performance. He also designs interventions to facilitate socio-cognitive processes related to mathematical and reading comprehension in English learners and professional development programs to enhance the sustainability of socio-cognitive mathematical and reading interventions.

Alba A. Ortiz, PhD, is Professor Emerita, Department of Special Education, in the College of Education at the University of Texas (UT) at Austin. She held the President's Chair for Education Academic Excellence, an honor bestowed by UT in recognition of her outstanding contributions as a teacher educator and researcher in the fields of special education and bilingual education. Dr Ortiz is a nationally recognized expert on the education of English learners with language and learning disabilities. A Past President of the Council for Exceptional Children, she is currently a co-editor of the *Bilingual Research Journal*.

Nydia Prishker, PhD, is a Postdoctoral Associate and Adjunct Instructor at New York University's Steinhardt School. Her research work focuses on quality and equity issues in the early care and education of children from diverse cultural, ethnic, and linguistic backgrounds. As a former certified bilingual classroom teacher, Dr Prishker understands the importance of how policies affect the practices of educators as they teach diverse populations. Her work aims to advocate for the reframing of policies to recognize the strengths of bi/multilingual children that enhance their education and well-being.

Maria Adelaida Restrepo, PhD, is Assistant Dean for Research and Professor in the College of Health Solutions at Arizona State University. She is director of the Bilingual Language and Literacy Laboratory, whose mission is to identify the best language assessment and intervention practices for bilingual children at risk of academic difficulties.

She specializes in oral language and emergent literacy development and the prevention of academic difficulties in bilingual children. Restrepo is a bilingual speech-language pathologist who has had ongoing funding for at least 18 years in projects focused on building oral language and literacy in preschool, kindergarten, and school-age children who speak Spanish as their native language. A former associate editor of *Language, Speech, and Hearing Services in Schools*, she reviews and publishes in a variety of journals in English and Spanish. She is a certified member of the American Speech-Language-Hearing Association. She was funded by a Fulbright Scholars grant to conduct a response to intervention project in Israel.

Rodolfo Rodriguez is a doctoral student at the University of North Texas at Denton with a research interest in young English learners with disabilities. He earned a Master's in early childhood special education from the University of Texas, Austin. Rodriguez is a practitioner with extensive experience: as a former bilingual early childhood special education teacher, he has served young English learners with special needs for several years. He has since provided leadership for various early childhood education programs, including Head Start, Early Head Start, Prekindergarten, and Early Childhood Special Education. He is currently a special education coordinator and supervises the early childhood special education services in the Garland Independent School District in Texas.

Sarah M. Salinas is a doctoral student at Arizona State University. She is a former special education teacher, reading intervention teacher, and community college instructor. Her research on special education policy and practice centers on understanding and improving how special and general educators think about policy, plan, and mediate learning opportunities for English learners with learning disabilities with an emphasis on reading and reading comprehension. She earned a Bachelor's degree in Political Science and Spanish Language and Literature at Southwestern University and a Master's degree at the University of Texas, San Antonio.

Sylvia Y. Sánchez, EdD, is an emerita faculty member of early childhood education at George Mason University in Virginia. She is known for her research on early bilingualism, integrated teacher education programs, cultural teaching dilemmas, and the use of family stories to prepare teachers to work with diverse children and their families. She co-founded the UTEEM Early Childhood Program, a triple license program that prepared early childhood teachers to work with culturally, linguistically, and ability-diverse young children and their families. With more than 40 years of experience in teaching, administration, research, and community work, she continues to be active on behalf of immigrant families and teachers through her publications and advocacy, including serving as a board member with Teaching for Change and with an organization working with asylum seekers.

Carol Scheffner Hammer, PhD, CCC-SLP, is Vice Dean of Research and Professor of Communication Sciences and Disorders at Teachers College, Columbia University. Her research focuses on cultural and environmental influences on young children's language and literacy development and on promoting preschoolers' school readiness through home- and classroom-based interventions, with an emphasis on dual language learners. Her work has been continually funded by US federal agencies since 2000, including the National Institutes of Health and the US Department of Education. Dr Hammer is past editor of the *American Journal of Speech-Language Pathology* and a Fellow of the American Speech-Language-Hearing Association.

Marlene Zepeda, PhD, is a Professor Emeritus in the Department of Child and Family Studies at California State University, Los Angeles. A former preschool and elementary school teacher, Dr Zepeda's scholarship focuses on dual language learning in Spanish-speaking preschool children and child development in Latino infants and toddlers. Her expertise also focuses on pedagogical practice and workforce development relevant to dual language learners. She has led a number of initiatives focused on the cultural and linguistic competencies needed in early educator teacher preparation. Currently, she is involved in a number of public policy efforts to support the rights of dual language learners for educational equity.

1 At the Intersection of Language, Learning, and Disability in the Education of Young Bilingual Children

Dina C. Castro and Alfredo J. Artiles

Young bilingual children continue to face the challenge of an education system that is not prepared to meet their needs. For decades, researchers have discussed the disproportionate representation of bilingual children in special education programs (Arreaga-Mayer & Perdomo-Rivera, 1996; Artiles & Ortiz, 2002; Mercer & Richardson, 1975; Rueda & Windmueller, 2006). However, this is an unresolved issue that has negative consequences on bilingual children's development and learning, especially for those from racial, ethnic and culturally minoritized and marginalized communities. Some progress has been made (Artiles *et al.*, 2010; National Research Council, 2017), but more remains to be done to address and eliminate the persistent barriers to providing equitable and effective services to bilingual children with disabilities. Those barriers include, but are not limited to, early education policies, accountability systems, and programming and instructional approaches that do not support bilingualism and do not consider the role of bilingualism in young children's development and learning. These are reflected in practices such as the use of culturally and linguistically biased assessment and referral practices and higher education programs that do not prepare professionals to serve bilingual children in general early education settings (Castro, 2014; Zepeda *et al.*, 2011).

Although limited, most research and policies in special education focusing on bilingual children has been conducted with school-age populations. There is a dearth of interdisciplinary research that considers the intersection between the fields of special education, bilingual education, and early childhood education. In this volume we discuss these and other barriers and propose next steps for an integrative and interdisciplinary perspective on early development and education research, policy and practices to address the pervasive challenges and identify opportunities in the education of young bilingual children with disabilities in the United States in the 21st century.

Terms Used in this Book

The term "young bilingual children" is used interchangeably with other terms in this book to refer to children from birth to 8 years of age who grow up exposed to two languages at home, the community and in early care and education programs. Other terms used in the various chapters include those commonly used in the fields of early childhood and elementary education to refer to this population in the United States. Those include "dual language learners," "English learners," "English language learners," and "limited English proficient." These terms are used because they are associated with specific language policies. The choice of the editors to use "young bilingual children" or "young bilingual learners" is related to how the processes of acquiring and learning in two languages are described in developmental science: the study of bilingualism and bilingual development and its implications for early care and education (National Research Council, 2017).

Related to the scope of the book, the focus is on young bilingual children with disabilities or with a higher probability of having language and communication delays or disorders, as well as cognitive, behavioral, and emotional disabilities. We do not focus on visual, physical, or other health impairments, which deserve an in-depth discussion that is not possible to include in this book.

Chapters in this Volume

In Chapter 2, "A Sociocultural, Integrative, and Interdisciplinary Perspective on the Development and Education of Young Bilingual Children with Disabilities," Dina C. Castro, Cristina Gillanders, Nydia Prishker, and Rodolfo Rodriguez present conceptual premises and empirical evidence in support of a sociocultural and integrative perspective when serving young bilingual children from birth to 8 years of age in early care and education, early intervention (EI) and special education programs. They argue that the unique experiences of young bilingual children at home, in their communities, and in society at large contribute to defining these children's development in a distinct way. Furthermore, the authors argue that the education of young bilinguals in the United States should move beyond an exclusive focus on English language acquisition to designing practices that take into consideration how children's bilingualism influences all developmental domains and learning processes. They discuss the need for shifting paradigms from a deficit to a strength-based approach in research, policy and early education practices with young bilingual children.

Chapter 3, "How Bilingualism Affects Children's Language Development," by Carol Scheffner Hammer and Maria Cristina Limlingan, focuses on developmental science related to bilingualism. Traditional approaches to developmental research have tended to view bilinguals as two monolinguals in one. This, in turn, has led to research in which the developmental outcomes of these children have been interpreted with reference to the performance of monolinguals. A major shortcoming of this approach is that it fails to take into account the extent to which the bilingual experience determines a particular developmental pathway for these children. This chapter discusses how bilingualism affects language development of children with disabilities. An understanding of the developmental characteristics of emergent bilinguals is essential for designing effective early intervention and educational approaches for these children.

Chapter 4, "Dual Language Learners in Early Intervention Programs: Issues of Eligibility, Access, and Service Provision," by Lillian Durán, focuses on bilingual children from birth to 3 years of age, discussing issues related to how young bilingual children are identified for services, including challenges faced by their families to find and access services. This chapter also discusses the availability of qualified early intervention providers and implementation of culturally and linguistically responsive early intervention services for very young children growing up bilingually.

Chapter 5, "Dual Language Learners with Disabilities in Inclusive Early Elementary School Classrooms," by Sarah L. Alvarado, Sarah M. Salinas, and Alfredo J. Artiles, centers on approaches to providing instruction to young bilingual children with disabilities in inclusive settings. Various current approaches are described, and their appropriateness and effectiveness are discussed. A related issue discussed is the opportunities provided in inclusive classrooms for young bilingual children with disabilities to become bilingual. Still today, there are professionals who conduct interventions only in the majority language (English) and base their recommendations on the outcomes of this focus. In this environment, parents give up on being able to communicate with their children fluently in their family's primary language, thus limiting opportunities for children to experience rich language environments.

Chapter 6, "Language Learning and Language Disability: Equity Issues in the Assessment of Young Bilingual Learners," by Maria Adelaida Restrepo and Anny P. Castilla-Earls, covers how the need to differentiate language learning from language disability is still a challenge for early interventionists and special educators. The limited availability of valid and reliable assessment instruments for bilingual children and assessment policies and procedures that do not take into account their bilingual development characteristics results in inaccurate identification, or no identification, of these children for early intervention and special education services. These challenges apply also to assessments conducted for progress monitoring and intervention planning purposes. This chapter presents an overview of these issues and outlines emerging findings that promise to advance this area of inquiry.

Chapter 7, "Learning from Sociocultural Contexts: Partnering with Families of Young Bilingual Children with Disabilities," by Cristina Gillanders and Sylvia Y. Sánchez, centers on the development of bilingual children and how development cannot be understood without considering the kinds of routine activities in which they engage within their family contexts. The demographic characteristics of the families of children growing up bilingually are frequently used as a proxy for the limitations that these families may experience in being able to provide support for their children's development. However, relying on demographic characteristics such as socioeconomic status or parental education can prevent researchers and educators from identifying family processes and routines that may constitute positive or protective factors to promote their children's development and learning. This chapter discusses these issues and their implications for building partnerships with families of young bilingual children with disabilities.

The implementation of early education practices that address the characteristics and needs of bilingual children with disabilities depends mostly on the preparation of their educators.

Chapter 8, "Preparing Teachers of Young Bilingual Children with Disabilities," by Norma A. López-Reyna, Cindy L. Collado, Mary Bay, and Wu-Ying Hsieh, discusses the knowledge, skills, and dispositions that should be the focus of teacher preparation and professional development intended to improve the quality of early intervention and special education services for young bilingual children with disabilities. This is particularly relevant in the context of inclusive classrooms serving these children. Also, the importance of increasing the cultural and linguistic diversity of the early childhood special education workforce is discussed.

In Chapter 9, "Language, Learning, and Disability in an Era of Accountability," Marlene Zepeda and Michael J. Orosco discuss the definition and assessment of program and classroom quality in the early grades (PreK-3) in the context of the current Quality Rating Improvement Systems that most states are currently implementing, as well as federal policies such as No Child Left Behind and the Common Core State Standards. Also, kindergarten entry assessments are discussed, focusing on the extent to which these and other accountability initiatives include indicators to assess educational practices that meet the needs of dual language learners with disabilities. Relevant to this discussion is how prepared early childhood programs, schools, and teachers are to serve their increasingly diverse child populations in early intervention and special education.

In Chapter 10, "Young Bilingual Children with Disabilities: Challenges and Opportunities for Future Education Policies and Research," Alba A. Ortiz discusses the main themes covered in this volume and outlines challenges and opportunities for federal legislation, identifies gaps, and presents recommendations for future research on this critical topic.

The discussions in the chapters of this volume provide readers with up-to-date information and critical perspectives with the purpose of bringing the early education of young bilingual children to the forefront of the debates at the intersection of early childhood education, special education, and bilingual education. Given the current state of knowledge, there is no justification for the persistence of policies and practices that negate young bilingual children with and without disabilities access to early intervention and early education that allows them to reach their full potential.

References

Arreaga-Mayer, C. and Perdomo-Rivera, C. (1996) Eco-behavioral analysis of instruction for at-risk language minority students. *Elementary School Journal* 96, 245–258.

Artiles, A.J. and Ortiz, A.A. (eds) (2002) *English Language Learners with Special Education Needs*. Washington, DC: Center for Applied Linguistics.

Artiles, A.J., Kozleski, E.B., Trent, S.C., Osher, D. and Ortiz, A. (2010) Justifying and explaining disproportionality, 1968–2008: A critique of underlying views of culture. *Exceptional Children* 76, 279–299. https://doi.org/10.1177/001440291007600303.

Castro, D.C. (2014) The development and early care and education of dual language learners: Establishing the state of knowledge. *Early Childhood Research Quarterly* 29, 693–698.

Mercer, J.R. and Richardson, J.G. (1975) Mental retardation as a social problem. In N. Hobbs (ed.) *Issues in the Classification of Children* (vol. 2, pp. 463–496). San Francisco, CA: Jossey-Bass.

National Research Council (2017) *Fostering School Success for English Learners: Toward New Directions in Policy, Practice, and Research*. Washington, DC: National Research Council.

Rueda, R. and Windmueller, M.P. (2006) English language learners, LD and over-representation. *Journal of Learning Disabilities* 39, 99–107.

Zepeda, M., Castro, D.C. and Cronin, S. (2011) Preparing teachers to work with young English language learners. *Child Development Perspectives* 5 (1), 10–14.

2 A Sociocultural, Integrative, and Interdisciplinary Perspective on the Development and Education of Young Bilingual Children with Disabilities

Dina C. Castro, Cristina Gillanders, Nydia Prishker, and Rodolfo Rodriguez

Language diversity has been a characteristic of societies around the world for millennia (Franceschini, 2013). Colonization and migration movements have contributed to the linguistic and cultural diversity in many communities. During the 21st century, the number of people leaving their communities in search of a better life for themselves and their families has increased dramatically. In 2015, 47 million or 19% of the world's total international migrants lived in the United States (United Nations, 2016). Bilingualism in the early years (birth to age 8) is found largely among children in immigrant families, the majority of whom are US citizens (Park *et al.*, 2018). However, there are also bilinguals among children of US born heritage language speakers (second generation and above) and children in indigenous families (Migge & Léglise, 2007). Bilingual children are a third (32%) of the US child population ages 0–8 and constitute a higher percentage in some states: 60% in California and 49% in Texas and New Mexico (Park *et al.*, 2017a, 2017b, 2017c, 2017d). Regarding bilingual children with dis/abilities, in 2013, 339,000 infants and toddlers (ages birth to 2 years), more than 745,000 children ages 3–5, and 5.8 million children and youth ages 6–21 were served under the Individuals with Disabilities Education Act (IDEA) of 2004 (US Department of Education, 2015).

The percentage of bilingual children enrolled in English language instruction educational programs (K-12) identified as having a dis/ability varies across states. Data available for the 2013-2014 school year show a national average of 12.8%, with percentages as high as 21% in New York, and 18% in Illinois, while some states have lower than the average percentages, such as Maryland with 5.6% and Texas with 7.6% (US Department of Education, 2020).

There is great variability in the languages spoken in the United States. In 2016, the US Census Bureau reported that more than 350 languages were spoken in the country by people 5 years of age and older. Among those speaking languages other than English, the five most spoken languages or groups of languages include Spanish (62%; with speakers from more than 20 countries), Chinese languages (4.7%; includes Mandarin, Cantonese and others), Native American languages (4.3%), Tagalog (2.7%), and Vietnamese (2.3%). The use of each of their two languages among bilingual families varies. For instance, a study conducted by Winsler and colleagues (2014) analyzed preferences in the use of home language and English in a national representative sample of immigrant families by country of origin and found that among Asian families, a larger percentage of Vietnamese families were bilingual (used both their home language and English) (66%) than Japanese families, the majority of whom used English only (80%). Among Latino families, more Mexican families tend to be bilingual (49%) than Puerto Rican (30%) and Cuban families (40%), with Puerto Rican families (living in the US mainland) using English only more (67%) than Mexican (32%) and Cuban (30%) families. Figure 2.1 shows the percentages of language(s) used (English and

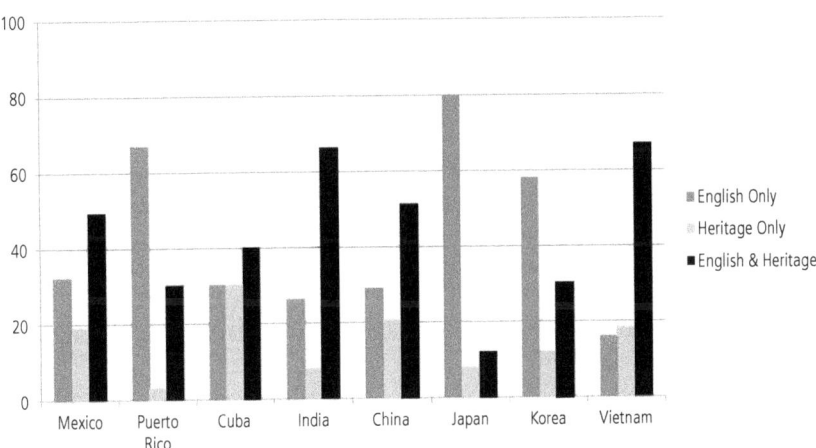

Figure 2.1 Language use among families of bilingual children in the United States by country of origin (Winsler et al., 2014)

another language, English only, and only another language) by immigrant families from eight countries.

In addition to this linguistic diversity, bilingual children are from diverse racial, ethnic, and cultural communities. In spite of this diversity, many research studies on child development and learning of bilingual children still use predominantly an English monolingual Eurocentric middle-class perspective. This means that bilingual children and families' characteristics are often compared to those of monolinguals. This deficit view ignores the complexities inherent to being bilingual and the richness of these children's experiences in the context of their families, communities, and early care and education settings. This deficit-oriented research then informs the development of early learning policies and curriculum approaches and programming in early childhood care and education, establishing "norms" and developmental expectations based on the mainstream/dominant culture's beliefs and practices (Pérez & Saavedra, 2017).

As a consequence, bilingual children from diverse racial, ethnic, and cultural communities, whose development and learning may not always conform with the established norm, may be seen as deficient. A demonstration of this perspective are accountability systems that currently govern early education, such as Kindergarten Entry Assessments (KEA) and national studies using assessment procedures and tools that do not take into account children's diverse characteristics and needs. They tend to report a school readiness gap affecting mostly children from racial, ethnic, and language minoritized communities (Espinosa & García, 2012; García, 2015).

This deficit perspective is reminiscent of prevalent views in special education (including early childhood special education) in which children who do not meet normative developmental standards are considered inherently disabled (Dalkilic, 2020) and are precluded from participating in educational opportunities reserved for those with "typical" development. Bilingual children with dis/abilities are in a double bind (Artiles, 2013), since they are excluded because they are members of linguistically, ethnically, and racially minoritized groups as well as because they are "biologically different". In special education the goal is to "remedy the *problem of disability* by reversing the physical, emotional, behavioral, and other, often pathologized, indicators of atypical development" (Dalkilic, 2020: 69). Similarly, for bilingual children, the mainstream goal is for them to learn English as fast as they can, ignoring their capabilities in their other language. This is particularly manifested in the under- or over-representation of children from minoritized groups among those diagnosed as having delays or dis/abilities (Zhang *et al.*, 2014). Specifically, bilingual children tend to be over- (or under-) identified as having language delays or disabilities (Artiles *et al.*, 2010; García & Ortiz, 2006). This seems to be an unresolved issue in the field, as evidenced by recent studies. For example, Yamasaki and Luk (2018) found disproportionate under-representation of bilingual children in grades 3–5 in the disability categories of autism spectrum disorder (ASD). Barrio *et al.* (2018) and Vega *et al.* (2016) also point to issues of cultural and linguistic differences as contributing factors to an overall under-identification of autism in young Latino children, with diagnosis typically happening at older ages. Other studies have found an over-representation of bilingual children, in particular, among those in the learning disabilities (LD) category (Rueda & Windmueller, 2006; Sanatullova-Allison & Robison-Young, 2016).

The lack of understanding of the cultural ways of thinking, speaking, and behaving explains in part the prevalence of over-representation of children of minoritized groups with diagnosis based on clinical judgement such as educable mental retardation, emotional/behavioral disorders, and learning disability. In contrast, diagnosis based on "biologically verifiable conditions – such as deafness or visual impairment – do not show disproportionality by ethnicity" (Harry & Klingner, 2007: 18). Years of research on sociocultural practices in different communities demonstrate that rather than a disability, children show varied "ways with words" (Heath, 1983). Assessments designed to diagnose their language proficiency are based on developmental milestones of English monolingual middle-class children and do not take into consideration these variations. In similar ways, bilingual children are usually assessed in only one language, and their competencies developed as a result of the use of two languages and practices in the home and community are ignored.

The concerns that motivated the writing of this book include (1) the prevalence of a deficit perspective, with monolingualism and Eurocentric, middle-class, and able-bodied culture as the "norm" in research on the development and learning of young bilingual children, both typically developing and those with dis/abilities; (2) the limited consideration of the unique features of young bilingual children's contexts of development in research with this population; and (3) the limited interdisciplinary research focusing on the intersection between the fields of early development and learning, bilingual education, and special education. In this chapter we propose a sociocultural theoretical perspective as an integrative and interdisciplinary approach in the study of the development and learning of young bilingual children with dis/abilities. Since we believe in the importance of a meticulous description of the context of these children's lives, we identify and discuss the unique developmental features and life experiences that need to be taken into consideration when designing and conducting research, and when developing policies targeting this population of young children.

A Sociocultural and Integrative Perspective: From Vulnerability to Resiliency

We argue that a shift from a deficit to an asset-based perspective is needed to advance research and policy about the development and learning of bilingual children from minoritized and marginalized communities, for both typically developing children and those with dis/abilities. An asset-based perspective would focus on the resiliency of these children and their families fighting to thrive in spite of societal structural inequities. A sociocultural-historical, integrative, and interdisciplinary approach to the development and learning of young bilingual children is needed that (1) recognizes the mutually defining nature of development, meaning that children are not passively "influenced" by sociocultural practices in their various contexts (i.e., family, early care and education, community), they are active participants in shaping their own development through their constant interactions in those contexts (Rogoff, 2003); (2) takes into consideration that bilingualism affects all domains of development, not only language (Comeau *et al.*, 2010); and (3) acknowledges that bilingualism is not a liability but can be an asset in the development and learning (Bialystok, 2009) of children in minoritized groups, as it is considered to be for children in majoritized groups. Research grounded in an asset-based paradigm would inform the development of policies focusing on young bilingual children with dis/abilities' characteristics and experiences, and guide the design of linguistically appropriate (i.e., curriculum and instruction supporting the goal of bilingualism) and culturally sustaining (Paris, 2012) early care and education and interventions for this growing population.

A sociocultural-historical theoretical perspective of development assumes not only that development is socially constructed (Vygotsky, 1978) but, also, that developmental competencies are mutually constituted from what children's individual characteristics bring to the situation and what is offered to them in that setting. Therefore, development is understood as a process in which the individual and the environment are mutually defined and developed (Rogoff, 2003). It recognizes that children develop through participation in their cultural communities, including their family, neighborhoods, and schools. Building on this perspective, Rogoff proposes that "culture is not an entity that influences individuals. Instead, people contribute to the creation of cultural processes and cultural processes contribute to create people" (2003: 5). Individuals act on their environments, and their environments act on them in a mutually defining process.

Other approaches (i.e., Bronfenbrenner, 1979; Whiting & Whiting, 1975) have also made important contributions to our understanding of child development, focusing on the interactions of children and families with the various settings in which they are involved, and the relations among those settings. However, it is important to notice that those theoretical perspectives still define cultural practices as independent entities that "influence" the child. In some cases, a bi-directional "influence" is acknowledged, but those influences are still defined as independent from each other (Rogoff, 2003). Following a sociocultural perspective of development, children approach developmental tasks in particular situations based on the cultural practices in which they have previously participated. Therefore, developmental competencies are not understood as being "influenced" by sociocultural practices. Rather, they are the result of the interaction between what children bring into the situation and what is being offered to them in the setting they are interacting with.

Conceptual frameworks have been proposed before for the study of the development and learning of children from racial and ethnic minoritized and marginalized communities, and those living in poverty (e.g., García-Coll *et al.*, 1996; McLoyd, 1990), and these can inform research and policy on bilingual children's development and learning. However, they do not incorporate and emphasize factors for understanding development when children are growing up as bilinguals, nor do they address the diversity within this population and the constellation of factors that are particular to their experiences. Furthermore, they more broadly address development across the lifespan, not focusing on the early childhood years.

Theoretical frameworks such as that by García-Coll and colleagues (1996) propose an integrative model of development that emphasizes the role of social class, culture, ethnicity, and race in shaping children's development and which incorporates elements from the culturally different model. Informed by this work, we assert that to further our understanding of the development and learning processes of bilingual children from minoritized and marginalized communities, it is necessary to acknowledge the role of social class, racism, prejudice, discrimination, and oppression as the macrosystem-level mechanisms that mediate the effects of social position and other contextual variables on these children's developmental and learning outcomes. Development and learning processes are profoundly affected by the individual's social position derived from the social stratification system of a given society (i.e., hierarchy of groups based on imputed relative worth). The invisibility of these societal conditions in developmental and educational research leads to misinterpretations and biased findings that may perpetuate inequities in the education and life experiences of bilingual children.

Recognizing the contributions of the theories and conceptual frameworks discussed above, we assert that a conceptual framework is needed to guide research on young bilingual children's development and learning that highlights variables and processes that are unique to their bilingual experience (e.g., bilingual and bicultural households, variation in parents' proficiency in L1 and L2, linguistically isolated communities). This is particularly critical for bilingual children with dis/abilities, since mainstream views emphasize the medical characteristics of the disability rather than the intersectionality of bilingualism, race and ethnicity, and disability in particular sociocultural contexts. A sociocultural perspective allows us to identify the unique characteristics of the practices in which bilingual children with dis/abilities participate. For example, in a study of Asian Muslim immigrant parents, Jegatheesan (2011) found that once their children were diagnosed with autism spectrum disorder, they believed in the importance of including their child fully in social life. They viewed themselves as being chosen for the special task of raising "God's child." Children were expected to participate in all everyday activities at home and in the community. This included participating in multilingual interactions with relatives and members of the community. Parents believed that children should learn English for school and therapy, native languages to interact with family members, and Arabic for participation in religious ceremonies. Examples such as this demonstrate that a sociocultural, integrative, and interdisciplinary perspective allows special educators and policy makers to understand the specific circumstances in which bilingual children with dis/abilities develop and learn. In the next section, we discuss societal, community, family, and early care and education contexts that provide unique experiences to young bilingual children. These should be taken into consideration when conducting research, developing policies, and designing and implementing practices/interventions with young bilingual children with disabilities.

Bilingual Children's Contexts of Development

Social contexts

The climate generated by national and state policies can affect children's lives and, therefore, not all children will experience life in the same way. For example, for bilingual children with immigrant parents, anti-immigrant policies can mean that they live in fear of their parents being deported. Most of them are US citizens suffering the uncertainties and stress affecting their undocumented immigrant parents (Yoshikawa, 2011). Parents with children with dis/abilities might be fearful of taking their children to be diagnosed, as they might perceive it as "coming out of the shadows." Due to immigration policies or family circumstances, transnationality becomes part of the experience of many young bilingual children. Transnational experiences can have negative consequences for children's socioemotional development and academic performance (Castro *et al.*, 2019; Sánchez-García *et al.*, 2012).

Early learning and education policies leading to segregation or limited access to high-quality education also can negatively affect young bilingual children's opportunities to develop and perform to their fullest potential. Examples are early education policies that place bilingual children in English-only general education classrooms, even when bilingual education programs are available; those children are growing up bilingually but are not given the opportunity to become fully bilingual and biliterate. This occurs because most bilingual education programs offered to bilingual children from racial and ethnic minoritized communities are subtractive (i.e., their goal is the acquisition of English, not to support bilingualism) (Castro & Prishker, 2019; Gándara & Escamilla, 2017). Findings from an analysis of Early Learning and Development Standards in 21 states and the District of Columbia conducted by Espinosa and Calderón (2015) showed that only one state (New Jersey) could be considered a Dual Language state (supporting the acquisition of English and the development and maintenance of children's home language). The majority of states (16) were classified as English Language Development states (no support provided for home language development), while the District of Columbia and 4 additional states were classified as English Immersion states. This is even more challenging for young bilingual children with dis/abilities, who are more likely than typically developing bilingual children to be placed in an English-only early intervention or special education program. This is based on the assumption that they will not be capable of developing and learning in two languages and that bilingualism will be detrimental to them. There is a body of research that demonstrates that this is a wrong assumption and that bilingualism is not detrimental for bilingual children with dis/abilities (Paradis, 2016).

It is likely that placing young bilingual children in English-only general instruction, and offering them special education only in English, will result in the arrested development or loss of their acquired home language abilities. Furthermore, for very young children (birth to 3 years of age) growing up in families speaking languages other than English, the risk of losing their home language before enrolling in a PreK program is high when bilingual child care and early intervention services are not available for their families. Research to support this assumption is scarce regarding access to and use of bilingual early care and education for very young children. However, an analysis of longitudinal data from a national representative sample (Espinosa et al., 2017) found that access to bilingual early care and education was high (87%) for young bilingual children at 9 months of age and that it diminished (40%) when they were 52 months old. Further research should be conducted to examine the impact of early learning policies on the development and learning of young bilingual children; in particular, infants, toddlers, and preschoolers.

The community and family

The presence and value of different languages in communities offer opportunities for increased and varied linguistic interactions for young bilingual children, which in turn will promote their bilingualism and biliteracy (Urzúa & Gómez, 2008). This is likely to happen in communities that are welcoming to immigrants. Communities that are hostile to immigrants, on the contrary, can create a detrimental environment for young bilingual children, when they perceive their home language and culture not being valued (Reese & Goldenberg, 2006). Similarly, communities have different perceptions and attitudes toward individuals with dis/abilities. Communities that welcome the presence of individuals with dis/abilities will create spaces in which these children can interact with other members of the community.

Examination of the family context should address family practices, values, and beliefs, including their beliefs about dis/abilities, access and preferences related to child care, and the role of extended family members. Parenting practices, particularly with young children, can differ quite extensively across cultural communities, with a variety of combinations between what researchers call warmth and control (Chao, 1994). Parents also induce different amounts of responsibility at different ages (Rogoff, 2003) and expect children to participate in cultural activities (e.g., sibling caregiving, food preparation, free play) in different ways and at different ages (Rogoff, 2003). Likewise, parents may have different conceptions of the diagnosis of disability and might engage their children in different cultural activities depending on their ideas of what they think is important for their child to learn and experience (see Gillanders & Sanchez, Chapter 7, in this volume). For instance, Riojas-Cortez (2011) describes how she engaged her son within the autism spectrum disorder in the important cultural practice of family celebrations. Throughout the years, her son felt more comfortable engaging with other family members, and the family members learned to understand his individual characteristics.

Variations in exposure to, and use of, each of their two languages exist among young children growing up in bilingual families and communities, and these will influence children's learning and the strategies used in instruction. Therefore, the amount and quality of exposure to and use of each of the two languages in their various environments should be documented when conducting research with these children (Byers-Heinlein *et al.*, 2019; Castro *et al.*, 2020).

Early care and education

Increased language diversity in the child population has meant that early care and education programs are serving more children who speak languages other than the majority language in their communities and who are growing up immersed in two or more cultures. According to Pérez and

Saavedra (2017), there has already been a push to expand the critical space to reconceptualize the field of early childhood care and education; however, these perspectives are specific to mainstream Eurocentric middle-class views and many times do not fully match the needs of bilingual children. Therefore, it is important to conceptualize a more equitable framework that fits the characteristics and circumstances of young bilingual children's lives. Pérez and Saavedra (2017) offer a perspective that relies on the everyday experiences of children of color to develop a curriculum that is equitable and socially just and challenges the deficit label that is often given to young bilingual children from minoritized communities.

There is general acceptance of how significant early childhood experiences are and how impactful they will be on young children's development and learning. These early experiences are especially important for young children with developmental delays or disabilities (Hebbeler *et al.*, 2012). In spite of its importance, the initial schooling experience of young bilingual children with dis/abilities is not often found in the research literature. If research on the development and early care and education of typically developing young bilingual children is limited (Castro, 2014), there is even more a dearth of research focusing on young bilingual children with dis/abilities, and research on what the families of these children experience (Hughes *et al.*, 2008). This is significant, considering that the number of bilingual children referred to special education programs is increasing (Cheatham & Barnett, 2017).

When we consider early learning experiences for bilingual children with dis/abilities, we must acknowledge when differences are due to a disability or to bilingual development. How these differences are addressed can affect the quality of their experiences and, in turn, their possibilities to develop, learn, and reach their full potential (Cheatham & Barnett, 2017; Liasidou, 2013; Rodriguez, 2009). This is relevant when designing interventions for these children, such as Response to Intervention or Recognition and Response. These approaches face challenges when teachers and other professionals involved are not knowledgeable about bilingual development and design interventions without considering children's experiences in their various contexts of development (see Zepeda & Orosco, Chapter 9, this volume).

Children with dis/abilities have less access to bilingual education than their typically developing counterparts. Findings from a study (de Valenzuela *et al.*, 2016) conducted in four countries Canada, the Netherlands, the United States, and the United Kingdom indicate that:

> Despite embracing a philosophy favoring inclusion, children with special needs at all sites were reported less likely than typically developing children to participate in language-in-education programs designed to promote bilingualism, especially if the child had a more severe disability or the language program involved a substantial percentage of instruction

in a minority language (i.e., immersion programs, dual language programs). (de Valenzuela *et al*., 2016: 67; quoted in Kay-Raining Bird, Trudeau *et al*., 2016)

Cioé-Peña (2017) explains that bilingual children with dis/abilities are at a greater disadvantage as a result of inadequate inclusion programs. Inclusion programs often create an intersectional gap for linguistically diverse children, that emerges from these "inclusive practices" "that meet either their academic needs or their linguistic needs but not both" (Cioé-Peña, 2017: 913).

Child Individual Characteristics

Individual characteristics, such as personality and motivation, have been identified as having a role in children's development, and specifically in bilingual language development. Personality dimensions such as extroversion and introversion have been found to encourage or inhibit second language learning (Zhang, 2008). Studies have found that extroverts do better than introverts on oral tasks when learning a second language, while introverts do better on written tests (Robinson *et al*., 1994) and vocabulary tests (van Daele *et al*., 2006). Another dimension of personality found to be related to language learning in bilingual children is their willingness to take risks in communicating when they are at early stages of learning a second language (Dewaele, 2012). Some researchers have argued that language learning also has a role in shaping individuals' personalities. Furthermore, the linguistic and cultural contexts in which children develop will have an effect on the formation of their personality, and that is more likely to occur in the early years of childhood and adolescence (Dewaele, 2012).

There is a large body of research on individuals' motivation to learn a second language, especially among sequential bilinguals. Scholars recognize that motivation to learn a second language involves not only "to acquire knowledge of the language but to identify with the target language community and adopt their distinct speech behaviours and styles" (Ushioda, 2012: 59). Thus, children's experiences related to their language backgrounds and abilities may increase or decrease their motivation to learn and use a language.

Developmental competencies and bilingual children with dis/abilities

As stated above, the bilingual and bicultural nature of children's development is a critical consideration when examining their developmental competencies. We have attempted to identify specific aspects of the cultural processes by which young bilingual children develop as participants of their cultural communities (Rogoff, 2003). We argue that participation in such sociocultural processes might result in developmental paths that differ from those of monolingual children in specific aspects of development, whereas they may be similar in others. As an example, reviews of the literature have found that when bilingual infants' vocabularies in their respective languages were compared to monolingual infants' vocabularies, bilingual children tended to have smaller vocabularies in each language. However, their conceptual vocabularies were comparable to those of their monolingual counterparts (Hammer *et al.*, 2014). Findings like these indicate that aspects of the developmental trajectories of young bilingual children are not equivalent to those of monolingual children. Bilingualism and specific sociocultural experiences might yield developmental competencies that are unique to the bilingual child population. Therefore, perspectives on development that focus on comparisons between monolinguals and bilinguals might miss important aspects of bilingual children's development or generate misinterpretations.

Following Rogoff (2003) and others, we seek to portray development of young bilingual children in an integrated framework in which culture, the bilingual experience, and the individual child cannot be isolated or viewed as separate entities. Therefore, the child's developmental competencies have to be viewed in relation to children's sociocultural settings. Research studies provide evidence of specific contextual factors on young bilingual children's development that need to be unpacked in order to understand these children's developmental and learning processes. For instance, a secondary data analysis of the Early Childhood Longitudinal Study – Birth Cohort (ECLS-B) found that, for young bilingual children, having an immigrant mother was associated with better cognitive outcomes and fewer behavior problems compared to young bilinguals with US-born mothers. Furthermore, for children whose mothers were born in the United States, ratings of problem behaviors were higher for monolingual English speakers than for young bilinguals (Winsler *et al.*, 2014). These findings are similar to those of other studies (Halle *et al.*, 2009) reporting that bilingual children tend to begin kindergarten with more social-emotional competencies than their monolingual English-speaking peers. Studies that examine immigrant mothers' child-rearing beliefs and practices can help elucidate bilingual children's social-emotional development when they begin kindergarten.

Not only their bilingual language development but also the cultural and racial/ethnic characteristics of their families, and the ways in which they interact with mainstream society, are going to define bilingual children's development and learning. As stated by García-Coll and colleagues (1996: 1907):

> The evaluation of meaningful developmental competencies will continue to involve important traditional skill areas such as cognitive, social, emotional, and linguistic skills. However, functional outcome measures

must also recognize manifestations of these skills that reflect competent adaptation to circumstances created by social stratification, the effects of racism and its concomitant processes, and the influence of segregation on the nature of the environments faced by children of color.

There is a need to broaden the view of children's competencies, to include aspects that are particularly of interest in the study of young bilingual children with dis/abilities.

The research literature on the development and learning of young bilingual children with developmental disabilities (DD) is smaller than that focusing on typically developing bilinguals; however, "the findings showing that children with developmental disabilities are indeed capable of dual language learning and that bilingualism is not harmful to their language development are clear and compelling" (Paradis, 2016: 79). A recent review of research (Kay-Raining Bird, Genesee *et al.*, 2016) found evidence that children with developmental disabilities are able to become bilinguals, although there will be differences, based on time and amount of exposure, between simultaneous and sequential bilinguals. Furthermore, a review conducted by the National Academies of Science, Engineering, and Medicine (NASEM, 2017: 353) concluded: "continued support for the home language through intervention or natural exposure helps develop that language while not hindering and even facilitating (through transfer of language skills) the learning of the second language (L2)".

In spite of the research evidence on the cognitive, language, social, emotional, and educational benefits of bilingualism (Collins *et al.*, 2011; de Abreu *et al.*, 2012; Fan *et al.*, 2015; Kay-Raining Bird, Trudeau *et al.*, 2016; Toppelberg, 2011), there is still a prevalent view among policy makers, practitioners, and parents that bilingualism can be detrimental for bilingual children with dis/abilities. Moreover, parents are discouraged from using their home language or are directly asked by educators and clinicians to support their children with developmental disabilities only in the majority or dominant language (Marinova-Todd *et al.*, 2016). The consequences may be, in fact, the opposite to that intended. Arrested development or complete loss of children's home language may cause further delays in their development and make communication between children and their family members difficult (NASEM, 2017). Some authors argue that the disconnect between the knowledge base, policies, and educational and intervention practices is rooted in structural and systemic factors, such as professional preparation (practitioners are not knowledgeable about how to serve young bilingual children), limited resources (no funds are allocated to hire bilingual specialized personnel – educator, speech pathologist, early interventionist), and service provision requirements that do not allow practitioners to make accommodations when serving bilingual children (e.g., not able to use assessments in both L1 and L2, or to use interpreters to gather information from parents in their first language) (Marinova-Todd *et al.*, 2016; Paradis, 2016).

Conclusion: At the Intersection of Language, Learning, and Disability

In this chapter, we discuss theoretical perspectives and empirical research on the development and learning of young bilingual children, both typically developing and those with dis/abilities. We argue that there is a lack of a comprehensive framework describing the development of these children that could guide relevant research questions, appropriate research methods, and interpretation of research findings. We propose a sociocultural, integrative, and interdisciplinary perspective to advance knowledge about the development and learning of young bilingual children with dis/abilities, one that considers the contexts of children's development, their bilingualism, and their dis/ability characteristics. Such an approach requires work at the intersection of language, learning, and dis/ability. Within this proposed perspective, we assert that research, policy, and practice focusing on the development and learning of young bilingual children with dis/abilities require an interdisciplinary approach involving a reconceptualization of the fields of early development and learning, bilingual education, and special education with consideration given to the unique characteristics of bilingual children and their sociocultural contexts of development, as discussed in previous sections and shown in Figure 2.2.

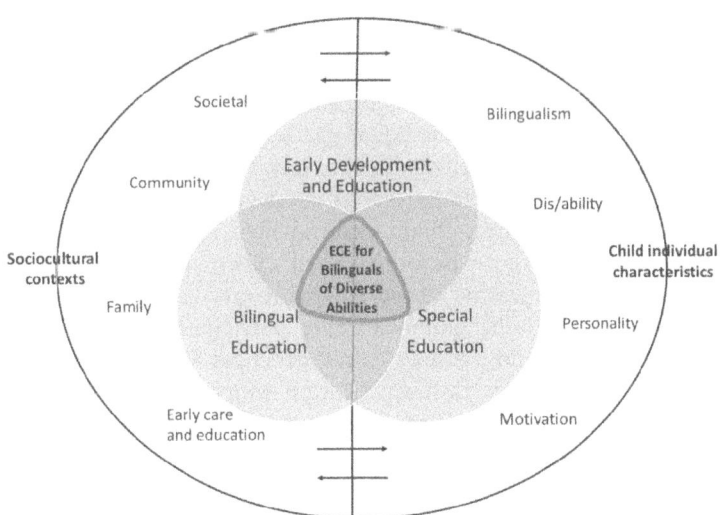

Figure 2.2 A sociocultural, integrative, and interdisciplinary perspective on early childhood education for bilingual children with diverse abilities

The intersectionality among being bilingual in a minoritized language, having a dis/ability, and being from a racial and/or ethnic minoritized group amplifies the impact of marginalization and discrimination on young bilingual children with dis/abilities in the early care and education systems, and society at large. The framework we propose has the goal of promoting equity in the early care and education of young bilingual children with dis/abilities. These children are in a sort of "limbo," from a theoretical and empirical research perspective, which is reflected in their invisibility in early care and education policies and practices.

The field of early development and education is still predominantly built on a conceptualization of child and childhoods that do not include or represent the experience of being bilingual in a minoritized situation, with all that is involved in it, culturally and socially. The challenge in the field of bilingual education, furthermore, lies in the emphasis on English language acquisition as a goal, with no support for bilingualism in most bilingual education program types made available to bilingual children (e.g., bilingual transitional programs, English as a second language), with the result that only a small percentage of bilingual children have access to dual language education. In addition, the knowledge base for bilingual education has been developed mostly from research with older bilingual children in public school settings, giving much less attention to young bilinguals, in particular those from birth to 5 years of age, who are served in a variety of early childhood care and education settings (i.e., child care, Head Start, Early Head Start, home-based care, parental care) with a variety of funding sources (i.e., private, for-profit, and non-profit; public, state, and federally funded).

Finally, research and practice in the field of special education are based on a medical model that sees children with diverse abilities in need of remediation or having a need to be normalized. Rather than designing environments that facilitate the equal participation of children with dis/abilities, special education environments seek to remedy the dis/ability in order to include the child in society. A sociocultural perspective on dis/ability allows practitioners to understand how bilingual children with dis/abilities bring to the classroom varied experiences that are beyond their dis/ability. Integrating these linguistic and cultural experiences in the classroom would enhance their participation and inclusion. Also, research informing policies and practices in special education programs is founded on Eurocentric and monolingual paradigms of child development, with most of the research targeting older school-age populations (Wang & Woolf, 2015).

As a consequence, we argue that there are major gaps related to what is known about the development and learning of young bilingual children (from birth to age 8) with dis/abilities. These gaps will need to be addressed in order to inform policies that promote equitable access to high-quality early intervention and early care and education for young bilingual children with dis/abilities. Below we share some examples of research questions for future studies, using this sociocultural, integrative, and interdisciplinary perspective:

- What are the family processes and practices that support the social and academic competencies of young bilingual children in transnational circumstances?
- How are teacher education programs preparing early childhood educators to promote the development and learning of bilingual children with dis/abilities?
- To what extent do bilingual children (from birth to 8 years of age), both typically developing and those with dis/abilities, have access to early care and education that supports bilingual development and is culturally sustaining?
- How is inclusion being implemented in classrooms serving young bilingual children with dis/abilities across program types (i.e., English-only general education and the different bilingual education models)?
- How and to what extent are accountability systems promoting high-quality early care and education that specifically responds to the linguistic and cultural experiences of bilingual children with dis/abilities?
- Which domains and practices are relevant indicators of high-quality early care and education for bilingual children with dis/abilities? And how are these being assessed?

It is imperative to shift from a focus on vulnerabilities to examining resilience, in research with young bilingual children with dis/abilities and their families. Recognizing their unique characteristics and experiences will make research more meaningful and relevant. This approach will, in turn, contribute to developing equitable early care and education policies and programs.

References

Artiles, A.J. (2013) Untangling the racialization of disabilities: An intersectionality critique across disability models. *Du Bois Review: Social Science Research on Race* 10 (2), 329–347.

Artiles, A.J., Kozleski, E.B., Trent, S.C., Osher, D. and Ortiz, A. (2010) Justifying and explaining disproportionality, 1968–2008: A critique of underlying views of culture. *Exceptional Children* 76 (3), 279–299. https://doi.org/10.1177/001440291007600303.

Barrio, B.L., Hsiao, Y.J., Prishker, N. and Terry, C. (2018) The impact of culture on parental perceptions about autism spectrum disorders: Striving for culturally competent practices. *Multicultural Learning and Teaching* 14 (1). https://doi.org/10.1515/mlt-2016-0010.

Bialystok, E. (2009) Bilingualism: The good, the bad, and the indifferent. *Bilingualism: Language and Cognition* 12 (1), 3–11.

Bronfenbrenner, U. (1979) *The Ecology of Human Development*. Cambridge, MA: Harvard University Press.

Byers-Heinlein, K., Esposito, A.G., Winsler, A., Marian, V., Castro, D.C. and Luk, G. (2019) The case for measuring and reporting bilingualism in developmental research. *Collabra: Psychology* 5 (1), 37.

Castro, D.C. (2014) The development and early care and education of dual language learners: Establishing the state of knowledge. *Early Childhood Research Quarterly* 29, 693–698.

Castro, D.C. and Prishker, N. (2019) Early childhood education for bilingual children and the road to multilingualism. In C.P. Brown, M.B. McMullen and N. File (eds) *The Wiley Handbook of Early Childhood Care and Education* (pp. 173–196). Chichester: Wiley Blackwell.

Castro, D.C., Prishker, N., Machuca Flores, S. and Gueta Solis, L.M. (2019) Education of transnational students: The voices of students and teachers from Jalisco, Mexico. Paper presented at the Conference on Education and Culture: Cross-Border Research, March 2019. Denton: University of North Texas.

Castro, D., Hammer, C., Franco, X., Cycyk, L., Scarpino, S. and Burchinal, M. (2020) Documenting bilingual experiences in the early years: Using the CECER-DLL Child and Family and Teacher Questionnaires. *Bilingualism: Language and Cognition* 23 (5), 958–963. doi:10.1017/S1366728920000401.

Castro, D.C., García, E.E., Espinosa, L., Genesee, F., Gillanders, C., Hammer, C.S., LaForett, D., Peisner-Feinberg, E. with Rivera, A., Martinez-Beck, I., DeCourcey, W. (2012) Conceptual framework for the study of young dual language learners' development. Paper presented at the Themed Meeting of the Society of Research on Child Development, Tampa, Florida.

Chao, R.K. (1994) Beyond parental control and authoritarian parenting style: Understanding Chinese parenting through the cultural notion of training. *Child Development* 65, 1111–9. 10.2307/1131308.

Cheatham, G.A. and Barnett, J.E. (2017) Overcoming common misunderstandings about students with disabilities who are English language learners. *Intervention in School and Clinic* 53 (1), 58–63.

Cioè-Peña, M. (2017) The intersectional gap: How bilingual students in the United States are excluded from inclusion. *International Journal of Inclusive Education* 21 (9), 906–919.

Collins, B.A., Toppelberg, C.O., Suárez-Orozco, C., O'Connor, E. and Nieto-Castañon, A. (2011) Cross-sectional associations of Spanish and English competence and well-being in Latino children of immigrants in kindergarten. *International Journal of the Sociology of Language* 208 (2011), 5–23.

Comeau, L., Genesee, F. and Mendelson, M. (2010) A comparison of bilingual and monolingual children's conversational repairs. *First Language* 30, 354–374. DOI:10.1177/0142723710370530.

Dalkilic, M. (2020) A capability-oriented lens. Reframing the early years education of children with disabilities. In F. Nxumalo and C.O. Brown (eds) *Disrupting and Countering Deficits in Early Childhood Education* (pp. 67–82). New York: Routledge.

de Abreu, P.M.E., Cruz-Santos, A., Tourinho, C.J., Martin, R. and Bialystok, E. (2012) Bilingualism enriches the poor enhanced cognitive control in low-income minority children? *Psychological Science* 23 (11), 1364–1371.

de Valenzuela, J., Kay-Raining Bird, E., Parkington, K., Mirenda, P., Cain, K., MacLeod, A. and Segers, E. (2016) Access to opportunities for bilingualism for individuals with developmental disabilities: Key informant interviews. *Journal of Communication Disorders* 63, 32–46. https://doi.org/10.1016/j.jcomdis.2016.05.005.

Dewaele, J. (2012) Personality: Personality traits as independent and dependent variables. In S. Mercer, S. Ryan, and M. Williams (eds) *Psychology for Language Learning: Insights from Research, Theory and Practice* (pp. 42–57). London & Basingstoke: Palgrave Macmillan.

Espinosa, L.M. and García, E. (2012) Developmental assessment of young dual language learners with a focus on Kindergarten entry assessments: Implications for state policies. Working Paper #1. Center for Early Care and Education Research-Dual Language Learners (CECER-DLL). Chapel Hill, NC: University of North Carolina, FPG Child Development Institute.

Espinosa, L. and Calderón, M. (2015) State early learning and development standards: How responsive are they to the needs of young dual language learners? Retrieved from http://scholar.aci.info/view/1495bde276b76db0388/1531aba332b00014c21.

Espinosa, L.M., LaForett, D.R., Burchinal, M., Winsler, A., Tien, H., Peisner-Feinberg, E. and Castro, D.C. (2017) Child care experiences among dual language learners in the US: Analyses of the Early Childhood Longitudinal Study-Birth Cohort. *AERA Open* 3 (2), 1–15. DOI:10.1177/2332858417699380.

Fan, S.P., Liberman, Z., Keysar, B. and Kinzler, K.D. (2015) The exposure advantage: Early exposure to a multilingual environment promotes effective communication. *Psychological Science* 26 (7), 1090–1097.

Franceschini, R. (2013) History of multilingualism. In C.A. Chapelle (ed.) *The Encyclopedia of Applied Linguistics* (pp. 1–9). New York, NY: Blackwell Publishing. doi:10.1002/9781405198431.wbeal0511.

Gándara, P. and Escamilla, K. (2017) Bilingual education in the United States. 10.1007/978-3-319-02258-1_33.

Garcia, A. (2015) How language and immigrant background influence pre-K participation and kindergarten readiness. New America, 7 January 2015. http://devedcentral.pantheon.io/prekparticipation/.

García, S.B. and Ortiz, A.A. (2006) Preventing disproportionate representation: Culturally and linguistically responsive pre-referral interventions. *TEACHING Exceptional Children* 38 (4), 64–68. https://doi.org/10.1177/004005990603800410.

García Coll, C., Lamberty, G., Jenkins, R., McAdoo, H.P., Crnic, K., Wasik, B.H. and Vázquez García, H. (1996) An integrative model for the study of developmental competencies in minority children. *Child Development* 67 (5), 1891–1914.

Halle, T., Forry, N., Hair, E., Perper, K., Wandner, L., Wessel, J. and Vick, J. (2009) *Disparities in Early Learning and Development: Lessons from the Early Childhood Longitudinal Study – Birth Cohort (ECLS-B)*. Washington, DC: Child Trends.

Hamann, E.T. and Zúñiga, V. (2008) Transnational students in Mexican schools. *Anthropology News*, 19.

Hammer, C.S., Hoff, E., Uchikoshi, Y., Gillanders, C., Castro, D.C. and Sandilos, L.E. (2014) The language and literacy development of young dual language learners: A critical review. *Early Childhood Research Quarterly* 29, 715–733.

Harry, B. and Klingner, J. (2007) Discarding the deficit model. *Educational Leadership* 64 (5), 16–21.

Heath, S.B. (1983) *Ways with Words: Language, Life, and Work in Communities and Classrooms*. Cambridge: Cambridge University Press.

Hebbeler, K., Spiker, D. and Kahn, L. (2012) Individuals with Disabilities Education Act's early childhood programs: Powerful vision and pesky details. *Topics in Early Childhood Special Education* 31 (4), 199–207. https://doi.org/10.1177/0271121411429077.

Hughes, M.T., Valle-Riestra, D.M. and Arguelles, M.E. (2008) The voices of families raising children with special needs. *Journal of Latinos and Education* 7 (3), 241–257.

IDEA (2004) Individuals with Disabilities Education Act, 20 U.S.C. § 1400 (2004).

Jegatheesan, B. (2011) Multilingual development in children with autism: Perspectives of South Asian Muslim immigrant parents on raising a child with a communicative disorder in multilingual contexts. *Bilingual Research Journal* 34 (2), 185–200.

Kay-Raining Bird, E., Genesee, F. and Verhoeven, L. (2016) Bilingualism in children with developmental disorders: A narrative review. *Journal of Communication Disorders* 63, 1–14.

Kay-Raining Bird, E., Trudeau, N. and Sutton, A. (2016) Pulling it all together: Maximizing bilingualism in children with developmental disabilities. *Journal of Communication Disorders* 63, 63–78.

Liasidou, A. (2013) Bilingual and special educational needs in inclusive classrooms: Some critical and pedagogical considerations. *Support for Learning* 28 (1), 11–16.

Marinova-Todd, S.H., Colozzo, P., Mirenda, P., Stahl, H., Kay-Raining Bird, E., Parkington, K. and Genesee, F. (2016) Professional practices and opinions about services available to bilingual children with developmental disabilities: An international study. *Journal of Communication Disorders* 63, 47–62. https://doi.org/10.1016/j.jcomdis.2016.05.004.

McLoyd, V.C. (1990) The impact of economic hardship on black families and children: Psychological distress, parenting, and socioemotional development. *Child Development* 61 (2), 311–346.

Migge, B. and Léglise, I. (2007) Language and colonialism. Applied linguistics in the context of creole communities. In M. Hellinger and A. Pauwels (eds) *Handbook of Language and Communication: Diversity and Change* (pp. 297–338). Handbooks of Applied Linguistics 9. Berlin: Mouton de Gruyter.

National Academies of Sciences, Engineering, and Medicine (NASEM) (2017) Promoting the educational success of children and youth learning English: Promising futures. Washington, DC: National Academies Press. doi.org/10.17226/24677.

Nores, M. and Barnett, W.S. (2009) Benefits of early childhood intervention across the world: (Under) Investing in the very young. *Economics of Education Review* 29 (2), 271–282.

Paradis, J. (2016) An agenda for knowledge-oriented research on bilingualism in children with developmental disorders. *Journal of Communication Disorders* 63, 79–84. dx.doi.org/10.1016/j.jcomdis.2016.08.002.

Paris, D. (2012) Culturally sustaining pedagogy: A needed change in stance, terminology, and practice. *Educational Researcher* 41 (3), 93–97. https://doi.org/10.3102/0013189X12441244.

Park, M., O'Toole, A. and Katsiaficas, C. (2017a) *Dual Language Learners: A National Demographic and Policy Profile*. Washington, DC: Migration Policy Institute.

Park, M., O'Toole, A. and Katsiaficas, C. (2017b) *Dual Language Learners: A Demographic and Policy Profile for California*. Washington, DC: Migration Policy Institute.

Park, M., O'Toole, A. and Katsiaficas, C. (2017c) *Dual Language Learners: A Demographic and Policy Profile for Texas*. Washington, DC: Migration Policy Institute.

Park, M., O'Toole, A. and Katsiaficas, C. (2017d) *Dual Language Learners: A Demographic and Policy Profile for New Mexico*. Washington, DC: Migration Policy Institute.

Park, M., Zong, J. and Batalova, J. (2018) *Growing Superdiversity among Young US Dual Language Learners and Its Implications*. Washington, DC: Migration Policy Institute.

Pérez, M.S. and Saavedra, C.M. (2017) A call for onto-epistemological diversity in early childhood education and care: Centering Global South conceptualizations of childhood/s. *Review of Research in Education* 41 (1), 1–29. https://doi.org/10.3102/0091732X16688621.

Reese, L. and Goldenberg, C. (2006) Community contexts for literacy development of Latina/o children. *Anthropology & Education Quarterly* 37 (1), 42–61.

Riojas-Cortez, M. (2011) Culture, play, and family supporting children on the autism spectrum. *Young Children* 66 (5), 94–99.

Robinson, D., Gabriel, N. and Katchan, O. (1994) Personality and second language learning. *Personality and Individual Differences* 16 (1), 143–157.

Rodriguez, D. (2009) Meeting the needs of English language learners with disabilities in urban settings. *Urban Education* 44 (4), 452–464.

Rogoff, B. (2003) *The Cultural Nature of Human Development*. Oxford: Oxford University Press.

Rueda R. and Windmueller, M.P. (2006) English language learners, LD, and overrepresentation: A multiple-level analysis. *Journal of Learning Disabilities* 39 (2), 99–107. doi: 10.1177/00222194060390020801.

Sanatullova-Allison, E. and Robison-Young, V.A. (2016) Overrepresentation: An overview of the issues surrounding the identification of English language learners with learning disabilities. *International Journal of Special Education* 31 (2), 145–151.

Sánchez-García, J., Hamann, E.T. and Zuñiga, V. (2012) What the youngest transnational students have to say about their transition from US schools to Mexican ones. *Diaspora, Indigenous, and Minority Education* 6 (3), 157–171. DOI:10.1080/15595692.2012.691135.

Toppelberg, C.O. (2011) Promover el bilingüismo: American children should learn Spanish, and so should American child psychiatrists. *Journal of the American Academy of Child & Adolescent Psychiatry* 50 (10), 963–965.

United Nations, Department of Economic and Social Affairs, Population Division (2016) *International Migration Report 2015: Highlights* (ST/ESA/SER.A/375).

Urzúa, A. and Gómez. E. (2008) Home style Puerto Rican: A study of language maintenance and use in New England. *Journal of Multilingual and Multicultural Development* 29 (6), 449–466.

US Census Bureau (2016) Language spoken at home. American Community Survey 1 year estimates. Retrieved from https://factfinder.census.gov/faces/tableservices/jsf/pages/productview.xhtml?pid=ACS_16_1YR_S1601&prodType=table.

US Department of Education (2015) *English Learner Toolkit for SEAs and LEAs*. Washington, DC: US Department of Education.

US Department of Education (2020) *The Condition of Education. English Language Learners in Public Schools*. Washington, DC: National Center for Education Satistics. Retrieved from https://nces.ed.gov/programs/coe/indicator_cgf.asp.

Ushioda, E. (2012) Motivation: L2 learning as a special case? In S. Mercer, S. Ryan and M. Williams (eds) *Psychology forLanguage Learning: Insights from Research, Theory and Practice* (pp. 58–73). Basingstoke: Palgrave Macmillan.

Van Daele, S., Housen, A., Pierrard, M. and De Bruyn, L. (2006) The effect of extraversion on oral L2 proficiency. In S.H. Foster-Cohen, M. Medved Krajnovic and J. Mihaljević Djigunović (eds) *EUROSLA Yearbook*, 6 (pp. 213–236). Amsterdam: John Benjamins. 10.1075/eurosla.6.13dae.

Vega, D., Arellano, J.I. and Carrillo, G.L. (2016) The under-identification of autism among Latino youth: Improving culturally competent training in school psychology programs. *Trainers' Forum* 34 (1), 42–53. Retrieved from https://libproxy.library.unt.edu/login?url=https://libproxy.library.unt.edu:2165/docview/2032395527?accountid=7113.

Vygotsky, L.S. (1978) *Mind in Society. The Development of Higher Psychological Processes*. Cambridge, MA: Harvard University Press.

Wang, P. and Woolf, S. (2015) Trends in bilingual special education teacher preparation: A literature review. *Journal of Multilingual Education* 6, 35–59.

Whiting, B.B. and Whiting, J.W. (1975) *Children of Six Cultures: A Psycho-cultural Analysis*. Cambridge, MA: Harvard University Press.

Winsler, A., Burchinal, M.R., Tien, H., Peisner-Feinberg, E., Espinosa, L., Castro, D.C., LaForett, D.R., Kim, Y.K. and De Feyter, J.J. (2014) Early developmental skills of diverse dual language learners: The roles of home language use, cultural heritage, maternal immigration, and sociodemographics in the ECLS-B. *Early Childhood Research Quarterly* 29, 750–764.

Yamasaki, B.L. and Luk, G. (2018) Eligibility for special education in elementary school: The role of diverse language experiences. *Language, Speech, and Hearing Services in Schools* 49 (4), 889–901. doi:10.1044/2018_LSHSS-DYSLC-18-0006.

Yoshikawa, H. (2011) *Immigrants Raising Citizens: Undocumented Parents and their Young Children*. New York, NY: Russell Sage Foundation.

Yoshikawa, H., Weiland, C. and Brooks-Gunn, J. (2016) Why does preschool matter? *The Future of Children* 26 (2), 21–35.

Zhang, Y. (2008) The role of personality in second language acquisition. *Asian Social Science* 4 (5), 58–59.

Zhang, D., Katsiyannis, A., Ju, S. and Roberts, E. (2014) Minority representation in special education: 5-year trends. *Journal of Child & Family Studies* 23 (1), 118–127. https://doi.org/10.1007/s10826-012-9698-6.

3 How Bilingualism Affects Children's Language Development

Carol Scheffner Hammer and
Maria Cristina Limlingan

Bilingual children across the world grow up with a wide range of language experiences, which vary with the amount of exposure they have to their two languages, the contexts in which they interact, and the languages used by the people with whom they interact. In addition, children's experiences differ based on the age at which they are exposed to the two languages on a regular basis. Some children are exposed to both their languages from birth and are simultaneous language learners. Others are sequential language learners, meaning that they are not exposed to a second language until they enter school. Often, bilingual children are learning their family's heritage language and a second language that is the majority language of the country in which they live. Regardless of whether children are simultaneous or sequential language learners, bilingual children vary greatly in their abilities to understand and speak their two languages. Some children will have stronger abilities in their heritage language and weaker abilities in the majority language. Others will have relatively equal abilities in their two languages. Still others will have stronger abilities in the majority language and weaker abilities in their heritage language.

In schools throughout the United States, bilingual children are typically compared to, and expected to perform like, monolingual children. There are at several reasons for this. First, the majority of children in classrooms are monolingual; however, this is changing. Currently, bilinguals constitute the fastest growing population entering the educational system in the United States. Approximately, 30% of children speak a language other than English at home (US Census Bureau, 2013).

Second, bilingual education in the United States is still a relatively new phenomenon. The first piece of federal legislation that attended to the educational needs of bilingual children, the Bilingual Education

Act (Title VII) of the Elementary and Secondary Education Act, was not passed until 1968. However, in more recent decades several states, including California, Arizona and Massachusetts, have passed English-only education laws, which have limited or eliminated education in children's heritage languages. Fortunately, some of these states have reversed that legislation.

Third, across grade levels and across states, many teachers have received limited training on bilingual children's development and how to support children's language skills. Only recently have some states begun to require all preservice teachers take a course on multiculturalism and multilingualism. However, many of these courses focus on demographics and broader cultural topics, as opposed to also providing teachers with information on how to support the language development of bilingual children. Thus, most teachers do not have the knowledge that they need.

Fourth, compounding the previously discussed problem, the preponderance of research on language development has focused on monolingual children. There is a paucity of research on bilingual children's language development. To illustrate this point, a recent review of literature on all areas of language and literacy from 2000 to 2011 found that only 182 articles were published in English on the development of bilingual children from birth through age 5 (Hammer et al., 2014). A companion review found only 25 studies investigating the effectiveness of classroom-based interventions for bilingual children in the United States during the same time period (Buysse et al., 2014). Due to the paucity of research on bilinguals, educators and researchers have a rather limited understanding of bilingual children's language development and how best to support their development.

Finally, few assessments are normed on bilingual children, and most of those that do exist are for Spanish speakers. Additionally, most tests of English language abilities are not normed on bilingual children. In the United States, only one test of English exists that has been normed on bilingual children, and, more importantly, the high-stakes state-level assessments are not standardized on bilingual samples. This lack of assessment instruments makes it difficult to study and understand bilingual children's development without using monolingual children as a reference group.

Although there are many reasons why bilingual children have been compared to monolinguals, bilinguals should not be expected to perform like monolinguals. As Grosjean (1989) asserted three decades ago, bilinguals are not two monolinguals in one. The purpose of this chapter is to support this point by presenting key findings on bilingual children's language development that illustrate how bilingualism affects young children's language skills, describe the characteristics of language disorders in bilingual children, and identify the factors that impact children's development. We conclude by discussing the implications of these findings for helping bilingual children. One caveat should be noted. Within the chapter, research that compares bilinguals to monolinguals is included. This is because researchers have had to use assessments standardized on monolinguals due to the lack of assessments for bilinguals. However, this research will be used to make the argument that educators and researchers should not expect bilingual development to mirror that of monolinguals.

Bilingual Children's Language Development

In this section, we summarize findings about bilingual children's language development, focusing on phonological, vocabulary, grammatical, and pragmatic development. We conclude the section by discussing research that has examined the relations between children's two languages.

Phonological development

Evidence shows that bilingual infants are able to discriminate between the speech sounds of their two languages (Bosch & Sebastián-Gallés, 2001), indicating that they have two language systems early in life. As the ability to produce sounds develops, bilingual toddlers' phonological or speech sound development progresses in a similar way to that of monolingual children in their more dominant language (Kehoe, 2002). Development of their less dominant language appears to occur at a slower pace. However, preliminary evidence suggests that bilingual toddlers may be at an advantage over monolinguals, as they are better able to learn complex speech sound patterns (Kovács & Mehler, 2009).

Bilingual children appear to catch up to monolingual children in their speech sound development in both languages during the preschool years. Children learning various languages such as Spanish, Russian, and Chinese, and growing up in different countries, have similarly sized speech sound repertoires as monolingual children who speak those languages (e.g., Fabiano-Smith & Barlow, 2010; Gildersleeve-Neumann & Wright, 2010; Lin & Johnson, 2010). Additionally, the accuracy with which bilingual children produce the speech sounds of their two languages is high, although accuracy tends to be higher for sounds that are shared between children's two languages (Fabiano-Smith & Goldstein, 2010).

Vocabulary development

Bilingual children's vocabularies are a good indication of language development, as research has found that early vocabulary development predicts later grammatical and cognitive skills (Conboy & Thal, 2006; Marchman *et al.*, 2004; Parra *et al.*, 2011; Tamis-LeMonda *et al.*,

2014). Several studies have shown that bilingual children's individual vocabularies are smaller to those of their monolingual peers when they are toddlers and when only one language is considered (Hoff et al., 2012; Place & Hoff, 2011; Poulin-Dubois et al., 2013; Vagh et al., 2009). For example, Poulin-Dubois et al. (2013) found that 24-month-old French-English bilinguals developed an expressive vocabulary size in their first language that was smaller than that of monolinguals. It is important to note that even though bilingual toddlers may have smaller vocabularies in each language, the size of their individual vocabularies is typically within the normal range of variation for monolingual children (Pearson et al., 1993; Vagh et al., 2009). Additionally, some studies have found no difference between bilingual toddlers' individual vocabulary size in their dominant language and monolinguals' vocabulary size. For instance, De Houwer et al. (2014) found no difference in the number of words produced by Dutch-French bilingual children at 13 and 20 months.

Additional evidence shows that bilingual children's vocabulary size is comparable to that of monolinguals when their conceptual vocabulary, which takes into account the number of concepts known across languages, is measured (Pearson et al., 1993; Poulin-Dubois et al., 2013). Recently, however, it has been argued that it may be more appropriate to measure bilingual children's total vocabulary or to determine the number of words produced in each language (Hoff et al., 2014). The rationale for favoring total vocabulary over conceptual vocabulary is that conceptual vocabulary scores may underestimate bilingual children's word knowledge (Core et al., 2013). For example, when calculating a conceptual score, a child would be given only one point for knowing "pan" in Spanish, as would a child who produced both "pan" and "bread." When calculating a total score, a child who produced both "pan" and "bread" would receive credit for both words, which acknowledges the fact that the child has learned the two phonological forms (i.e., sound combinations) as well as the semantic representations of the words in their two languages. Core et al. (2013) demonstrated how 22–30-months old Spanish-English bilingual children's vocabulary size and average rate of growth was similar to that of their monolingual peers when total vocabulary was used as a measure. However, when conceptual vocabulary was used, both bilingual children's vocabulary sizes and rate of growth were found to be significantly smaller and slower than total vocabulary scores. Thus, total vocabulary may be a preferable method for determining vocabulary size, particularly during the toddler period, when it is possible to capture more systematically children's individual word knowledge.

As children enter the preschool years, differences in their vocabulary development emerge between bilingual groups and monolinguals depending on the socioeconomic status (SES) and the type of input that children receive. For example, studies of bilingual children in Head

Start, a preschool program in the United States that serves children from low-SES homes, have shown that Spanish-English speaking bilinguals begin and end preschool with vocabulary scores in their individual languages that are below those of their monolingual peers (e.g., Hammer *et al.*, 2008; Tabors *et al.*, 2003). However, when studying children from high-SES families, Hoff and colleagues (2014) found that Spanish-English bilingual children with two native Spanish-speaking parents showed higher gains in their total vocabulary from 22 to 48 months of age than bilingual children with only one native Spanish-speaking parent.

Differences have also been found among bilinguals' development depending on when they were first exposed to English on a regular basis. Hammer *et al.* (2008) demonstrated that sequential language learners had higher rates of growth in both Spanish and English than simultaneous language learners during two years in preschool.

Grammatical development

In comparison with studies of children's phonological and vocabulary development, relatively few studies have investigated the grammatical development of bilingual children. The extant research has shown that bilingual children learn the grammatical rules of their two languages and do not confuse the rules. For example, children who speak a language where a subject is not required to be expressed once the referent has been established (e.g., Spanish, Catalan, and Italian) did not have difficulty learning that subjects needed to be expressed in their other language (e.g., English) (Juan-Garau & Pérez-Vidal, 2000; Serratrice *et al.*, 2004; Silva Corvalán, 2007).

Also, bilingual children generally acquire the morphemes in their languages in the same order as monolinguals (Bland-Stewart & Fitzgerald, 2001; Nicoladis & Marchak, 2011). However, one study investigating Spanish-English bilingual children's acquisition of English morphemes found some differences in the order of acquisition in comparison to monolingual norms (Davison & Hammer, 2012). Although bilingual children's grammatical development follows the same general progression as monolinguals, bilingual children's development may be slower than that of monolinguals. For example, Schwartz *et al.* (2015) found that the Russian morphological development of 4–5-year-old bilingual children who spoke various second languages was qualitatively similar to the development of 3–4-year-old monolingual children.

As all children learn language, they make production errors. Research has shown that the grammatical errors made by typically developing bilingual children who are in the process of acquiring English produce errors in verb morphology that are similar to the errors produced by English-speaking monolingual children with developmental language disorder (has now replaced specific language impairment in the research literature) (Paradis *et al.*, 2011). This makes determining which children truly have a language disorder challenging; however, errors produced by children with language disorders will persist over time.

Bilingual children's grammatical development in each language is strongly influenced by the degree of exposure they have to each language. A recent study by Thordardottir (2015) demonstrated that French-English bilingual children who had equal exposure to their two languages had morphological skills that were similar to monolingual children who spoke their respective languages. Children who did not have equal exposure to their languages demonstrated unequal morphological skills, with their skills being stronger in the language to which they had more exposure.

Pragmatic development

Although bilingual children's pragmatic development has not received much attention, there is evidence to suggest that differences exist in the way that bilingual children use pragmatic cues to understand a speaker's message in comparison to monolingual children (e.g., Brojde *et al.*, 2012; Yow & Markman, 2011). Early on, bilingual children begin to understand that they are learning multiple language systems and realize that they need to adapt their language to meet the needs of their conversational partners, who will have varying levels of language proficiency. It is theorized that this additional awareness heightens bilinguals' sensitivity to pragmatic cues, such as gestures, facial expression, and tone of voice, so they are able to better understand a speaker's communicative intentions.

When pragmatic cues are congruent with the verbal message of the speaker, both monolingual and bilingual children can use these cues to understand what their conversational partner is trying to say (Yow & Markman, 2011). However, communication becomes more challenging when children have access to multiple cues simultaneously or when the verbal message is inconsistent with the non-linguistic cues the speaker is displaying. For example, Yow and Markman (2011) found that while both monolingual and bilingual children were able to judge emotions when a speaker's content and tone of voice were consistent, bilingual children were better at judging emotion in situations when the content conflicted with the speaker's tone of voice. Additionally, Brojde *et al.* (2012) found that when there were conflicting cues, bilingual children were more likely to attend to pragmatic cues compared to monolingual children, who used object property cues regardless of whether the other cues were consistent or not. Additional evidence from Groba and colleagues (2018) shows that at a neurological level, bilingual children process pragmatic cues differently from monolingual children, with bilingual children having heighted sensitivity to these cues during word learning. Thus, bilingual children appear to have an advantage in the area of pragmatics.

Relations between children's languages

As suggested in earlier sections of this chapter, bilingual children have two language systems, and these systems are developed early in life. Evidence from this comes from studies on children's early phonological, lexical, grammatical, and pragmatic development. A number of studies on children's phonological development have shown that children's speech sound systems are separate (e.g., Fabiano-Smith & Barlow, 2010; Fabiano & Goldstein, 2010; Gildersleeve-Neumann et al., 2009; Goldstein et al., 2005); however, these studies have also identified cross-linguistic effects between the two languages. This means that some characteristics of one language can be observed when a child is speaking in the other language. Studies have suggested that the dominant language has greater effects on the non-dominant language than vice versa but that these effects disappear over time (Fabiano-Smith & Barlow, 2010; Gildersleeve-Neumann & Wright, 2010; Lin & Johnson, 2010).

Additionally, studies of children's vocabulary development have demonstrated that bilingual children may learn words in each language that represent a single concept, thus demonstrating the presence of two language systems (Pearson et al., 1995; Schelletter, 2002). If children had only one system, they would only need to learn a single word for a given concept. However, it should be noted that children's semantic representation of a concept may differ in each language, because of cultural and linguistic differences between the two languages. Findings from studies of children's grammatical and pragmatic development also support the conclusion that children have two language systems. These studies have shown that children can learn and apply grammatical and pragmatic rules of their two languages appropriately (e.g., Comeau et al., 2007; Serratrice et al., 2004; Silva-Corvalán, 2007).

Complementing these findings are the results of studies on coding switching, which have shown that bilingual children use adult-like structural constraints of their two languages when constructing utterances containing both languages (Paradis et al., 2011). However, language dominance appears to affect children's code switching, with children using their stronger language to fill in gaps in their weaker language (Bernardini & Schylter, 2004). Related to this, children may code switch as a compensatory strategy by using a vocabulary word from one language when they do not know the word in the language that they are currently speaking (Wei & Lee, 2001).

The Language Interdependence theory of Cummins (1979) proposes that children's abilities in one language may transfer to their other language once a level of proficiency in a language has been reached. Cummins posited that bilinguals have common cross-linguistic proficiencies that underlie the surface structures that they produce. These relations may be language independent, meaning that there are underlying cognitive-linguistic skills that are independent of the structure of the language and function similarly across languages. An example of language independent skills is phonological sensitivity, which has been shown to transfer across languages regardless of their structure (Durgunoğlu et al., 1993). Relations may also be language dependent, meaning that the skills are shared across languages that have similar features. An example of language dependent skills includes grammatical structure, where transfer is dependent on the degree of similarity of the structures of the two languages being spoken (Edele & Stanat, 2016). For instance, Spanish and English are similar in that both languages use articles before nouns (e.g, a/un, the/el or la), use pronouns that differ based on gender (e.g., he/él, and she/ella) and number (e.g., he/él, they/ellos, and she/ella they/ellas), and mark nouns as being singular or plural (e.g., dog/dogs, perro/perros). These similarities in the grammatical structures allow for transfer. Mandarin, however, differs from Spanish and English in that pronouns are rarely used in spoken language and, when they are, the word for he and she is the same. Additionally, nouns are not marked as being plural to indicate more than one. As a result, transfer of these structures is not possible, because these structures do not exist in Mandarin.

Language Disorders in Bilingual Children

Having discussed typical language development, we now discuss language disorders in bilingual children. Research in this area has focused on children with specific language impairment and children with developmental disorders. Before beginning this discussion, it is important to highlight that there is no evidence that bilingualism causes language disorders in children. Children with language disorders would have a disorder whether they were monolingual or bilingual (Kohnert, 2013).

Developmental language disorder in bilingual children

Developmental language disorder (DLD) is a deficit in language learning in the presence of typical cognitive abilities and hearing. Approximately 7% of monolingual children have DLD, and it is reasonable to assume that the same percentage of bilingual children would be affected with the disorder, although no studies have systematically explored this question (Kohnert, 2013).

An underlying deficit in processing language is thought to be the main cause of DLD, which results in difficulties in expressive and receptive language. Deficits in morphosyntactic or grammatical skills are the primary characteristic of the disorder. The nature of grammatical errors produced by speakers of various languages reflects the characteristics of the particular language spoken. For example, English-speaking children with DLD have difficulty with verbal morphology (e.g., third person singular –s; e.g., *says*). This is because English has a sparse verb morphology, which means that English has only a few inflected verb morphemes. Because there are few morphemes used to inflect verbs, these morphemes are not highly salient and are likely to be omitted. In contrast, Spanish has a richer morphology than English, in which all verbs are marked for person, number, mood, and tense, making the morphemes highly salient. Spanish-speaking children with DLD do not have problems with verb morphology given the saliency of the Spanish verb morphology. Instead, Spanish-speaking children with DLD experience problems with less salient morphemes, such as articles and clitic pronouns (Restrepo & Gutiérrez-Clellen, 2012).

In general, studies of the characteristics of DLD in bilingual children show that bilingual children with DLD produce morphosyntactic errors that are similar to their monolingual peers with DLD who speak the children's respective languages (e.g., Armon-Lotem *et al.*, 2015; Bedore & Peña, 2008; Kay-Raining Bird, 2016; Restrepo & Gutiérrez-Clellen, 2012). This holds for both simultaneous learners and sequential learners, once sequential learners have received sufficient exposure to the second language (Paradis *et al.*, 2011). Additionally, the gap between the language skills of bilingual children with DLD and their bilingual peers with typical development is similar to the gap between the skills of monolingual children with DLD and their peers with typical development.

Similar to monolingual children with DLD, bilingual children with DLD may have difficulty with vocabulary development, having shallow semantic representations and poorly linked semantic networks (Bedore & Peña, 2008). They can also have difficulty producing narratives. Specifically, children may not provide sufficient background information and may have problems expressing temporal, causal, spatial, or referential relations to create coherence (Gutiérrez-Clellen, 2012). Children with DLD also display difficulties performing non-linguistic cognitive processing tasks (Kohnert, 2013); however, their pragmatic and code-switching abilities are often not affected (Gutiérrez-Clellen *et al.*, 2009).

Language disorders in bilingual children with developmental disorders

The two most commonly studied developmental disorders in bilingual children are Down syndrome (DS), a genetic disorder affecting all areas of development, and autism spectrum disorders (ASD), a pervasive disorder affecting social and communication abilities. Although there is a paucity of research on bilingual children with developmental disorders, the extant research has demonstrated that the language development of bilingual children with DS and with ASD is very similar to that of monolingual children with these disorders. Similar to children with SLI, learning two languages does not delay the language development of bilingual children with DS and ASD (e.g., Kay-Raining Bird, 2016; Marinova-Todd & Mirenda, 2016).

Factors that Affect Bilingual Children's Language Abilities

A number of factors affect bilingual children's language abilities. First and foremost, children's experience with language, which includes their exposure to and usage of their two languages, influences their abilities in each language. Furthermore, characteristics of the family and the home literacy environment also play a role. These factors are discussed in the sections that follow.

Bilingual children's language experiences

As mentioned earlier, the abilities of bilingual children in their two languages can vary greatly. These differences are largely due to the age that the children were first exposed to their second language, as well as the frequency of exposure to and usage of their two languages on an ongoing basis.

Age of exposure has been found to affect both the level of children's abilities in their two languages and the growth of the two languages. For example, a longitudinal study of bilingual preschoolers found that children who were exposed to both Spanish and English from birth (e.g., simultaneous learners) began preschool with higher abilities in English and lower abilities in Spanish than their peers who were not exposed to English until school entry at age 3 (e.g., sequential learners). However, sequential learners exhibited faster rates of vocabulary growth in both Spanish and English than simultaneous learners (Hammer *et al.*, 2008). Similarly, Golberg *et al.* (2008) found that later exposure to English, the children's second language, was associated with faster vocabulary growth rates in English.

Additionally, the amount of each language used by various family members and teachers when talking with children has a strong effect on children's language abilities. Studies have demonstrated that children from low-income homes whose mothers spoke more Spanish than English to them had higher abilities in Spanish as compared to children whose mothers spoke less Spanish to them, and that children whose mothers spoke more English to them had higher English language abilities than children with less exposure to English (Bohman *et al.*, 2010; Hammer *et al.*, 2012; Place & Hoff, 2011; Quiroz *et al.*, 2010). Similar results have been found for children from high-income homes (Hoff et al., 2012).

Also, continued usage of more Spanish than English or all Spanish by mothers during the preschool and kindergarten years has been shown to result in faster Spanish vocabulary growth than when mothers used more English or all English with their bilingual children. However, continued usage of more or all English did not result in higher rates of English vocabulary or emergent literacy growth. It was thought that if children had sufficient exposure to English in their preschool and kindergarten classrooms, usage of English at home did not result in faster English growth as compared to children whose mothers spoke primarily Spanish to them (Hammer et al., 2009).

Studies have also shown that the amount of Spanish and English that fathers speak to their children has an impact on their language abilities (Hammer et al., 2012). Specifically, Hammer et al. (2012) found that fathers' Spanish usage positively impacted children's Spanish vocabulary abilities, with fathers' language usage being the largest contributor to children's Spanish abilities out of a number of factors, including maternal language usage. Complementing this finding, Veltman (1983) reported that when fathers spoke English and mothers spoke Spanish, children living in the United States were more likely to be English monolinguals, whereas when mothers spoke English and fathers spoke Spanish, only 20% of children were English monolinguals.

Whether or not parents are native speakers of a language seems to impact their influence on children's language development. A longitudinal study of high-income families showed that children with two native Spanish-speaking parents showed steeper gains in total vocabulary between 24 and 48 months of age than children with one native Spanish-speaking parent. When considering children's Spanish and English vocabularies separately, children with two native Spanish-speaking parents had greater growth in Spanish vocabulary, whereas children with one native Spanish-speaking and one native English-speaking parent showed consistently higher English vocabularies (Hoff et al., 2014).

Although few studies have examined the role of language exposure provided by siblings, preliminary evidence suggests that having an older sibling affects the younger sibling's language skills. Bridges and Hoff (2014) found that young bilingual children with school-age bilingual siblings had smaller Spanish vocabularies and larger English vocabularies than young bilingual children who did not have older bilingual siblings.

Children's language abilities can also be affected by settings outside the home, and, in particular, the school setting. Initial evidence shows that teachers' usage of children's heritage language in the classroom supports children's vocabulary development in that language (Hammer *et al.*, 2012). Additionally, several studies conducted in the United States have demonstrated that teacher usage of the majority language negatively impacts children's heritage language abilities (Hammer *et al.*, 2012).

In addition to language exposure, a small body of evidence indicates that children's usage of their languages also affects their language development. Specifically, Bohman *et al.* (2010) showed that bilingual kindergartners who used more English than Spanish had more advanced semantic and morphosyntactic abilities in English, and children who used more Spanish than English exhibited greater Spanish language abilities. Additionally, Hammer *et al.* (2012) found that children's usage of English with their fathers and teachers and usage of Spanish with their mothers had the largest impact on children's English and Spanish vocabularies, respectively, than other factors that were considered, including children's language exposure. Bohman *et al.* (2010: 339) hypothesized that "using a language forces the learner to process the language in a way that only hearing it does not."

Characteristics of the family and home

Emerging research has shown that a number of familial factors influence bilingual children's development. As would be expected, maternal education is one of those factors. Several studies have shown that higher maternal education is related to higher English language development (Bohman *et al.*, 2010; Golberg *et al.*, 2008; Hammer *et al.*, 2012). Surprisingly, when studied in conjunction with other factors, including maternal education, paternal education has not been found to make a significant contribution to children's language development. Additionally, contrary to expectations, maternal and paternal education has not been found to be related to children's heritage language abilities, when studying children from Spanish-speaking children in the United States (Hammer *et al.*, 2012). It is thought that higher education may reflect that mothers were more likely to have attended school in the United States. As a result, the mothers are more familiar with the educational system, which places importance on English, and thus, mothers are more likely to speak English to their children.

Additionally, the generational status of the family, or the number of generations that have lived in the United States, has been found to relate to bilinguals' abilities to speak their languages. Several large-scale studies have shown that individuals from the first generation sustain their usage of their heritage language, with a subset acquiring English over time. Individuals in the second generation often acquire both Spanish and English, whereas individuals in the third generation use English as their primary language, with many having lost their heritage language (Hurtado & Vega, 2004; Portes & Hao, 1998; Veltman, 1983). Focusing more specifically on young children's language development, a more recent study showed that generational status had an impact on children's Spanish vocabulary development. Children from families who arrived more recently had stronger Spanish abilities than children whose families had been living in the United States for two or more generations. Generational status, however, did not play a role in their English vocabulary (Hammer *et al.*, 2012).

Mothers' English language proficiency also appears to impact bilingual children's language abilities, although this factor has received relatively little attention in the research literature. One study conducted in Wales found that parents' proficiency in their two languages was related to the language(s) used by parents and children when speaking to one another (Gathercole & Thomas, 2007). In the United States, another study found that mothers' self-rated English proficiency was positively related to children's English vocabulary and negatively related to children's Spanish vocabulary (Hammer *et al.*, 2012).

There is also early evidence that maternal depression can negatively affect children's language growth, particularly in their heritage language. Two studies, one conducted in the United States with Spanish-English speaking preschoolers (Cycyk *et al.*, 2015) and one conducted in Germany with Turkish-German speaking school-aged children (Willard *et al.*, 2019), found that maternal depressive symptomology slowed children's rate of growth of their heritage language vocabulary. In general, it is thought that mothers who are depressed provide children with fewer opportunities to interact with them, and, when they do interact with their children, their manner can be more abrupt and irritable, which in turn negatively impacts language development. In should be noted that the study involving Spanish-English speaking children also investigated children's development of the majority language and found no impact on children's English development. It was hypothesized that the children, who attended schools where English was the language of instruction, received sufficient support in English from teachers and peers that their mothers' depression did not negatively affect their English abilities.

In addition to maternal and family characteristics, the home literacy environment also promotes children's language development. Multiple studies have found that the frequency of book reading, telling stories, taking children to the library and engaging them in language and emergent literacy activities promotes children's vocabulary, comprehension, and narrative skills (Bitetti & Hammer, 2016; Farver *et al.*, 2006; Gonzalez & Uhing, 2008; Lewis *et al.*, 2016).

Implications

As has been illustrated throughout this chapter, aspects of bilingual children's language development are distinct from those of monolingual children. This has implications for educators and researchers. First, given that bilingual children are developing skills in two languages rather than just one, comparisons should not be made between bilinguals and monolinguals. As discussed, it is important to remember that in some areas of language, bilingual children's language development may progress at a different rate than monolinguals, and that bilinguals' development may follow a slightly different progression. This, however, does not mean that bilinguals' development is deficient or problematic. Children are simply becoming bilingual. In other areas, such as pragmatics, bilingual children may be at an advantage over monolingual children, and certainly, they are at an advantage over monolinguals overall, because they are learning two languages. Having knowledge of two languages provides them with great occupational and economic opportunities, among many advantages. Thus, knowing two or more languages should be celebrated.

Second, because bilingual children have two separate language systems starting very early in life, they are not confused by learning two languages and can use their abilities in one language to support the development of their other language. Because of this, bilingual children should not be discouraged from using their two languages. Instead, they should be encouraged to learn both languages and should receive high quality language instruction in both languages to assist them in doing so. This applies to bilingual children who are typically developing, as well as to children with language disorders. Being bilingual does not change the nature of the language disorder nor does it affect children's abilities to learn two languages (Kay-Raining Bird, 2016). Discouraging bilingual children with language disorders from speaking one of their languages does not improve their abilities in their remaining language, nor does it remediate the disorder (Kohnert, 2013). Importantly, bilingual children need both of their languages to communicate in their schools, homes, and communities. Taking away their heritage languages may impede their ability to interact with family and members of their community. This, in turn, may harm their relationships with those individuals and may negatively impact children's cultural identities (Patterson, 2016).

Third, if concerns exist about an individual child's development, that child's skills should be compared to a normative sample of bilingual children who speak the same languages. Tests normed on monolinguals should not be used. Admittedly, this recommendation is difficult to follow because of the lack of tests that are standardized on bilingual children; however, methods for assessing bilingual children are discussed in Chapter 6.

Finally, to understand bilingual children's language development, it is essential that information about their language experiences and their families' characteristics be gathered, because these factors affect their abilities in their two languages. This is true when working with children in educational programs as well as when including groups of children in research projects. In order to determine to whom research findings apply, well described samples are required. Specifically, it is critical to obtain information on families about the ages at which children were first exposed to their languages on a regular basis and the current amount of exposure and usage that children experience when speaking with parents, siblings, grandparents, and teachers. Once rapport has been established with families, it is helpful to learn about the mother's level of education, generational status, and language proficiency as well as the frequency with which family members engage children in language and literacy activities. Such information can greatly assist in understanding children's language development and potential differences between children's skills in their two languages, in determining whether children have language disorders, and in understanding differences among bilingual children. Additionally, it is important to look for signs of maternal depression and to make referrals as appropriate, because maternal depression can affect children's language development and mothers' overall well-being and parenting skills. Through all this information, a better understanding of bilinguals' development can be achieved.

References

Armon-Lotem, S., de Jong, J. and Meir, N. (2015) *Assessing Multilingual Children: Disentangling Bilingualism from Language Impairment*. Bristol: Multilingual Matters.

Bedore, L.M. and Peña, E.D. (2008) Assessment of bilingual children for identification of language impairment: Current findings and implications for practice. *International Journal of Bilingual Education and Bilingualism* 11 (1), 1–29.

Bernardini, P. and Schlyter, S. (2004) Growing syntactic structure and code-mixing in the weaker language: The Ivy Hypothesis. *Bilingualism: Language and Cognition* 7 (1), 49–69.

Bitetti, D. and Hammer, C.S. (2016) The home literacy environment and the English narrative development of Spanish-English bilingual children. *Journal of Speech, Language and Hearing Research* 59, 1159–1171.

Bland-Stewart, L.M. and Fitzgerald, S.M. (2001) Use of Brown's 14 grammatical morphemes by bilingual Hispanic preschoolers: A pilot study. *Communication Disorders Quarterly* 22, 171.

Bohman, T.M., Bedore, L.M., Peña, E.D., Mendez-Perez, A. and Gillam, R.B. (2010) What you hear and what you say: Language performance in Spanish–English bilinguals. *International Journal of Bilingual Education and Bilingualism* 13 (3), 325–344.

Bosch, L. and Sebastián-Gallés, N. (2001) Evidence of early language discrimination abilities in infants from bilingual environments. *Infancy* 2, 29–49.

Bridges, K. and Hoff, E. (2014) Older sibling influences on the language environment and language development of toddlers in bilingual homes. *Applied Psycholinguistics* 35 (2), 225–241.

Brojde, C., Colunga, E. and Ahmed, S. (2012) Bilingual and monolingual children attend to different cues when learning new words. *Frontiers in Psychology* 3.

Buysse, V., Peisner-Feinberg, E., Páez, M., Hammer, C.S. and Knowles, M. (2014) Effects of early education programs and practices on the development and learning of dual language learners: A review of the literature. *Early Childhood Research Quarterly* 29 (4), 765–785.

Comeau, L., Genesee, F. and Mendelson, M. (2007) Bilingual children's repairs of breakdowns in communication. *Journal of Child Language* 34 (1), 159–74.

Conboy, B.T. and Thal, D.J. (2006) Ties between the lexicon and grammar: Cross-sectional and longitudinal studies of bilingual toddlers. *Child Development* 77, 712–735.

Core, C., Hoff, E., Rumiche, R. and Señor, M. (2013) Total and conceptual vocabulary in Spanish-English bilinguals from 22 to 30 months: Implications for assessment. *Journal of Speech, Language and Hearing Research* 56, 1637–1649.

Cummins, J. (1979) Linguistic interdependence and the educational development of bilingual children. *Review of Educational Research* 49, 222–251.

Cycyk, L.M., Hammer, C.S. and Bitetti, D. (2015) Maternal depressive symptomatology, social support, and language development of bilingual preschoolers from low-income households. *American Journal of Speech-Language Pathology* 24, 411–425.

Davison, M.D. and Hammer, C.S. (2012) Development of 14 English grammatical morphemes in Spanish-English preschoolers. *Clinical Linguistics and Phonetics* 26, 728–742.

De Houwer, A., Bornstein, M.H. and Putnick, D.L. (2014) A bilingual-monolingual comparison of young children's vocabulary size: Evidence from comprehension and production. *Applied Psycholinguistics* 35, 1189–1211.

Durgunoğlu, A., Nagy, W. and Hancin-Bhatt, B. (1993) Cross-langauge transfer of phonological awareness. *Journal of Educational Psychology* 85, 453–465.

Edele, A. and Stanat, P. (2016) The role of first-language listening comprehension in second-language reading comprehension. *Journal of Educational Psychology* 108, 163–180.

Fabiano-Smith, L. and Barlow, J.A. (2010) Interaction in bilingual phonological acquisition: Evidence from phonetic inventories. *International Journal of Bilingual Education and Bilingualism* 13, 81–97.

Fabiano-Smith, L. and Goldstein, B.A. (2010) Early-, middle-, and late-developing sounds in monolingual and bilingual children: An exploratory investigation. *American Journal of Speech-Language Pathology* 19, 66–77.

Farver, J.A.M., Xu, Y., Eppe, S. and Lonigan, C.J. (2006) Home environments and young Latino children's school readiness. *Early Childhood Research Quarterly* 21, 196–212.

Gathercole, V. and Thomas, E. (2007) Factors contributing to language transmission in bilingual families: The core study – adult interviews. In V. Gathercole (ed.) *Language Transmission in Bilingual Families in Wales* (pp. 59–182). Bangor: University of Wales/Welsh Language Board.

Gildersleeve-Neumann, C.E. and Wright, K.L. (2010) English speech acquisition in 3- to 5-year-old children learning Russian and English. *Language, Speech and Hearing Services in Schools* 41 (4), 429–444.

Gildersleeve-Neumann, C., Peña, E.D., Davis, B.L. and Kester, E.S. (2009) Effects on L1 during early acquisition of L2: Speech changes in Spanish at first English contact. *Bilingualism* 12, 259–272.

Golberg, H., Paradis, J. and Crago, M. (2008) Lexical acquisition over time in minority first language children learning English as a second language. *Applied Psycholinguistics* 29, 41–65.

Goldstein, B.A., Fabiano, L. and Washington, P.S. (2005) Phonological skills in predominantly English-speaking, predominantly Spanish-speaking, and Spanish-English bilingual children. *Language, Speech and Hearing Services in Schools* 36, 201–18.

Gonzalez, J.E. and Uhing, B.M. (2008) Home literacy environments and young Hispanic children's English and Spanish oral language: A communality analysis. *Journal of Early Intervention* 30, 116–139.

Groba, A., Houwer, A.D., Mehnert, J., Rossi, S. and Obrig, H. (2018) Bilingual and monolingual children process pragmatic cues differently when learning novel adjectives. *Bilingualism: Language and Cognition* 21 (2), 384–402. Published online by Cambridge University Press 25 May 2017.

Grosjean, F. (1989) Neurolinguists, beware! The bilingual is not two monolinguals in one person. *Brain and Language* 36, 3–15.

Gutiérrez-Clellen, V. (2012) Narrative development and disorders in bilingual children. In B. Goldstein (ed.) *Bilingual Language Development and Disorders in Spanish-English Speakers* (pp. 233–250). Baltimore, MD: Brookes Publishing.

Gutiérrez-Clellen, V., Simon-Cereijido, G. and Leone, A. (2009) Codeswitching in bilingual children with specific language impairment. *International Journal of Bilingualism* 13, 91–109.

Hammer, C.S., Lawrence, F.R. and Miccio, A.W. (2008) Exposure to English before and after entry into Head Start: Bilingual children's receptive language growth in Spanish and English. *International Journal of Bilingual Education and Bilingualism* 11, 30–56.

Hammer, C.S., Davison, M.D., Lawrence, F.R. and Miccio, A.W. (2009) The effect of maternal language on bilingual children's vocabulary and emergent literacy development during Head Start and kindergarten. *Scientific Studies of Reading* 13, 99–121.

Hammer, C.S., Komaroff, E., Rodriguez, B.L., Lopez, L.M., Scarpino, S.E. and Goldstein, B. (2012) Predicting Spanish-English bilingual children's language abilities. *Journal of Speech, Language and Hearing Research* 55, 1251–1264.

Hammer, C.S., Hoff, E., Uchikoshi, Y., Gillanders, C., Castro, D.C. and Sandilos, L.E. (2014) The language and literacy development of young dual language learners: A critical review. *Early Childhood Research Quarterly* 29, 715–733.

Hoff, E., Rumiche, R., Burridge, A., Ribot, K.M. and Welsh, S.N. (2014) Expressive vocabulary development in children from bilingual and monolingual homes: A longitudinal study from two to four years. *Early Childhood Research Quarterly* 29, 433–444.

Hoff, E., Core, C., Place, S., Rumiche, R., Senor, M. and Parra, M. (2012) Dual language exposure and early bilingual development. *Journal of Child Language* 39, 1–27.

Hurtado, A. and Vega, L. (2004) Shift happens: Spanish and English transmission between parents and their children. *Journal of Social Issues* 60, 137–155.

Juan-Garau, M. and Pérez-Vidal, C. (2000) Subject realization in the syntactic development of a bilingual child. *Bilingualism: Language and Cognition* 3, 173–191.

Kay-Raining Bird, E. (2016) Bilingualism and children with Down syndrome. In J.L. Patterson and B.L. Rodríguez (eds) *Multilingual Perspectives on Child Language Disorders* (pp. 49–73). Bristol: Multilingual Matters.

Kehoe, M. (2002) Developing vowel systems as a window to bilingual phonology. *International Journal of Bilingualism* 6, 315–334.

Kohnert, K. (2013) *Language Disorders in Bilingual Children and Adults* (2nd edn). San Diego, CA: Plural Publishing.

Kovács, Á.M. and Mehler, J. (2009) Flexible learning of multiple speech structures in bilingual infants. *Science* 325, 611–612.

Lewis, K., Hammer, C.S., Sandilos, L., Sawyer, B. and Mendez, L. (2016) Relations among the home language and literacy environment and children's language abilities: A study of Head Start dual language learners and their mothers. *Early Education and Development* 27, 478–494.

Lin, L.C. and Johnson, C.J. (2010) Phonological patterns in Mandarin-English bilingual children. *Clinical Linguistics & Phonetics* 24, 369–386.

Marchman, V.A., Martínez-Sussmann, C. and Dale, P.S. (2004) The language-specific nature of grammatical development: Evidence from bilingual language learners. *Developmental Science* 7, 212–224.

Marinova-Todd, S. and Mirenda, P. (2016) Language and communication abilities in bilingual children with autism spectrum disorders. In J.L. Patterson and B.L. Rodríguez (eds) *Multilingual Perspectives on Child Language Disorders* (pp. 31–48). Bristol: Multilingual Matters.

Nicoladis, E. and Marchak, K. (2011) Le carte blanc or la carte blanche? Bilingual children's acquisition of French adjective agreement. *Language Learning* 61, 734–758.

Paradis, J., Nicoladis, E., Crago, M. and Genesee, F. (2011) Bilingual children's acquisition of the past tense: A usage-based approach. *Journal of Child Language* 38, 554–78.

Parra, M., Hoff, E. and Core, C. (2011) Relations among language exposure, phonological memory, and language development in Spanish-English bilingually developing 2-year-olds. *Journal of Experimental Child Psychology* 108, 113–125.

Patterson, J.L. (2016) Child language disorders across languages, cultural context and syndromes. In J.L. Patterson and B.L. Rodríguez (eds) *Multilingual Perspectives on Child Language Disorders* (pp. 1–30). Bristol: Multilingual Matters.

Pearson, B.Z., Fernández, S.C. and Oller, D.K. (1993) Lexical development in bilingual infants and toddlers: Comparison to monolingual norms. *Language Learning* 43, 93–120.

Pearson, B.Z., Fernández, S.C. and Oller, D.K. (1995) Cross-language synonyms in the lexicons of bilingual infants: One language or two? *Journal of Child Language* 22, 345–368.

Place, S. and Hoff, E. (2011) Properties of dual language exposure that influence 2-year-olds' bilingual proficiency. *Child Development* 82, 1834–1849.

Portes, A. and Hao, L. (1998) E pluribus unum: Bilingualism and loss of language in the second language. *Sociology of Education* 71, 269–294.

Poulin-Dubois, D., Bialystok, E., Blaye, A., Polonia, A. and Yott, J. (2013) Lexical access and vocabulary development in very young bilinguals. *International Journal of Bilingualism* 17 (1), 57–70.

Quiroz, B.G., Snow, C.E. and Jing Zhao (2010) Vocabulary skills of Spanish-English bilinguals: Impact of mother-child language interactions and home language and literacy support. *International Journal of Bilingualism* 14, 379–399.

Restrepo, A. and Gutiérrez-Clellen, V. (2012) Grammatical impairments in Spanish-English bilingual children. In B. Goldstein (ed.) *Bilingual Language Development and Disorders in Spanish-English Speakers* (pp. 213–232). Baltimore, MD: Brookes Publishing.

Schelletter, C. (2002) The effect of form similarity on bilingual children's lexical development. *Bilingualism* 5, 93–107.

Schwartz, M., Minkov, M., Dieser, E., Protassova, E., Moin, V. and Polinsky, M. (2015) Acquisition of Russian gender agreement by monolingual and bilingual children. *International Journal of Bilingualism* 19, 726–752.

Serratrice, L., Sorace, A. and Paoli, S. (2004) Crosslinguistic influence at the syntax-pragmatics interface: Subjects and objects in English-Italian bilingual and monolingual acquisition. *Bilingualism* 7, 183–205.

Silva-Corvalán, C. (2007) Early Spanish-English bilingualism: Theoretical issues, empirical analyses. *Southwest Journal of Linguistics* 26, 1–19.

Tabors, P.O., Páez, M. and López, L.M. (2003) Dual language abilities of bilingual four-year olds: Initial findings from the early childhood study of language and literacy development of Spanish-speaking children. *NABE Journal of Research and Practice* 1, 70–91.

Tamis-Lemonda, C.S., Song, L., Luo, R., Kuchirko, Y., Kahana-Kalman, R., Yoshikawa, H. and Raufman, J. (2014) Children's vocabulary growth in English and Spanish across early development and associations with school readiness skills. *Developmental Neuropsychology* 39, 69–87.

Thordardottir, E. (2015) The relationship between bilingual exposure and morphosyntactic development. *International Journal of Speech-Language Pathology* 17, 97–114.

US Census Bureau (2013) School enrollment in the United States: Census Bureau Report. https://www.census.gov/library/publications/2013/demo/p20-571.html.

Vagh, S.B., Pan, B.A. and Mancilla-Martinez, J. (2009) Measuring growth in bilingual and monolingual children's English productive vocabulary development: The utility of combining parent and teacher report. *Child Development* 80, 1545–1563.

Veltman, C. (1983) Anglicization in the United States: Language environment and language practice of American adolescents. *International Journal of the Sociology of Language* 44, 99–114.

Wei, L. and Lee, S. (2001) L1 development in an L2 environment: The use of Cantonese classifiers and quantifiers by young British-born Chinese in Tyneside. *International Journal of Bilingual Education and Bilingualism* 4, 359–382.

Willard, J., Cycyk, L., Bitetti, D. and Hammer, C.S. (2019) Mothers' depressive symptoms and their children's Turkish heritage language vocabulary development. *International Journal of Bilingualism* 23, 71–86.

Yow, W.Q. and Markman, E.M. (2011) Bilingualism and children's use of paralinguistic cues to interpret emotion in speech. *Bilingualism* 14, 562–569.

4 Dual Language Learners in Early Intervention Programs: Issues of Eligibility, Access, and Service Provision

Lillian Durán

Young Dual Language Learners

Young children who speak a language other than English are one of the fastest-growing populations in the United States (National Academies of Sciences, Engineering, and Medicine, 2017). These children are often referred to as dual language learners, because they will need to maintain their home language or languages to communicate with their families and will also learn English as they begin participating in early education programs or attend kindergarten. Dual language learners are a diverse group and include children born in and outside the United States and born to parents both who are native born and immigrants. More than one-quarter of American children under the age of 5 have at least one immigrant parent, and the number of young children of immigrants rose from 2.9 million in 1990 to 5.6 million in 2018 (Migration Policy Institute, 2018). As these children grow and develop, they will be an important sector of the labor market and represent an important source of cultural and linguistic capital in the United States (Fortuny *et al.*, 2010; Murphey *et al.*, 2014).

Dual language learners are a heterogenous population, which creates challenges in developing effective programming, since a "one size fits all" approach to the delivery of services to the dual language learner population is unlikely to be effective or meet all their needs. Children grow and develop within the family context, and this context includes the family's culture and language. Not only do dual language learners come from many different countries and cultural backgrounds, but they also are exposed to a wide variety of languages. More than 350 different languages are spoken in the United States (US Census Bureau, 2015), and the timing and amount of exposure to children's home languages also varies considerably (Phillips & Lonigan, 2014). Some children are simultaneously bilingual, meaning that they are exposed to their family's home language or languages and English in their homes. Other young children are sequential bilinguals and may only be exposed to their family's home language and then formally introduced to English through early education programs (Paradis et al., 2011). Ultimately, this variation in language background leads to a broad range of language proficiency in both home languages and English. This necessitates that programs attend to children's home language exposure so that they can address the linguistic needs of children who have different levels of proficiency in their home language and English.

Importantly, being bilingual does not cause a language delay, but young children in the United States who speak languages other than English at home face challenges when they enter early childhood programs, because our systems and educational approaches are poorly designed in terms of meeting their needs (Jacoby & Lesaux, 2016). Many longitudinal studies provide evidence that young dual language learners demonstrate low levels of language and early literacy development in both their home language and English (Hoff et al., 2014; Jackson et al., 2014; Páez et al., 2007). However, it is important to critically examine the social factors that may contribute to this finding, such as limited support for their home language in school and community, higher incidences of poverty in immigrant and non-English speaking populations, and low quality educational settings (Franco et al., 2019; National Academies of Sciences, Engineering, and Medicine, 2017). This results in a gap in kindergarten readiness between dual language learners and their white monolingual peers and greater risk of identification of developmental delays and later diagnosis of learning disabilities (Marcella et al., 2014).

We also know that socioeconomic status (which includes income and education) has a profound effect on children's development (Chaudry & Wimer, 2016). In 2018, there were 26.9 million children under the age of 18 living in low-income families (i.e., with family incomes below 200% of the federal poverty threshold). Of them, 8.5 million, or 32% were children of immigrants. Children of immigrants were more likely to be in low-income families (47% of the 18 million) compared to children of US-born parents (36% of the 51.5 million) (Batalova et al., 2020). Although the educational attainment of immigrants has been on the rise overall, there are still many immigrant populations who have a high school degree or less (Krogstad & Radford, 2018). These socioeconomic discrepancies between native-born and immigrant parents create differences in the resources and opportunities that are available to these families.

Despite these social barriers, however, immigrant families have many important strengths. Despite increased challenges on socioeconomic indicators, immigrants and their children seem to fare better than second- or third-generation immigrant populations on some metrics. Better prenatal practices of expectant mothers who are immigrants have been found to lead to higher birth weights. Immigrants also tend to have more two-parent households, which leads to more social and economic stability, potentially leading to the higher social-emotional and behavioral outcomes in preschool-aged children of immigrants that have been documented (Administration for Children and Families, 2015a; Coll & Marks, 2012).

In summary young dual language learners as a group are generally marginalized ethno-linguistic minority populations that experience multiple risk factors increasing the likelihood that their development will be adversely affected (Garbarino & Ganzel, 2000). Additionally, early childhood education personnel are often inadequately prepared to work successfully with culturally and linguistically diverse families (Genesee, 2008; Sawyer et al., 2018) and several studies document the fact that culturally and linguistically diverse families often feel isolated from, and uninvolved in, the special education process (Durán et al., under review; Rispoli et al., 2018; Wolfe & Durán, 2013). Given the significant challenges often faced by these families, early intervention (EI) programs need to work holistically with families to create environments that are welcoming and supportive. Families should feel valued and heard in order to support and foster collaborative relationships between EI professionals and families and promote optimal outcomes in the young children served.

Early Intervention Professionals

The majority of early intervention professionals are monolingual English speakers and are limited in their ability to deliver culturally and linguistically appropriate services (Kidd et al., 2008; Whitebook et al., 2018). We do know, however, some key focus areas that should be included in early intervention teacher training programs. Zepeda et al. (2011) describe the competencies that teachers need to have to work effectively with young dual language learners. These competencies include: knowledge of language development generally and, more specifically, bilingual development; the ability to implement effective practices when teaching dual language learners; an understanding of the link between language and culture; accurate information about dual language assessment practices; and strategies for engaging in culturally and linguistically appropriate services to provide adequate opportunities for meaningful involvement of families in their child's early education experience.

Not only do teachers need to be aware of appropriate practices: they also need to have the dispositions necessary to be motivated to implement effective practices and change or adapt their current practices if need be. The Alliance for a Better Community, in collaboration with the National Council of La Raza, published the following seven core principles that should guide practice with dual language learners (Lopez et al., 2012):

(1) children have the right to a high-quality, linguistically and culturally competent education;
(2) knowing more than one language benefits an individual's cognitive, social, and emotional development;
(3) development of the first language is critical in the development of the second language;
(4) socio-emotional development of young children is central for language learning;
(5) family engagement and involvement contribute to positive child outcomes, positive home interactions, and increased student success;
(6) effective teaching for dual language learners is founded on a strength-based approach to learning; and
(7) reflective practice is a central component of teacher preparation and ongoing development.

Together, the practice competencies, as well as the guiding principles, provide important direction for next steps in preservice and in-service teacher training.

Early Intervention Programs for Infants and Toddlers

Early intervention programs are charged with providing effective and timely services to the diverse range of families in the United States. Children from birth to age 3 who are at-risk or have documented delays or disabilities are served primarily by two federal programs. Children who meet eligibility criteria for developmental delay or disability are served under Part C of the Individuals with Disabilities Education Act, 20 U.S.C, 1400 (2004). Children whose families meet federal poverty guidelines are served by Early Head Start programs. Head Start also has a mandate to ensure that 10% of children enrolled are identified with a disability. There is, therefore, some overlap between the populations served through Part C and Early Head Start.

Individuals with Disabilities Education Act (IDEA) – Part C

Part C of IDEA governs the services provided to children under the age of 3 who are experiencing developmental delays in one or more of the following developmental areas: cognition, physical (including vision and hearing), communication, social/emotional, and adaptive. Part C eligibility is determined by each state's definition of developmental delay and includes children with established physical or mental conditions with a high probability of resulting in developmental delay and includes conditions such as chromosomal abnormalities; genetic or congenital disorders; sensory impairments; inborn errors of metabolism; disorders reflecting disturbance of the development of the nervous system; congenital infections; severe attachment disorders; and disorders secondary to exposure to toxic substances, including fetal alcohol syndrome (IDEA, 2004). States may choose to include children at risk for disabilities in the eligible group.

Children qualify for services by undergoing an evaluation process that involves standardized testing, parent reports, informed clinical opinion, and natural observation. Regulations also require native language assessment and the inclusion of families in the evaluation process (IDEA, 2004). The majority of children are served under the developmental delay category in Part C, which involves documenting a developmental delay in one or more of five developmental areas (communication, cognition, motor, social-emotional, adaptive). Children can also qualify for services if they have a diagnosed physical or mental condition that has a high probability of resulting in developmental delay (IDEA, 2004). Family-centered services delivered in natural settings are a cornerstone of Part C programming (IDEA, 2004). In 2011, 86.6% of children enrolled received services primarily through home visiting programs, with 7.4% in community-based settings, with the remaining 6% described as being in "other settings" (Office of Special Education and Rehabilitative Services, 2018). Professionals involved in delivering Part C services include Early Childhood Special Education (ECSE) teachers, speech and language pathologists, service coordinators, and occupational and physical therapists (Office of Special Education and Rehabilitative Services, 2018). In 2018, Part C early intervention served 338,569 children nationwide; 52% were identified as White, 27% as Hispanic/Latino, 3% as Asian, 12% as Black or African American, 0.7% as American Indian or Alaskan Native, 0.2% as Native Hawaiian or Pacific Islander, and 5.1% as mixed race (Office of Special Education and Rehabilitative Services, 2018). At this point, the Office of Special Education Programs (OSEP) does not collect data on children's home languages or the number of dual language learners enrolled in Part C programs. Given that states are not required to report these data, this information is currently also not collected at the state level. State data collection is often driven by what is needed for federal reporting. However, within each of these racial/ethnic categories there are likely to be dual language learners, especially in the Latino population.

Effectiveness of Part C programs

There is currently no data publicly available on the specific outcomes of dual language learners enrolled in Part C programs. However, the National Early Intervention Longitudinal Study (NEILS in Hebbeler *et al.*, 2007) was initiated with a nationally representative group of families entering Part C services in the 1997–1998 school year and longitudinally followed 3, 338 children and families through kindergarten. Data sources included family interviews, service records, service provider surveys, and kindergarten teacher surveys. Outcomes were analyzed at 36 months and during children's kindergarten year. At 36 months, findings from the NEILS indicated that 71–76% of children receiving Part C services demonstrated greater than expected growth in social relationships (getting along with children and adults), use of knowledge and skills (thinking, reasoning, problem solving, early literacy, and math skills), and taking action to meet needs (feeding, dressing, self-care, and following rules related to health and safety) (Goode *et al.*, 2011; Hebbeler *et al.*, 2007). Between 54% and 62% of the children receiving Part C services exited the program functioning within age expectations in these three areas. Seventy-six percent of families reported that Early Intervention services had a lot of impact, with 20% reporting some impact. A notable caveat, however, is that families in the NEILS were only interviewed in English, and this limits what we know about the experiences of families that speak languages other than English receiving Part C services (Hebbeler *et al.*, 2007).

Early Head Start

Early Head Start serves pregnant women, and children under the age of 3, who meet federal poverty guidelines. The goal of Early Head Start is to provide early, continuous, intensive, and comprehensive child development and family support services (Office of Head Start, 2015). Services are provided through both home- and center-based services that focus on early childhood development, health and nutrition, and parenting skills. In 2018, 39% of children served by Early Head Start were identified as Hispanic/Latino, 30% as Black/African American, 26% as White, 0.2% as American Indian/Alaskan Native, and 0.2% as Asian, with the remaining population falling in bi-racial, unspecified, or other categories. Twenty-seven percent of children served by Early Head Start speak a language other than English at home, but the majority of parents have resided in the United States for six years or more. Of the population of dual language learners, 79% come from homes where Spanish is spoken. In 2018, 14% of Early Head Start enrollment consisted of children with disabilities (Office of Head Start, 2018).

There are many more data available specific to the experiences of dual language learners and their families receiving Early Head Start services versus Part C services. This information is aggregated in the *Report to Congress on Dual Language Learners in Head Start* (Administration for Children and Families, 2015b). More than half of home visitors serving dual language learners are Hispanic, and the majority have five or more years of experience, with associate's or bachelor's degrees in early childhood education. Nearly 80% of parents of dual language learners in Early Head Start reported that they attended group activities for parents, and 57% specifically attended parent education meetings and workshops related to child development. The majority of dual language learners are served in home-based programs, but the characteristics of home visits varied slightly between families of dual language learners and non-dual language learners. Specific activities were reported to occur less during home visits with the families of dual language learners. For example, 61% of families who spoke languages other than English at home, vs. 75% of English-speaking families, reported that their home visit included the provision of education or information. Only 35% of bilingual and multilingual families, vs. 49% of English-speaking families, reported that their home visit included evaluation/feedback on parent-child interactions. Finally, 68% of English-speaking families, vs. 59% of bilingual and multilingual families, reported that their home visitor assessed their child or observed parent-child interactions.

Effectiveness of Early Head Start programs

The best data available on the efficacy of Early Head Start programs are provided by the Early Head Start Family and Child Experiences Study (Baby FACES) (Administration for Children and Families, 2015a). The study was conducted with a nationally representative sample of infants enrolled in Early Head Start in 2009, and used a longitudinal cohort design, with data collected until children left or aged out of the program (at age 3). Data sources included annual interviews with parents, home visitors and teachers, interviews and self-administered surveys with program directors, home visit observations, and direct classroom observations. Also, direct child assessments, video-recorded parent-child and assessor-child interactions, and weekly service logs were gathered. This study provided rich descriptive data on the population of dual language learners being served, the Early Head Start workforce, and the quality of home visits and parent participation. For example, we know that dual language learners demonstrate significant gains in pre-academic, social-emotional, and language and early literacy skills from Head Start preschool participation (Administration for Children and Families, 2015b; Bloom & Weiland, 2015; Williams, 2015).

Limitations of early intervention programs

The science of early childhood development demonstrates that the most effective interventions are individualized to meet the child's and family's needs, delivered through high-quality programs with well-trained personnel, and provided at a level of sufficient intensity and duration to make a difference (Shonkoff & Phillips, 2000). Given the high level of need of young dual language learners and their families, early intervention programs should be intensive, culturally and linguistically responsive, and individualized to meet child and family characteristics. However, it is clear that early intervention programs fall short in providing a bilingual and multicultural workforce that more closely represents the populations being served and that has the training necessary to be effective (Administration for Children and Families, 2015b; Banerjee & Luckner, 2010; Zepeda et al., 2011).

It is also unfortunate that Latino and other immigrant families have lower participation rates in early intervention programs. Nores (2015), in a report published by the National Institute of Early Education Research (NIEER), used data from the Early Childhood Longitudinal Study-K to disentangle trends in participation in early childhood programs among groups of children (Whites, Asians, Hispanics, dual language learners, and children with immigrant backgrounds). Hispanic children, dual language learners, and children with immigrant backgrounds each had lower rates of participation in either center-based or Head Start pre-K programs than their White and Asian peers. About 50% of each of these subgroups of children were not enrolled in pre-K, compared with about 30% for White and Asian children. Around 60% of native-born Hispanic children were enrolled in pre-K compared to only about 45% of immigrant Hispanic groups.

In two recent studies, dual language learners have also been found to be under-identified for early childhood special education services in several southern states and across the United States (Morgan et al., 2012; Morrier & Gallagher, 2012). Researchers hypothesize several reasons why this may be a trend. Given a lack of training, teachers may avoid conducting assessments with dual language learners, because they are concerned that they may not be able to distinguish delay from typical differences associated with children acquiring two languages. Families may also have barriers in locating programs and finding the local resources to refer their children for services. Whatever the case may be, it appears that young children who are dual language learners are not accessing special education services at a rate that would be expected, and changes are needed in practice to ensure equal access and opportunity to participate in early intervention programs when necessary.

Differences in participation rates between native-born and immigrant children have been documented in other populations as well: for example, 31% of all 3-year-old children born to immigrants are enrolled in pre-school, versus 37% of children of native-born families (Fortuny et al., 2010). We also know that according to the 40th Annual Report to Congress on the implementation of IDEA, children who are identified as Hispanic/Latino, American Indian/Alaskan Native, and Asian were slightly less likely than those in all other racial groups to be served under IDEA, Part C (Office of Special Education and Rehabilitative Services, 2018). Although the under-enrollment of dual language learners (DLLs) in early intervention (EI) and pre-K programs is a complicated issue, some reasons might include limited resources for accessing the programs, a poor fit between service delivery systems and the needs of these children and families, an ineffective Child Find program in these communities, concerns regarding participation and releasing of personal information and compromised immigration status and possible deportation, and a lack of availability of programs in their neighborhoods (Cycyk & Durán, 2020; Fortuny et al., 2010; Yoshikawa, 2011).

Recommendations for Improvement of Early Childhood Programs

The Latino Policy Forum in Illinois recently published a report focused on the state of infant and toddler services in the Latino community in Illinois and provided recommendations for improvement. The *Primeros Pasos* report, developed with 12 early childhood providers serving the Latino community, concluded with seven primary recommendations that mirror what has also been suggested in national reports (Vigil et al., 2013):

Recommendation 1: Increase funding and facilities and the expansion of services in the communities of greatest need and growth.

Recommendation 2: Hire and retain more highly qualified bilingual and bicultural EI professionals and increase professional development opportunities especially focused on providing culturally and linguistically responsive services.

Recommendation 3: Increase and strengthen relationships with higher education faculty with expertise in bilingual development and cultural diversity.

Recommendation 4: Improve outreach efforts to Latino families and promote awareness of the importance of parent engagement and the services available to infants and toddlers in the community.

Recommendation 5: Improve the ability of EI systems to provide services to children in high-need areas in a timely manner and strengthen the process of transition between Part C and Part B services.

Recommendation 6: Strengthen and expand community-based partnerships and linkages between providers of infant and toddler services.

Recommendation 7: Develop systems that collect and make available comprehensive data on infants and toddlers and service providers and the quality of services provided to dual language learners in publicly funded programs.

Although these recommendations were developed for the Latino community in one state, they provide a useful and comprehensive list to guide future improvements in early intervention service delivery systems to infants and toddlers who are dual language learners more generally.

Future Directions: Policy

The first step in improving the development of policy that best meets the needs of dual language learners and their families is to gather data on the number of dual language learners being served in early intervention programs nationally, their language backgrounds, home characteristics, and immigration and socioeconomic status. Such data will inform policy makers on the populations being served. This is especially relevant for Part C, since we currently have no information about dual language learners specifically being served. States and early education programs cannot tailor policies and instruction to support diverse young learners if data are not collected on children's linguistic backgrounds and other relevant demographic characteristics.

Head Start published a report, *Dual Language Learners: What Does It Take?* (US Department of Health & Human Services, 2008), that outlines comprehensive service delivery and program components that should be in place to best serve dual language learner populations. Part C programs need similar guidance from the federal Office of Special Education Programs (OSEP), and more of an emphasis should be placed on providing culturally and linguistically responsive services to infants and toddlers identified with disabilities. As it stands now, there is little federal special education guidance to states regarding dual language learners and no systematic data collection efforts in place to begin to describe the number or distribution of dual language learners served under Part C.

Another step in improving policy is facilitating a change in the public rhetoric about young children who speak languages other than English. This is one of the fastest-growing populations in the United States, and our economic and social stability as a nation depends on this next multilingual and multicultural generation accessing the support they need to be successful and productive members of society. This means that policies need to be developed that facilitate the growth and quality of early intervention programs that are prepared to meet the needs of bilingual and multicultural children and their families. It is well established that providing high-quality early education is an effective approach to improving the outcomes of at-risk populations (Bakken *et al.*, 2017). Funding streams need to be available to invest in these children and families early on to prevent school failure and compromised life outcomes.

Future Directions: Programs

In Part C programs there is evidence that dual language learner populations may be under-enrolled, and more effort may be necessary to locate, recruit, and retain children and families who speak languages other than English in service delivery programs (Garcia, 2015). Targeted community outreach, hiring bilingual and bicultural staff, producing recruitment materials in languages other than English, and developing relationships with key community partners are some avenues to increasing the enrollment of dual language learners in early intervention programs. There should also be targeted professional development that addresses the needs of families with pending immigration status, so that these families are not made to feel vulnerable when accessing services (Cycyk & Durán, 2020). There is evidence that there may be systemic barriers reducing their participation.

A report by the Migration Policy Institute that focused on immigrant parents and early childhood programs suggested that, for immigrant families with young children, combining adult English as a Second Language (ESL) classes with infant care and family literacy might be one approach to improving child outcomes and participation (Park & McHugh, 2014). Early education and adult education are interlocking issues in these communities: helping families to acquire higher levels of education and increased English proficiency will allow for greater economic opportunity and participation in society. This, in turn, will reduce the risks faced by children in immigrant families that result from the higher rates of poverty and lower educational attainment of their families. Addressing the developmental needs of young DLLs by holistically considering the needs of the family within the context of their community might improve long-term outcomes beyond those programs that focus exclusively on child development (Williams, 2014).

In this same report it was also recommended that programs should expand effective parenting support programs in immigrant communities (Park & McHugh, 2014). This is not to insinuate that immigrants are less skilled at parenting: it simply addresses the reality that there is a higher incidence of poverty, a history of trauma relating to experiences of war, violence, sexual assault, and resource scarcity in their home countries, and the associated ongoing life stressors in this population (Park & McHugh, 2014; Yoshikawa, 2011). Effective parenting practices are central to healthy child development. Many immigrant parents may also be undergoing a process of acculturation, and there can be significant challenges associated with raising a child within a new social milieu. Low levels of English proficiency and literacy have also been found to limit the participation of many immigrant families in their child's early childhood education, which may, in turn, exclude them from participating in parenting classes currently offered by programs such as Head Start or community education to the English-speaking community (Park & McHugh, 2014; Williams 2014). Therefore, targeted parenting programs that are developed in languages other than English and that are culturally responsive to specific immigrant communities by reflecting their beliefs and values regarding discipline, child development, and the role of family in education, need to be developed to more adequately and effectively address the needs of these families. Parenting programs cannot simply have a "one-size-fits-all" approach given the complex relationships between language, culture, previous life experiences, and parenting practices.

It is also imperative that early intervention programs recruit, hire, and retain more bilingual and bicultural staff to more effectively serve diverse populations across the United States. Although Head Start has made significant progress in the availability of Spanish-speaking staff, there are more than 140 languages spoken by children in Head Start (Administration for Children and Families, 2015b). The number of bilingual service providers working through Part C service delivery systems is not even available. However, there is evidence that the early childhood workforce is far from achieving the level of diversity found in children from birth through age 4 served in early childhood programs nationally (Build Initiative, 2015; Whitebook *et al.*, 2018).

More targeted and effective professional development opportunities also need to be provided to practitioners already working in the field. Early intervention practitioners need information on bilingual development, appropriate bilingual assessment procedures, dual language intervention, working with interpreters, building culturally responsive relationships with families, and the importance of home language maintenance and the negative consequences of home language loss (Anderson, 2012; Banerjee & Luckner, 2010; Zepeda *et al.*, 2011). Resources such as the *The New Voices: Nuevas Voces Guide to Cultural and Linguistic Diversity in Early Childhood* (Castro *et al.*, 2011) and *Many Languages, Building Connections* (Nemeth, 2012) can provide solid support for, and guidance in, these professional development efforts, but trainers and coaches are needed to provide not only presentations, but ongoing technical assistance to translate new knowledge into practice.

Future Directions: Research

To date, little to no research has been conducted investigating the outcomes of dual language learners from Part C programs. As a field we know little about what practices are most effective from birth to age 3 and what we can do to increase the efficacy of home visiting practices. This leaves practitioners with little guidance to bridge evidence to practice and to increase the likelihood that their involvement will significantly improve child and family outcomes. Ultimately, early intervention is centered on the premise that early identification and the delivery of targeted services will result in meaningful improvements in a child's development. At this point more research is needed to fully understand early intervention practices that are most effective with dual language learners.

We also need more information about how we can better prepare the early childhood workforce to work successfully and effectively with dual language learners and their families. Current evidence suggests that early intervention professionals often feel insecure about their own abilities when working with dual language learners and recognize the need for more training (Banerjee & Luckner, 2010; Kidd et al., 2008). Few researchers have undertaken the systematic study of practices that lead to important improvements in preservice or in-service teachers' knowledge, skills, or attitudes when working with dual language learners. More work needs to be completed to better understand this process of teacher learning and the changes in dispositions that will lead to important changes in practice (Kidd et al., 2008; Mancilla-Martinez & Lesaux, 2014).

We also only have emerging evidence about the best process for the early identification of delay or disability with children from birth to age 3. What we do know is that in preschool it is important to assess children in both their home language and English in order to accurately measure their ability (Division for Early Childhood, 2014; Peña & Halle, 2011). Preschool-aged children in the United States usually have some exposure to both languages, and, in order to better complete educational planning, it is important to know more about their abilities in each language. Birth to age 3, however, represents an earlier stage in development, and little is known about the best approach to assessment both for determining eligibility for special education services under Part C and for ongoing progress monitoring. We need more research that systematically investigates best approaches to assessment that maps onto early developmental milestones and can provide evidence-based guidance to practitioners.

What we do know is that it is important to gather multiple sources of data across natural settings to make informed decisions about children's need for special education (Durán et al., 2011). Language samples, family interviews, questionnaires (e.g., the Ages and Stages Questionnaires), direct observation in natural settings, and monitoring progress over time, can all provide more accurate information about a child's development rather than a one-time assessment that is interpreted into a language other than English. When an assessment is translated and administered by an interpreter, the standard scores are no longer valid; it is important to recognize the limitations of this approach to assessment. Therefore, more research is necessary to investigate alternatives to empirically explore which approaches provide the most accurate information to reduce the likelihood of disproportionate representation in special education.

Developmentally, we also do not have enough information to understand typical growth trajectories of infants and toddlers who are dual language learners. There is a growing body of growth trajectory studies but more information is needed and on a wider range of languages and social contexts (Durán & Wackerle-Hollman, 2018). Future developmental studies should include children who speak languages other than Spanish and with more systematic documentation of exposure to English and their home language. Given the heterogeneity of the dual language learner population in the United States, we need large sample sizes that include diverse linguistic populations in order to more accurately develop growth trajectory models that can be used as a reference when we are considering individual children's development. This research would serve as an invaluable resource for practitioners and researchers alike.

Summary and Conclusion

Bilingualism is an asset in our highly globalized economy. There has been a significant growth in the number of preK-6th grade dual language immersion programs in the United States, focused both on dual language learners maintaining their home languages while learning English and on English-speaking children learning a second language (Boyle *et al.*, 2015). This has become an attractive option for many monolingual English-speaking families because of the increased awareness of the benefits of bilingualism (Williams, 2017). However, as a society, we also need to value and nurture the linguistic resources of young children in the United States who naturally speak languages other than English at home. A shift in thinking changes these young children from being labeled as "limited English proficient" to being considered as "emergent bilinguals" (García, 2009). The first five years of life set the stage for lifelong learning and are a critical period in the acquisition of any language (Golinkoff *et al.*, 2019). Early intervention programs have the responsibility of serving some of America's most vulnerable children. This responsibility also comes with an important opportunity to improve developmental trajectories and ultimately long-term outcomes. At no other point in development are children so malleable, with brains literally wired for change (Shonkoff & Phillips, 2000). The quality of the investment we make today in America's youngest and most diverse population will ultimately pay off for all of us for generations to come.

References

Administration for Children and Families (ACF) (2015a) *The Faces of Early Head Start: A National Picture of Early Head Start Programs and the Children and Families they Serve*. OPRE Report #2015-29. Washington, DC: Office of Planning, Research, and Evaluation, Administration for Children and Families, US Department of Health and Human Services.

Administration for Children and Families (ACF) (2015b) *Report to Congress on Dual Language Learners in Head Start and Early Head Start Programs*. Washington, DC: US Department of Health and Human Services.

Anderson, R.T. (2012) First language loss in Spanish-speaking children: Patterns of loss and implications for clinical practice. In B.A. Goldstein (ed.) *Bilingual Language Development and Disorders in Spanish-English Speakers* (pp. 187–212). Baltimore, MD: Brookes Publishing.

Bakken, L., Brown, N. and Downing, B. (2017) Early childhood education: The long-term benefits. *Journal of Research in Childhood Education* 31 (2), 255–269.

Banerjee, R. and Luckner, J. L. (2010) Assessment practices and training needs of early childhood professionals. *Journal of Early Childhood Teacher Education* 34, 231–248.

Batalova, J., Blizzard, B. and Bolter, J. (2020) *Frequently Requested Statistics on Immigrants and Immigration in the United States*. Washington, DC: Migration Policy Institute. Retrieved on 2-22-20 from https://www.migrationpolicy.org/article/frequently-requested-statistics-immigrants-and-immigration-united-states#Demographic,%20Educational,%20and%20Linguistic%20Characteristics.

Bloom, H.S. and Weiland, C. (2015) *Quantifying Variation in Head Start Effects on Young Children's Cognitive and Socio-emotional Skills Using Data from the National Head Start Impact Study*. New York, NY: MDRC. https://www.mdrc.org/sites/default/files/quantifying_variation_in_head_start.pdf.

Boyle, A., August, D., Tabaku, L., Cole, S. and Simpson-Baird, A. (2015) Dual language education programs: Current state policies and practices. Washington, DC: American Institutes for Research.

Build Initiative (2015) Addressing the workforce diversity gap. Retrieved from: http://www.buildinitiative.org/TheIssues/DiversityEquity/Workforce.aspx.

Castro, D.C., Ayankoya, B. and Kasprzak, C. (2011) *The New Voices: Nuevas Voces Guide to Cultural and Linguistic Diversity in Early Childhood*. Baltimore, MD: Paul H. Brookes Publishing Company.

Chaudry, A. and Wimer, C. (2016) Poverty is not just an indicator: The relationship between income, poverty, and child well-being. *Academic Pediatrics* 16 (3), S23–S29.

Coll, C.G.E. and Marks, A.K.E. (2012) *The Immigrant Paradox in Children and Adolescents: Is Becoming American a Developmental Risk?* (pp. xiv–328). Washington, DC: American Psychological Association.

Cycyk, L.M. and Durán, L. (2020) Supporting young children with disabilities and their families from undocumented immigrant backgrounds: Recommendations for program leaders and practitioners. *Young Exceptional Children* 23 (4), 212–224. doi:1096250619864916.

Division for Early Childhood (2014) DEC recommended practices in early intervention/early childhood special education. Retrieved from http://www.dec-sped.org/recommendedpractices.

Durán, L. and Wackerle-Hollman, A. (2018) A review of dual language and literacy growth. In D. Baker (ed.) *Second Language Acquisition: Methods, Perspectives and Challenges* (pp. 39–62). Hauppauge, NY: Nova Science Publishing.

Durán, L., Cheatham, G., Santos, A. (2011) Evaluating young dual language learners: Gathering and interpreting multiple sources of data to make informed decisions. *Young Exceptional Children. Thirteenth Monograph: Gathering Information to Make Informed Decisions: Contemporary Perspectives about Assessment in Early Intervention and Early Childhood Special Education*. Missoula, MT: Division of Early Childhood.

Durán, L., Cycyk, L. and Batz, R. (under review) Voces de la gente: Perspectives of Spanish-speaking Latinx families on early intervention and early childhood special education. *Topics in Early Childhood Special Education*.

Fortuny, K., Hernandez, D.J. and Chaudry, A. (2010) *Young Children of Immigrants: The Leading Edge of America's Future*. Brief No. 3. Washington, DC: Urban Institute.

Franco, X., Bryant, D.M., Gillanders, C., Castro, D.C., Zepeda, M. and Willoughby, M.T. (2019) Examining linguistic interactions of dual language learners using the Language Iinteraction Snapshot (LISn). *Early Childhood Research Quarterly* 48, 50–61.

Garbarino, J. and Ganzel, B. (2000) The human ecology of early risk. In J.P. Shonkoff and S. J. Meisels (eds) *Handbook of Early Childhood Intervention* (pp. 7–93). Cambridge: Cambridge University Press.

Garcia, A. (2015) *How Language and Immigrant Background Influence Pre-K Participation and Kindergarten Readiness*. New America. Blog post, January 2015. Retrieved from https://www.newamerica.org/education-policy/edcentral/prekparticipation/. http://devedcentral.pantheon.io/prekparticipation/

García, O. (2009) Emergent bilinguals and TESOL: What's in a name? *TESOL Quarterly* 43 (2), 322–326. Retrieved February 23, 2020, from www.jstor.org/stable/27785009.

Genesee, F. (2008) Early dual language learning. *Zero to Three* 29 (1), 17–23.

Golinkoff, R.M., Hoff, E., Rowe, M.L., Tamis-LeMonda, C.S. and Hirsh-Pasek, K. (2019) Language matters: Denying the existence of the 30-million-word gap has serious consequences. *Child Development* 90 (3), 985–992.

Goode, S., Diefendorf, M. and Colgan, S. (2011) *The Outcomes of Early Intervention for Infants and Toddlers with Disabilities and their Families*. Chapel Hill, NC: National Early Childhood Technical Assistance Center.

Hebbeler, K., Spiker, D., Bailey, D., Scarborough, A., Malik, S., Simeonsson, R., Singer, M. and Nelson, L. (2007) *Early Intervention for Infants and Toddlers with Disabilities and their Families: Participants, Services, and Outcomes: Final Report of the National Early Intervention Longitudinal Study (NEILS)*. Menlo Park, CA: SRI International.

Hoff, E., Rumiche, R., Burridge, A., Ribot, K.M. and Welsh, S.N. (2014) Expressive vocabulary development in children from bilingual and monolingual homes: A longitudinal study from two to four years. *Early Childhood Research Quarterly* 29 (4), 433–444.

IDEA (2004) Individuals with Disabilities Education Act, 20 U.S.C. § 1400 (2004).

Jackson, C.W., Schatschneider, C. and Leacox, L. (2014) Longitudinal analysis of receptive vocabulary growth in young Spanish English-speaking children from migrant families. *Language, Speech, and Hearing Services in Schools* 45 (1), 40–51.

Jacoby, J. and Lesaux, N. (2016) Language and literacy instruction in preschool classes that serve Latino dual language learners. *Early Childhood Research Quarterly* 40, 77–86.

Kidd, J.K., Sánchez, S.Y. and Thorpe, E.K. (2008) Defining moments: Developing culturally responsive dispositions and teaching practices in early childhood preservice teachers. *Teaching and Teacher Education* 24 (2), 316–329.

Krogstad, J.M. and Radford, J. (2018, September 14) Education levels of US immigrants are on the rise. *Fact Tank: News in the Numbers*. Washington, DC: Pew Research Center.

Lopez, A., Zepeda, M. and Medina, O. (2012) *Dual Language Learner Teacher Competencies (DLLTC) Report*. Los Angeles, CA: Alliance for a Better Community.

Mancilla-Martinez, J. and Lesaux, N.K. (2014) Bilingual teachers in early Head Start/Head Start. *NHSA Dialog* 17 (3).

Marcella, J., Howes, C. and Fuligni, A.S. (2014) Exploring cumulative risk and family literacy practices in low-income Latino families. *Early Education and Development* 25, 36–55.

Migration Policy Institute (2018) *Children in US Immigrant Families*. Retrieved from https://www.migrationpolicy.org/programs/data-hub/charts/children-immigrant-families.

Morgan, P.L., Farkas, G., Hillemeier, M.M. and Maczuga, S. (2012) Are minority children disproportionately represented in early intervention and early childhood special education? *Educational Researcher* 41 (9), 339–351.

Morrier, M.J. and Gallagher, P.A. (2012) Racial disparities in preschool special education eligibility for five southern states. *Journal of Special Education* 46 (3), 152–169.

Murphey, D., Guzman, L. and Torres, A. (2014) *America's Hispanic Children: Gaining Ground, Looking Forward*. Bethesda, MD: Child Trends Hispanic Institute.

National Academies of Sciences, Engineering, and Medicine (2017) *Promoting the Educational Success of Children and Youth Learning English: Promising Futures*. Washington, DC: National Academies Press.

Nemeth, K.N. (2012) *Many Languages, Building Connections: Supporting Infants and Toddlers Who Are Dual Language Learners*. Lewisville, NC: Gryphon House.

Nores, M. (2015) *Early Childhood Choices and Hispanic Families*. NIEER. Retrieved from http://www.nieer.org/sites/nieer/files/Early%20childhood%20choices%20and%20Hispanic%20families.pdf.

Office of Head Start (2015) *Early Head Start*. Retrieved from http://eclkc.ohs.acf.hhs.gov/hslc/tta-system/ehsnrc/about-ehs#about.

Office of Head Start (2018) *Early Head Start Services Snapshot*. Retrieved from https://eclkc.ohs.acf.hhs.gov/sites/default/files/pdf/no-search/service-snapshot-ehs-2018-2019.pdf.

Office of Special Education and Rehabilitative Services (2018) *40th Annual Report to Congress on the Implementation of the "Individuals with Disabilities Education Act," 2018*. ERIC Clearinghouse.

Páez, M.M., Tabors, P.O. and López, L.M. (2007) Dual language and literacy development of Spanish-speaking preschool children. *Journal of Applied Developmental Psychology* 28 (2), 85–102.

Paradis, J., Genesee, F. and Crago, M. (2011) *Dual Language Development and Disorders: A Handbook on Bilingualism and Second Language Learning*. Baltimore, MD: Brookes Publishing.

Park, M. and McHugh, M. (2014) *Immigrant Parents and Early Childhood Programs: Addressing Barriers of Literacy, Culture, and Systems Knowledge*. Washington, DC: Migration Policy Institute.

Peña, E.D. and Halle, T.G. (2011) Assessing preschool dual language learners: Traveling a multiforked road. *Child Development Perspectives* 5 (1), 28–32.

Phillips, B. and Lonigan, C. (2014) Symposium: Early language and literacy skills among Spanish-speaking dual-language learners. Home environment predictors of language minority preschool children's English and Spanish skills. Society for the Scientific Study of Reading Conference, Santa Fe, New Mexico, July 2014.

Rispoli, K.M., Hawley, L.R. and Clinton, M.C. (2018) Family background and parent-school involvement for at-risk preschool children with disabilities. *Journal of Special Education* 52 (1), 39–49.

Sawyer, B., Atkins-Burnett, S., Sandilos, L., Scheffner Hammer, C., Lopez, L. and Blair, C. (2018) Variations in classroom language environments of preschool children who are low income and linguistically diverse. *Early Education and Development* 29 (3), 398–416.

Shonkoff, J.P. and Phillips, D.A. (2000) *From Neurons to Neighborhoods: The Science of Early Childhood Development*. Washington, DC: National Academies Press.

US Census Bureau (2015) Census Bureau Reports at Least 350 Languages Spoken in US Homes. https://www.census.gov/newsroom/press-releases/2015/cb15-185.html.

US Department of Health & Human Services (2008) *Dual Language Learning: What Does It Take?* Office of Head Start, Administration for Children and Families. https://www.buildinitiative.org/Portals/0/Uploads/Documents/Dual%20Language%20Learning%20-%20What%20Does%20It%20Take.pdf.

Vigil, J., Pacione-Zayas, C. and Puente, S. (2013) *Primeros Pasos: Strengthening Programs that Support Illinois Infants and Toddlers*. Chicago, IL: Latino Policy Forum.

Whitebook, M., McLean, C., Austin, L.J. and Edwards, B. (2018) *Early Childhood Workforce Index 2018*. Berkeley, CA: Center for the Study of Child Care Employment, University of California at Berkeley.

Williams, C. (2014) Building on immigrants' strengths to improve their children's early education. New America. Blog post, June 5, 2014. Retrieved from https://www.newamerica.org/education-policy/edcentral/building-immigrants-strengths-improve-childrens-educations/.

Williams, C. (2015) Head Start works particularly well for dual language learners. *New America.* Blog post, April 3, 2015. Retrieved from https://www.newamerica.org/education-policy/edcentral/headstartdlls/.

Williams, C. (2017) The intrusion of white families into bilingual schools. *The Atlantic.* Retrieved from https://www.theatlantic.com/education/archive/2017/12/the-middle-class-takeover-of-bilingual-schools/549278/.

Wolfe, K. and Durán, L.K. (2013) Culturally and linguistically diverse parents' perceptions of the IEP process: A review of current research. *Multiple Voices for Ethnically Diverse Exceptional Learners* 13 (2), 4–18.

Yoshikawa, H. (2011) *Immigrants Raising Citizens: Undocumented Parents and their Children.* New York, NY: Russell Sage Foundation.

Zepeda, M., Castro, D.C. and Cronin, S. (2011) Preparing early childhood teachers to work with young dual language learners. *Child Development Perspectives* 5 (1), 10–14.

5 Dual Language Learners with Disabilities in Inclusive Early Elementary School Classrooms

Sarah L. Alvarado, Sarah M. Salinas, and Alfredo J. Artiles

This chapter synthesizes research on teaching and learning for dual language learners with disabilities (DLLsWD) in pre-kindergarten (pre-K) through third grade. DLLsWD constitute a growing subgroup of the K-12 population, with a vast degree of demographic diversity whose educational needs may be overlooked or misunderstood. Teaching and learning in early childhood inclusive classrooms require a wide-ranging lens through which school personnel can account for students' multiple linguistic and cognitive strengths and needs (National Academies of Sciences, Engineering, and Medicine, 2017). This work also requires attention to be paid to the legal and ethical obligations that school personnel must consider in order to address DLLsWD needs (Kangas, 2018). Unfortunately, the education of these students is fraught with misconceptions, such as: "(1) Students with disabilities cannot be bilingual, (2) students with disabilities should not be bilingual, (3) English should be the only instructional language, (4) pull-out services are the best, and (5) families will value bilingualism" (Cheatham & Barnett, 2017: 60). The NAS (2017) reported research evidence that dispels these misunderstandings and identified approaches to nurture bilingualism, a point we address subsequently in this chapter.

We start by noting three important caveats about this knowledge base (National Academies of Sciences, Engineering, and Medicine, 2017). First, although there are sizable bodies of empirical work on dual language learners and students with disabilities, there is a dearth of research on DLLsWD. Second, we signal a theoretical shift in this research. Research on learners with disabilities has historically emphasized instructional approaches grounded in behavioral and cognitive perspectives, while the scholarship on DLLs tends to draw from sociocultural and linguistic perspectives. Throughout the chapter, we use the term "social organization of learning" to mark the shift from an emphasis on teaching to the simultaneous consideration of teaching, learning, and sociocultural contexts, thus recognizing the situated nature of learning (Cole, 1996; Greeno & Engeström, 2014; Trent et al., 1998). Although this is still an under-represented perspective in the research with DLLsWD, there are interesting developments in literacy and bilingual education research that can enrich the knowledge base on DLLsWD. Third, key information about inclusive education models, definitions, or features, is not reported consistently in the studies consulted to create this overview. This is a limitation of this literature.

In this chapter, we outline two core principles that underlie effective teaching and learning literacy models for DLLsWD: the critical importance of building on children's strengths, particularly the first language (L1) to develop a second language (L2), and the central role of local contexts in the design and implementation of effective educational models for DLLsWD. We begin by stressing core principles of teaching and learning that promote students' multilingualism and cognitive development. Next, we review research on teaching and instructional approaches for DLLsWD. We discuss the possibility of organizing learning that is responsive to DLLsWDs' needs through empirically based work which values students' backgrounds using a culturally and linguistically responsive learning lens. We end with a brief conclusion on the social organization of learning for DLLsWD in inclusive programs.

Foundational Principles of Teaching and Learning for DLLsWD

In this section we review foundational work which builds on what DLLsWD bring to the early childhood classroom. We highlight research that builds on student and family linguistic and cultural strengths. These efforts center on the development of children's multilingualism towards the goals of helping them develop linguistically in one or more languages. This work also outlines the approaches to foster L1 and L2 learning through collaboration between schools, students, and families. This expansive approach is also the means by which school personnel can organize learning and teaching for all content areas.

Toward bilingualism and biliteracy: Building on L1 to learn L2

Asset-based approaches are a foundational idea in the education of DLLsWD. In this work, school personnel build on students' linguistic and cultural backgrounds as they are considered assets for instruction. To do this work, Cloud (2002) emphasized the importance of recognizing students' linguistic home and school repertoires. Consideration of families' language use is critical for the design of learning contexts that address students' needs (Cloud, 2002). Other key considerations also include (a) the student's immediate and future needs and desired goals for each language; (b) the student's development in each language, which includes consideration of which language might better support learning; and (c) the degree to which the student's special education needs impact learning and language development, in distinct subjects (e.g., literacy, math). Rather than viewing students' linguistic resources as a deterrent to learning, school personnel foster learning by recognizing students' personal histories and experiences as strengths and use that knowledge to organize student learning.

Debunking myths to foster bilingualism

School personnel and families may hold misconceptions about DLLs' capabilities to develop bilingualism and about their education (National Academies of Sciences, Engineering, and Medicine, 2017). Cheatham *et al.* (2012) reviewed comparison studies examining the impact of bilingualism, bilingual instruction, and interventions for students with disabilities. Reviewing a range of studies spanning several decades, Cheatham and colleagues' findings reinforced the possibility that DLLsWD can develop in both (or multiple) languages. Cheatham *et al.* reassured that DLLsWD "can be bilingual without consequences to their communication, cognition, and behavior and that some evidence exists of advantages of being bilingual" (Cheatham *et al.*, 2012: 7). In their review, Cheatham and colleagues concluded that, for students with disabilities, home and second language interventions, as welcoming and "promoting" bilingualism, are a critical component of "culturally and linguistically appropriate services for bilingual students with disabilities" (Cheatham *et al.*, 2012: 2). Noting earlier work, and connecting language use and development to home, Cheatham and colleagues reiterated this position:

> At a minimum, special educators can no longer simply advise families to stop speaking their home language with a student who has a disability. Discussions with families about the importance of the home language and potential for home-language loss can occur with regard to student competencies and family priorities ... Focusing only on English could result in isolating children from the multitude of contexts in which they live and learn. (Cheatham *et al.*, 2012: 7)

Similarly, Soto and Yu (2014) confirmed the benefits of bilingual instruction for students who require augmentative and alternative communication. Additional research support that challenges these myths include (National Academies of Sciences, Engineering, and Medicine, 2017: 361–362):

(1) There is no evidence that DLLs/ELLs get confused or are overwhelmed or have additional difficulties with negative consequences from two (or more) languages;
(2) code-switching is a normal grammatical and communicatively effective behavior in all DLLs/ELLs;
(3) sequential bilinguals with L1 tend to perform more poorly on standardized tests of second language (L2) ability (but similarly on narrative structure measures). However, their performance in L2 tends to approximate or equal that of monolinguals with LI when exposure to L2 has occurred for six years or longer and the two languages are similar, a finding consistent with research showing that ELLs in general education become proficient in English more quickly than those with disabilities; [and]
(4) research findings suggest that speaking the home language facilitates social interaction, and in turn language and social development.

As such, empirical support for bilingualism and biliteracy among DLLsWDs is clear. In this chapter, we highlight examples by which school professionals can organize learning to foster asset-based approaches aimed at addressing students' linguistic and special education needs.

Supporting L1 and L2 learning in inclusive programs

Student language and learning needs can be fostered through school practices that involve all personnel and multiple program aspects (Kangas, 2018). For instance, regardless of whether parents, school systems, or policies support bilingualism, school personnel can ensure that school documents, letters, or other forms of communication are offered to parents in their home language (Artiles & Ortiz, 2002; Kangas, 2018; Ortiz & Yates, 2001; Staples & Diliberto, 2010). For example, a "purposefully designed IEP [individualized education program]" can further support both language and special education needs and involves parent input (Cheatham & Barnett, 2017: 61). School personnel can specify which goals will be achieved in the general, special education classroom, or in both settings, in the targeted language, and how linguistic development will be supported. To illustrate, if a student has a goal of learning 25 sight words, the target language (or languages) should be noted, keeping in mind students' overall learning goals. Targeting sight words, for example, the IEP would stipulate the student's goals for reading sight words in English and Spanish. We note that although particular language goals might commonly be perceived as the responsibility of general education teachers, the education of DLLsWD in inclusive classrooms involves the work of all school personnel; thus, collaboration among staff and disciplines is key (Cheatham & Barnett, 2017; Ortiz & Yates, 2001). School professionals can support student learning by offering instruction and assessments in the students' home language and in English, whenever possible (Abedi, 2006, 2010; Barrera & Liu, 2006). Since instruction and assessment may be contextually driven, we reiterate the need for school personnel to engage in critical praxis (reflection and action, Hoffman-Kipp *et al.*, 2003) to plan for DLLsWD learning. This means that, depending on the local context, social contexts for learning may be designed to align with, and build from, students' and families' repertoires, which will require school staff to reflect on what is relevant and meaningful for the students.

In addition, inclusive education for DLLsWD needs to rely on the contributions of language and learning experts in schools, which has implications for collaborative work (Ortiz & Artiles, 2010). These professionals can include specialists, such as bilingual teaching assistants, monolingual and bilingual service providers, such as speech-language pathologists, and occupational therapists (Hoover *et al.*, 2008). For instance, second language acquisition experts can help colleagues understand the ways to support L2 learning (Klingner *et al.*, 2014; Turnbull *et al.*, 2015). A bilingual staff member could assist teachers in translating work for students or in providing one-on-one language support to students whose English is limited. Other collaborative means of support might involve linguistic specialists observing students in other classes to inform the planning of interventions or providing feedback to teachers to address particular student learning needs. Collaborative work also involves partnerships among colleagues to brainstorm solutions to student struggles and create plans for L1 and L2 support or development.

Fostering L1 and L2 through collaborative arrangements with families

Involving the parents of DLLsWD in their children's learning is a legal and ethical matter (McCray & García, 2002). School personnel can help families of DLLsWD feel welcomed through their actions and attitudes (Ruiz, 1991; Soto & Yu, 2014; Staples & Diliberto, 2010). In a review of research and policy literature of 20 states with the largest number of DLLs, Burr *et al.* (2015) reiterated parents' rights and their role in special education processes. Throughout the identification, placement, or re-evaluation processes, parents could offer support in multiple key decisions. Burr and colleagues also emphasized parents' roles as key players in instructional decisions related to students' developmental, cultural, and linguistic needs. For example, parents may provide critical information about language use, family health, immigration experiences, or their acculturation to the US education system (when relevant) (Burr et al., 2015; McCray & García, 2002). In this way, school professionals should recognize and value multiple forms of knowledge and view parents and families as collaborators with key information about their children's learning.

School staff can also foster student learning through embracing families' cultural and linguistic assets. For instance, the families of DLLsWD might feel appreciated when school personnel establish after-school activities or training for parents in their home language(s). Further support might include school-based activities (e.g., school events, forms, and fliers sent home) that support home languages vis-à-vis providing translations or opportunities for families to use the home language after school. Other means of supporting bilingual development include encouraging parents to read to their children in their home language for enjoyment or homework assignments, where parents can act as partners in bi-literacy development (Soto & Yu, 2014; Staples & Diliberto, 2010). Cheatham and Barnett (2017) highlighted the benefits of bilingualism as a mediator of inclusive practices, since DLLsWD can participate in routine family activities at home and the community. For instance, fostering bilingualism includes encouraging families to support the use of multiple languages at home, even in contexts where DLLsWD may not have access to bilingual education (Cheatham & Barnett, 2017).

While we stress the importance of bilingualism, we acknowledge that there is considerable diversity among families in their beliefs and positions about bilingualism, bilingual instruction, and learning. Indeed, not all parents have the same views pertaining to second language instruction (Staples & Diliberto, 2010). For example, while some parents may support bilingualism entirely or partially, others may believe it is their responsibility to teach their children their home language, while the school is responsible for teaching English (Cheatham & Barnett, 2017). In cases where families do not embrace bilingual instruction at school, school personnel can still be respectful and responsive to the needs of DLLsWD and their families in other ways. Al Khateeb et al. (2015) highlighted the importance of considering parents' varied perceptions of the school system, preferred methods of communication, as well as language barriers that often impeded their full involvement in the schooling processes.

Respecting and recognizing family values requires building a rapport to develop the lines of communication between schools and families (Staples & Diliberto, 2010). To improve parent and school collaboration and communication, Staples and Diliberto proposed the use of multiple modes of communication, beyond traditional means (i.e., report cards, progress reports). School personnel in the early childhood classroom might also consider the benefits and use of more interactive tools, such as journals, as a communication medium, where teachers can send daily notes home to students' parents and families. Used this way, daily communication journals might also include information about students' behaviors, learning, language successes, or struggles during the day. The communication journals may also offer a place for parents to write down and share their responses, comments, or feedback related to student learning. Phone calls home are another widely used means of communication when a student is absent or sending materials home in the parents' dominant language (Staples & Diliberto, 2010). In cases where school personnel do not speak the students' home language, school leaders can support teachers by providing resources (e.g., language specialists from the school community) to assist teachers in communicating in the L1.

School personnel can also provide support to DLLsWD and their families by sharing research-based practices that support learning. For instance, families may be unaware of research that supports bilingual instruction for students, may not know that bilingual instruction is offered or available to their child, or may also hold common misunderstandings, similar to those held by school staff (Cheatham & Barnett, 2017). In any case, school personnel can support students and families by offering their expertise and knowledge about best instructional approaches in designing learning for DLLsWD so that parents can make informed decisions.

The foundational principles outlined in the preceding sections are critical to providing meaningful educational opportunities for DLLsWD. However, the application of these principles should take into account important contextual influences that mediate educational success.

Teaching and Learning for DLLsWD: Sociocultural Contexts Matter

A key contextual consideration in the design of effective programs for DLLsWD is the identification of an educational model to address the needs of this population. Cheatham and Barnett (2017) recommended that school personnel nurture bilingualism by developing and supporting dual language and bilingual models. Dual language programs aim to maintain students' home language(s) while they are learning the L2 (Lindholm-Leary & Howard, 2008). Dual language programs (also referred to as two-way immersion) consist of instruction taking place in both the home language (e.g., Spanish) and English, with 50% of instruction in one language, across disciplines. The other half of the day consists of instruction in the alternative language (Lindholm-Leary & Howard, 2008), typically with the primary goals of developing bilingualism and biliteracy. Program models may vary in the percentage of time spent in target languages during the school day, depending on local practices (National Academies of Sciences, Engineering, and Medicine, 2017). Not all programs are the same, however, as funding, the linguistic diversity of the school population, the policy climate at the district and state levels, staff capacity, and parental and school leadership support, constitute contextual mediators that shape implementation.

In Arizona and Massachusetts, for example, DLLsWD may not qualify for dual language instruction due to students' inadequate levels of English language proficiency, driven by restrictive language policies. However, since DLLsWD instruction requires attention to linguistic and special education needs, as stipulated by federal law, school personnel can work together and advocate bilingual instruction. School staff may also face challenges due to the multiplicity of languages represented in schools (Pew Research Center, 2018). The diversity of languages will likely impact the design of two-way immersion programs due to the challenges associated with choosing a manageable number of home languages to include in such programs.

In addition, teacher capacity is a central consideration. Ortiz and Robertson (2018) summarized the necessary core teacher competencies in teaching DLLsWD (see Appendix 5.1) and outlined three areas to develop teacher competencies: language factors, learning development and individual differences, and literacy foundations. Within these three areas, consideration of contextual factors is a requirement. For instance, school personnel might be highly knowledgeable about assessments or interventions but may not understand cultural variability among families (even those from the same ethnic group), which affects language use, e.g., variations in dialects, which may have an impact on students' language use.

Babich defined dialect as a "subclass or variety within a language. It is a systematic way in which one speaker or a group of speakers in a language differs from other speakers of the same language" (Babich, 1987: 89). This scholar extended the notion of dialect to "members of differing social classes, religious, ethnic, cultural, or vocational groups – even the two sexes" (Babich, 1987: 89). Babich offered three guidelines that teachers can follow in the classroom. Teachers can (1) encourage children to be sensitive to the communication of others, which might include a dialectical variation, to develop the "appropriateness of communication behavior"; (2) suspend value judgment from the ways individuals speak, especially when communication patterns are associated with specific personal or cultural characteristics; and (3) expand students' "repertoire of dialects," by recognizing language diversity within and across groups (Babich, 1987: 93).

It is critical that educators use linguistic differences in schools and classrooms productively. Typically, teachers face at least two scenarios: (a) they use a language that students are not familiar with, due to dialectical variation; or (b) children may produce language that teachers are not familiar with (Fillmore & Snow, 2000). It is in the best interest of teachers and students to draw upon this linguistic diversity as a resource for learning, while keeping in mind that dialectical variation exists within members of apparently similar subgroups of students (e.g., Spanish or English speakers), and that those differences may directly impact learning, language use, or learning outcomes (Babich, 1987; Fillmore & Snow, 2000; Solano-Flores, 2006; Terry et al., 2012).

Assessment plays a significant role in the social contexts of learning, particularly becausethe assessment results of DLLsWD may be confounded by their language backgrounds (Abedi, 2010). This has implications for assessments at all levels, including large-scale assessments (Liu et al., 2017), assessments to measure student learning difficulties (Barrera & Liu, 2006), and classroom assessments of learning. Liu and colleagues (2017) highlighted how large-scale assessment practices need to account for students' multiple needs and consider language and special education needs together. Liu et al., stressed five guiding principles for large-scale assessment practices: (1) content standards that do not differ from those used with students who are not second language learners; (2) assessment items that are developed directly from content, do not include bias, and do not deviate from the measured construct; (3) informed specifications related to assessment decisions as spelled out in the students' IEP (individualized education program); (4) knowledgeable decisions based on IEP team input to make individual student accommodations; and (5) use of reports that outline how students were supported during large-scale assessments.

Next, we summarize various instructional models grouped under the broad category of culturally responsive approaches.

Culturally Responsive Approaches for DLLsWD

Foundational principles for the work of DLLsWD include instructional approaches that attend to students' multiple needs. Embracing student needs requires the work of culturally and linguistically responsive learning (CRL) as well as comprehensive instructional approaches (González & Artiles, 2015; Klingner et al., 2015; Lesaux & Harris, 2013; Linan-Thompson & Cavazos, 2017). Enveloped within the family of responsive teaching, culturally sustaining pedagogy (CSP) (Paris, 2012) is a promising emerging model that extends culturally responsive pedagogy (Alim et al., 2017; Waitoller & King Thorius, 2016). Though we did not locate CSP empirical work targeting young DLLsWDs, we illustrate some possibilities when uniting CSP with other instructional approaches. For example, Waitoller and King Thorius (2016) offered the possibility of cross-pollinating culturally sustaining pedagogy (CSP) and universal design for learning (UDL), a promising approach for improving educational opportunities for culturally and linguistically diverse learners. This concept of cross-pollination as part of CSP and UDL aligns with many of the practices we cover in this chapter, since it extends culturally responsive learning and teaching (CRL) by building on students' assets and invoking critical reflectivity. These conceptualizations align with work we illustrate in the subsequent section, such as embracing students' backgrounds and building on students' cultural and linguistic assets (e.g., Cheatham & Barnett, 2017; King Thorius et al., 2013; Linan-Thompson & Cavazos, 2017). Cross-pollinating both CSP and UDL also bears similarities to previous work in emphasizing that learning must be differentiated (e.g., scaffolding), because it is based on UDL's three guiding principles. Next, we illustrate the family of CRL approaches we identified in the DLLsWD literature.

Comprehensive and culturally responsive literacy approaches

A core assumption of these approaches is that DLLs need balanced or comprehensive approaches to literacy instruction (Lesaux & Harris, 2013). González and Artiles explained that a balanced literacy approach:

> attends to the cognitive and sociocultural dimensions of literacy that most researchers have examined, albeit in isolated fashion, while adding resource pedagogies as a way to respond to heterogeneous Latina/o cultures ... Bringing culturally sustaining processes into special education standpoints provides a powerful turn in how we attend to the cultural aspect of literacy research – treating culture as a fluid and vital mediator in the learning process. (González & Artiles, 2015: 26)

As such, a more holistic method also embodies the essential components of culturally and linguistically responsive pedagogy for DLLsWD. This perspective builds on the scholarship that has been used in general education (Klingner *et al.*, 2014; Gay, 2002; Huerta, 2011; Kea & Trent, 2013; Ladson-Billings, 1991, 2014; Lucas *et al.*, 2008; Nieto, 2015). Teachers who embrace this standpoint understand that learners bring assets from their homes and communities. For example, King Thorius and colleagues pointed out that culturally and linguistically responsive interventions in inclusive classrooms are:

(1) *Relevant:* Teachers use the cultural knowledge and prior experiences of diverse students to make learning more appropriate and effective; teaching to and through the strengths of DLLs.
(2) *Multi-faceted:* Teacher goals are to develop a variety of forms of literacies in DLLs, to provide opportunities to participate in critical inquiry about their world, and to work for social change. Multiple literacies include language-based, mathematical, scientific, historical, cultural, and political aspects.
(3) *Explicit:* DLLs receive direct instruction in basic literacy skills required in order to fully participate in the dominant culture. (King Thorius *et al.*, 2013: 54)

Designing instruction for DLLsWD requires connecting with students in culturally responsive ways (King Thorius *et al.*, 2013; Linan-Thompson & Cavazos, 2017). Culturally responsive practices in inclusive classrooms may include books or materials that resonate with students' sociocultural experiences as well as exposing them to other cultures. Examples of these might include the use of characters, themes, or settings that are familiar to students (Cloud, 2002). For instance, through literacy practices, teachers can use books and themes that are written in students' home languages, including themes and topics familiar to students and families. In addition, attention to language development is critical in the education of DLLsWD. In this regard, Linan-Thompson and Cavazos explained that effective language instruction includes the use of "(a) comprehensible language, (b) scaffolding, (c) visuals, (d) pre-teaching of and multiple exposures to new vocabulary, (e) sheltered content instruction, (f) cooperative learning, (g) peer tutoring, and (h) multimodal and culturally relevant instruction" (Linan-Thompson & Cavazos, 2017: 260–261). For instance, teachers could organize reading or writing experiences with more or less experienced readers within small, guided, or paired groups to assist with cognitively more challenging activities. Additionally, teachers could pair students strategically according to varying levels of language proficiency in one or more languages. Through reading aloud to students, the teacher could introduce comprehension strategies to model fluency and understanding, adapting instruction based on small-group or individual needs. Teachers may also incorporate videos, field trips, hands-on demonstrations, or other multi-sensory activities that could help students understand the texts being read, on topics they may have never experienced before. For example, if a student has never been to the ocean, a video on ocean pollution or a visit to an artificial or real-life beach could help learning become more meaningful, build comprehension, and develop vocabulary.

Culturally responsive and comprehensive learning approaches also extend into other content areas. For example, culturally responsive approaches in inclusive classrooms include use of story problems for mathematics instruction, which is often missing for students with disabilities (Lambert & Tan, 2017). Employing culturally responsive mathematics instruction, teachers can have students write or illustrate their own math story word problems either individually or with the help of others (e.g., peers or adults). DLLsWD can work alongside peers to write math problems using themes, names, and language(s) familiar to students. In an early childhood classroom, teachers can have DLLsWD use pictures and sentence patterns to create simple to more complex word problems. Teachers can use sentence starters to provide patterns to guide students in creating their own story problems and sharing their work with others, integrating several subjects to tackle multiple learning areas.

Vocabulary instruction

Lesaux and Harris (2013), as well as Klingner and colleagues (2015), noted a rather small research base that informs vocabulary development for younger DLLs (see August *et al.*, 2009; Klingner *et al.*, 2015, for a review). Vocabulary development, which includes introducing words within the context of instruction (e.g., fictional trade books, articles), illustrates meaningful learning through "planned, ongoing encounters with words – receptive and productive – using different modes (reading, writing, discussion, debate, structured play, etc.)" (Lesaux & Harris, 2013: 77). More explicitly, Klingner and colleagues emphasized the importance of vocabulary development that can be embedded throughout students' learning day to promote students' linguistic and cognitive development. Strategies to foster vocabulary development might take place before, during, or after reading activities, such as during read alouds, guided reading groups, or shared readings, those intended to develop comprehension or foundational skills, and across multiple subjects and learning situations (see Klinger *et al.*, 2015, for a summary of vocabulary development strategies). By utilizing these specific vocabulary practices, teachers can build a foundation that will support students' comprehension of reading texts when vocabulary strategies are also used in conjunction with strategies to support reading comprehension.

Next, we offer other "dynamic," rather than "static" (Lesaux & Harris, 2013: 78) processes for developing reading comprehension.

Reading comprehension through strategy instruction

Building on foundational work targeting middle school students who struggled with comprehension, Brown *et al.* (1984), among others, extended the idea of *reciprocal teachin*g, proposing that learning is a shared, mutual experience. Namely, strategic instruction relates to "instructional approaches designed to help students become strategic readers by applying a set of strategies before, during, and after reading … [identified as] multicomponent reading strategy" (Klingner *et al.*, 2015: 172). Although the research reviewed by Klingner and colleagues highlights mostly empirical work in middle school grades or above, reading strategy instruction offers a multi-component approach that helps enhance vocabulary as well as improve comprehension for learners in all grades. Klingner and colleagues identified some of these components as providing students with opportunities to discuss texts based on targeted words from shared book reading experiences, connecting students' background knowledge with class work. To illustrate, teachers can emphasize reading strategies to assist students in deciphering unknown words within texts. In a shared reading experience, for example, the teacher could model skipping the word and reading to the end of the sentence, using picture clues, or looking at the first letter to figure out unknown words.

Researchers state that while instructional strategies have been found to bring promising results for students of all abilities and needs, teachers should exercise caution with the use of learning strategies that are applied too generally across settings (Hoover & Collier, 2004; Lesaux &

Harris, 2013). Pointing out the work of "McKeown *et al.* (2009)", Lesaux and Harris illustrated this tendency, offering words of caution:

> For example, standard practice has been to teach a "set" of strategies to be applied generically across texts (e.g., finding a main idea, making predictions, drawing inferences), without necessarily attending to the nuanced process of constructing meaning from text in real time, focusing especially on its content. (Lesaux & Harris, 2013: 78)

In essence, this model of reading instruction emphasizes the dynamic nature of reading, in which students develop literacy through connecting content and personal experiences to texts. Lesaux and Harris emphasized that "reading instruction occurs in the context of knowledge and language building and is anchored in rigorous and engaging texts," such as through "metacognitive prompts that require students to reflect on and talk about their reasoning processes and also be connected to opportunities to promote deep comprehension through writing" (Lesaux & Harris, 2013: 78). Similarly offering words of caution in addressing the sociocultural and learning needs of DLLsWD, Hoover and Collier (2004) reiterated this point, emphasizing that instructional strategies students can be distracted by stimuli used to teach the strategy in the first place. For example, in teaching a strategy to build comprehension, a teacher might use a visual image of an object that is not familiar to the students.

Next, we specify other interactive and multi-component (Klingner *et al.*, 2015) approaches to literacy instruction, involving students in assisting others in learning, a social and interactive process in inclusive classrooms.

Peer-assisted learning and flexible grouping

One approach to building reading comprehension, and a form of strategy instruction (Klingner *et al.*, 2015), relies on peer-assisted learning strategies (PALS). Klingner and colleagues (2015) summarized PALS as focused on reading fluency and comprehension, a "structured class-wide peer tutoring model [in which] students read together in pairs, taking turns being the 'coach' and the reader. As the reader reads, the coach provides corrective feedback. Points are awarded for good reading and coaching" (Klingner *et al.*, 2015: 174). This approach has been used in first through sixth grade and is not limited to students with disabilities (Calhoon *et al.*, 2007; Klingner *et al.*, 2015; Rivera *et al.*, 2009; Saenz *et al.*, 2005).

King Thorius and Santamaría Graff (2018) extended the use of PALS to encompass more culturally and linguistically responsive tactics. For example, rather than emphasize individual or group competition, teachers could emphasize the importance of community achievement, as opposed to rewarding individuals or groups for learning outcomes. King Thorius and Santamaría Graff illustrated the importance of being responsive to classroom cultural diversity:

> In line with experiences of some historically underserved groups, working cooperatively toward a common goal may provide greater extrinsic motivation for certain students than actively competing against one another for individual or team points (Arzubiaga, Rueda, & Monzó, 2002). Whereas competition creates the implicit binary classification of winner/loser in traditional PALS' team activities, collectivism encourages students to work together, advocate for one another, and attain reading goals for the good and fun of the entire class. (King Thorius & Santamaría Graff, 2018: 167)

In sum, organizing learning in culturally responsive ways requires critical reflection and action to decide what may best suit students' needs (Hoffman-Kipp *et al.*, 2003). We conclude, as King Thorius and Santamaría Graff pointed out, PALS may be productive in some classes, but not in other cases. As such, we emphasize that this work requires organizing learning in ways that respond to students' sociocultural and special education needs.

Other collaborative approaches have been used with this population that involve other grouping structures. For instance, Linan-Thompson and Cavazos (2017) emphasized flexible grouping formats in the work of teaching DLLsWDs. Flexible grouping is defined as a way of organizing students based on group and lesson goals. In flexible grouping formats, student learners are divided into small groups that typically have between three and five students. Teachers can then plan instruction and the use of different learning strategies based on the needs of each individual group, which allows for the use of necessary scaffolds to address the learning needs of DLLsWD. Further, these group approaches provide opportunities for students to engage in both paired-partner and independent practice (Linan-Thompson & Cavazos, 2017). As with other examples, however, school personnel must use teacher praxis, as well as consider contextual variables when deploying these strategies and grouping approaches.

Scaffolding

CRL approaches and pedagogy include the actions, methods, and practices that school personnel engage in to maximize students' multiple learning needs. Often associated with Vygotsky's (1978) social theory, scaffolding is learning "guided by others" (Stone, 1998: 351, as cited in van de Pol *et al.*, 2010). Educational researchers define scaffolding as "what a teacher, adult assistant, or more capable peer does when working with a student to solve a problem, carry out a task, or achieve a goal which would be beyond their unassisted efforts" (as cited in Santamaría et al., 2002: 135). Scaffolding techniques are strategies to help expand students' level of development until such a point in time that a student is more capable of solving a task or learning a concept on her or his own. Scaffolds, and the process of using scaffolding, represent temporary support structures that are removed when no longer needed (Santamaría et al., 2002). Based on previous empirical work (e.g., Englert & Mariage, 1996), targeting third grade DLLsWD, Santamaría et al. (2002) identified four scaffolding techniques: (1) mediated scaffolds, (2) task scaffolds, (3) materials scaffolds, and (4) comprehensible input, as follows:

Mediated scaffolds

The teacher, the teacher's aide, or a more proficient peer helps to make information accessible to the student. Assistance is gradually withdrawn, and responsibility is systematically transferred to the student. For example, a teacher-directed series of mini-lessons on adjectives could help a student understand the process of adjective use.

Task scaffolds

These scaffolds shape the ways a task is carried out. They allow students with learning disabilities to focus on their learning process and strategies by reducing the information that they must generate independently. In language arts, for example, the students might be given pictures on cue cards that depict the steps they need to follow to complete an activity. Eventually, the students will be able independently to compose summaries, stories, or descriptions without the cue cards.

Materials scaffolds

Materials scaffolds are strategically designed advanced organizers (e.g., story maps, paragraph frames, and sentence starters) that gradually provide less and less support, resulting in the students' ability to create a product with little or no support. Eventually, students are given opportunities to work with these scaffolds independently.

Comprehensible input

A concept that seems compatible with scaffolding strategies is comprehensible input (Krashen, 1982). Developed to explain one aspect of second language acquisition, comprehensible input is language used in ways that make it understandable and meaningful to the language learner. Comprehensible input can be viewed as a scaffolding strategy that enables students to more readily acquire a second language within a well-supported zone of proximal development. For example, in presenting the concept of simple fractions, a teacher might pair key vocabulary (e.g., whole, half, and quarter) with concrete demonstrations using manipulatives.

As we have pointed out, school personnel can design and implement culturally responsive learning instructional approaches that foster learning through the actions of adults, adults and students, as well as between students. Next, we turn to systemic efforts to address DLLsWD multiple learning needs.

Contemporary models: Tiered support systems

After IDEA's reauthorization in 2004, tiered frameworks such as response to intervention and multi-tiered systems of support were endorsed to address students' learning needs (Jimerson *et al.*, 2016). School personnel can support the learning needs of DLLsWD through early intervening services, as well as tiered intervention frameworks (National Academies of Sciences, Engineering, and Medicine, 2017).

The terms "response to intervention" and "multi-tiered systems of support" are often used interchangeably, as there are similarities between them (e.g., tiered levels, academic support); however, their functions are distinct. According to Vaughn and Fuchs (2006), response to intervention came from the National Research Council's 1982 report (as cited in Pullen *et al.*, 2019). Response to intervention aims to address students' academic struggles, whereas multi-tiered systems of support is a broader framework and includes students' emotional and behavioral well-being. It also includes professional development for adults, targeting school-wide reform improvement efforts (e.g., behavioral interventions, curricular, or environmental factors) (Pullen *et al.*, 2019).

In essence, school personnel do not wait until students are failing but, rather, through close monitoring of student progress within multi-tiered systems of support contexts, teachers address students' linguistic and special education learning needs. Multi-tiered systems of support models are used in inclusive programs and have also been noted as useful for DLLs with and without disabilities (Carta *et al.*, 2016; Cheatham & Barnett, 2017).

The multi-tiered systems of support model is based on the premise that all students receive research-based instructional practices in the general education classroom, also considered Tier 1 (Fuchs & Fuchs, 2006). School personnel document student progress over time in a systematic fashion (Fuchs & Fuchs, 2006; Lesaux & Harris, 2013). When students do not meet learning goals, school personnel respond with targeted instruction in the next tier of support; these interventions are more intense and focused on the specific needs of struggling learners. In the inclusive classroom, teacher practices might involve the use of more intensive interventions (Tier 2), such as small-group instruction grounded in research-based intervention programs for struggling students. Frequent assessments, through progress monitoring and learning benchmarks, continue to be used over time. When students' learning trajectories do not improve at Tier 2, more intensive interventions are provided. Student unresponsiveness might result in learners participating in more intense interventions (e.g., Tier 3), through the use of more focused instruction (e.g., one-on-one instruction).

Due to the unique needs of DLLs who struggle with literacy learning or have disabilities, researchers have recommended (as well as cautioned about) the use of multi-tiered systems of support models – emphasizing the need to employ culturally responsive multi-tiered systems of support (Artiles & Kozleski, 2010; Bal et al., 2018; García & Ortiz, 2008). Drawing from Alexander's (1996) model of "good practice," King Thorius and colleagues outlined this work as requiring political, pragmatic, conceptual, value, and empirical considerations (King Thorius et al., 2013: 51). García and Ortiz's (2008) illustration of a culturally and linguistically responsive tiered intervention model is an example of the multiple environmental, legal, and instructional factors that need to be considered (see Appendix 5.2). King Thorius and colleagues summarized this work as (1) recognizing that learning may be shaped by local structural forces or historical tendencies within local schools; (2) considering that local processes and school practices may restrict or foster learning; (3) teaching that involves "essential elements" that require consideration of learning, curriculum, and the "relationships between them;" (4) school personnel beliefs and values about students; and (5) effective instructional practices based on empirical evidence (King Thorius et al., 2013: 51).

The use of culturally and linguistically responsive multi-tiered systems of support presumably would open more opportunities to examine closely the conflation of students' learning difficulties that are due to a disability vs. due to second language learning. For instance, the strategic use of multi-tiered systems of support should include careful consideration of the practices and benefits for particular (sub-)groups of students (Orosco & Klingner, 2010). Klingner and Edwards (2006) emphasized the need for school personnel to consider for *whom* practices might be beneficial. Similarly, King Thorius and colleagues (2013) concluded that culturally relevant literacy intervention research should fulfill three criteria: (1) provide explicit, small-group instruction; (2) incorporate authentic texts and purposes for using texts; and (3) recognize DLLs' "cultures and languages as a basis for understanding themselves and others" (King Thorius et al., 2013: 54). King Thorius and Sullivan (2013) cautioned that tiered intervention frameworks may have unintentional consequences, since students' low performance or lack of progress could be associated with the possibility of a cognitive deficit rather than other environmental factors (e.g., insufficient opportunities to learn). In turn, without careful use of multi-tiered systems of support, school personnel could "perpetuate one of the very problems it was designed to prevent" (King Thorius & Sullivan, 2013: 79).

Conclusion

In this chapter, we synthesized the limited research base on instructional approaches for the social organization of learning for DLLsWD. This work requires a "new vision of critical, situated reflection [that] must include both technical and political content and be based on a dialogic approach," identified as "praxis" or reflection and action (Hoffman-Kipp *et al.*, 2003: 248). This means that there is not a one-size-fits-all approach for learning: the consideration of individual differences and contextual influences is necessary. An important way to provide such education is culturally responsive literacy practices which acknowledge students' home experiences and knowledge. In other words, the social organization of learning for DLLsWD demands distancing away from deficit-oriented perspectives.

The social organization of learning in inclusive classrooms also entails cultural-historical, practical, and legal considerations. For example, multiple laws govern how teaching and learning should be designed and assessed for DLLsWD (Kangas, 2018). This means that teachers are responsible for attending to DLLsWD language development and language use among and within sub-groups, while keeping in mind that their special education needs equally matter. In short, the education of DLLsWD requires attention to their intersectional needs (González *et al.*, 2015).

Appendix 5.1: Teacher Core Competencies (Ortiz & Robertson, 2018)

Language and Linguistics	Learner Development and Individual Differences	Literacy Foundations
Understand theories of native language (L1) and English (L2) acquisition.	Understand the nature of individual differences.	Understand the inter-relations among oral language, reading, and writing and the importance of integrating them in instruction.
Understand development of social and academic language among English Learners (ELs) and non-ELs.	Understand that individuals possess a variety of group (e.g., culture, language, social class) and individual characteristics (e.g., ability/disability).	Understand the developmental stages of literacy and/or biliteracy development.
Understand the basic patterns and structures of language.	Understand the heterogeneity of ELs and the characteristics and needs of sub-groups.	Understand similarities and differences between L1 and L2 literacy development.
Understand developmental and dialectical variations.	Understand the characteristics of ELs with language and/or literacy disabilities.	Understand essential components of L1 and L2 reading instruction, including teaching for cross-linguistic transfer.
Recognize similarities and differences between L1 and L2 and cross-linguistic influences.	**Educational Contexts**	Understand similarities and differences in literacy instruction for ELs and non-ELs.
Understand the importance of oral language development in the context of literacy instruction.	Understand basic theories, philosophies, program models, and practices used in educating ELs, including language instruction educational programs (LIEPs) and general and special education programs.	Apply relevant theory, research, policies, and practices in the selection and design of developmentally appropriate, research-based language and literacy instruction for ELs.
Value and promote bilingualism and biliteracy.	Understand the characteristics of schools and learning environments that support ELs' oral language and literacy development.	**Assessment**
Cultural Variability	Understand approaches to supporting ELs with language or learning difficulties or disabilities, including multi-tiered systems of support and response to intervention.	*General principles*
Understand the nature of culture and cultural variability.	Understand local, state, and national language and literacy performance standards.	Understand the purposes, types, and appropriate uses of formal and informal language and literacy assessments.
Understand factors that influence cultural identity.	Know state and federal laws, regulations and policy regarding entry and exit criteria for LEPs.	Evaluate instruments and procedures for linguistic and cultural bias.
Understand how cultural identity influences communication, behavior, interaction, and learning processes.	Know state and federal laws, regulations, and policy regarding referral, assessment, eligibility determinations, and individualized education program planning for ELs.	Select and administer formal and informal language and literacy assessments, aligned to the curriculum, to inform instruction and monitor progress.
Demonstrate cultural self-awareness.	Understand and apply universal design principles to create learning environments that accommodate learning differences.	Document oral language skills in L1 and L2, separately and together.
Understand the sociocultural context of teaching and learning.		Document literacy skills in L2, and in L1 if the student has received L1 instruction, separately and together.
Recognize and address cultural conflicts, stereotypes, and deficit thinking.		Evaluate student responses to language and literacy instruction in L1 and/or L2 using multiple measures.
Recognize the influence of organizational culture(s) on school practices and on teaching and learning.		Understand the impact of assessment modifications and adaptations on performance of ELs.
Value the linguistic and cultural knowledge and resources ELs acquire in their homes and communities.		
Create learning environments that value diversity and validate student's cultural identity and experiences in the teaching-learning process.		

Language and Linguistics	Learner Development and Individual Differences	Literacy Foundations
Understand assessment procedures used when ELs are referred to special education for language- and/or literacy-related difficulties.	Select and use curricula, instructional materials, technology, and strategies that respond to students' cultural backgrounds and to a range of language and literacy levels.	Collaborate with others to increase the knowledge base of best practices for ELs.
Data-based decision-making	Provide instruction and/or intervention that is meaningful, culturally and linguistically responsive, and at the student's instructional level(s) in L1 and/or L2.	Establish respectful and mutually beneficial relationships with EL families and communities, and with professional colleagues.
Identify consistent patterns of strengths and difficulty in the language(s) ELs speak and those in which they have received language and/or literacy instruction.		Participate effectively in problem-solving team processes.
Interpret present performance in relation to past performance and development of L1 and/or L2 language and literacy skills over time.	Teach language and literacy skills in L1 and/or L2 using approaches that are interactive and student-centered.	Actively engage family members in decision-making affecting their children's education.
Interpret results of language and literacy assessments in each language separately, and together, to identify strengths and needs within and across languages.	Provide frequent and appropriate feedback to enhance language and literacy achievement of ELs.	Understand the roles of interpreters and translators, and how to use their services.
	Employ flexible grouping to address the needs of individual ELs, groups, and the whole class.	Understand the roles and responsibilities of paraprofessionals and how to support their work.
Identify factors that promote or inhibit mastery of L1 and/or L2 language and literacy skills.	Apply knowledge of language and literacy difficulties and disabilities in differentiating instruction.	**Professional and Ethical Practice**
Utilize assessment results to plan L1 and/or L2 language and literacy instruction/intervention.	Facilitate transfer of language and literacy skills across languages and across home and school contexts.	Engage in self-evaluation about language and literacy instruction, considering personal assumptions and biases about ELs, language, culture, and ability/disability.
Compare the language and literacy skills of ELs to true peers in identifying students who need additional intervention or who should be considered for special education referral.	Critically evaluate current research related to best practices in L1 and/or L2.	Critically evaluate current research related to best practices in language and literacy for ELs and ELs with language- and/or literacy-related difficulties or disabilities.
Evaluate the effectiveness of instructional approaches for ELs and modify as needed.	**Collaboration**	Advocate linguistically and culturally responsive policies and practices at the local, state, and national levels.
Instruction/Intervention	Understand models and strategies for consultation and collaboration.	
Provide instruction that is aligned to state, and/or national language and literacy standards for ELs.	Work to develop a common philosophy among colleagues that reflects best practices for language and literacy instruction, and joint responsibility for the success of ELs.	Engage in ongoing professional development focused on language and literacy instructions for ELs.
Integrate language and literacy instruction guided by assessment and progress monitoring data.	Develop effective communication strategies in working with EL families, colleagues, and support personnel.	Participate in professional organizations engaged in advocacy for ELs.

Appendix 5.2: Framework for Culturally and Linguistically Responsive Tiered Interventions (García & Ortiz, 2008)

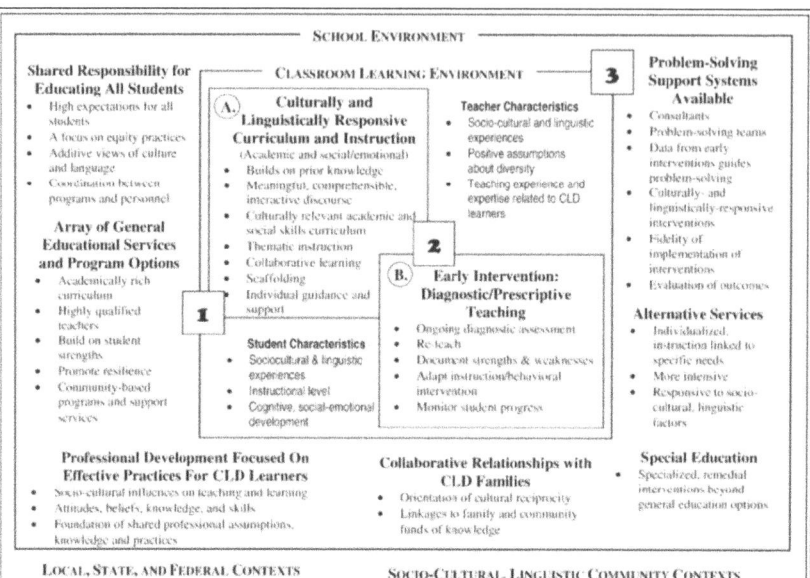

Source: García, S. & Ortiz, A. (2008) A framework for culturally and linguistically responsive design of response-to-intervention models. *Multiple Voices for Ethnically Diverse Exceptional Learners* 11 (1), 24–41. Reprinted by permission of SAGE Publications, Inc.

Note

The first and second author recognize funding from the US Department of Education, Office of Special Education Programs, Grant #H325D130065. The third author recognizes the support of the Equity Alliance. The opinions expressed here do not necessarily reflect the positions or policies of the US Department of Education.

References

Abedi, J. (2006) Psychometric issues in the ELL assessment and special education eligibility. *Teachers College Record* 108, 2282–2303. Retrieved from https://www.ncaase.com/docs/Abedi_TCRE782_2006.pdf.

Abedi, J. (2010) English language learners with disabilities: Classification, assessment, and accommodation issues. *Journal of Applied Testing Technology* 10 (2), 1–30. Retrieved from http://www.jattjournal.com/index.php/atp/article/view/48353.

Alexander, R. (1996) In search of good primary practice. In P. Woods (ed.) *Contemporary Issues in Teaching and Learning* (pp. 52–72). New York, NY: Routledge.

Alim, H.S., Baglieri, S., Ladson-Billings, G., Paris, D., Rose, D.H. and Valente, J.M. (2017) A *Harvard Educational Review* forum: Responding to "Cross-pollinating culturally sustaining pedagogy and universal design for learning: Toward an inclusive pedagogy that accounts for dis/ability." *Harvard Educational Review* 87 (1), 4–25. https://doi.org/10.17763/1943-5045-87.1.4.

Al Khateeb, J.M., Al Hadidi, M.S. and Al Khatib, A.J. (2015) Addressing the unique needs of Arab American children with disabilities. *Journal of Child and Family Studies* 24 (8), 2432–2440. https://doi.org/10.1007/s10826-014-0046-x.

Artiles A.J. and Ortiz A.J. (eds) (2002) *English Language Learners with Special Needs: Identification, Placement, and Instruction*. Washington, DC and McHenry, IL: Center for Applied Linguistics and Delta Systems Company, Inc. Retrieved from https://files.eric.ed.gov/fulltext/ED482995.pdf.

Artiles, A.J. and Kozleski, E.B. (2010) What counts as response and intervention in RTI? A sociocultural analysis. *Psicothema* 22 (4), 949–954. Retrieved from https://www.redalyc.org/pdf/727/72715515062.pdf.

Arzubiaga, A., Rueda, R. and Monzó, L. (2002) Family matters related to the reading engagement of Latino children. *Journal of Latinos and Education* 1 (4), 231–243. doi:10.1207/S1532771XJLE0104_3.

August, D., Shanahan, T. and Escamilla, K. (2009) English language learners: Developing literacy in second-language learners.Report of the National Literacy Panel on Language-Minority Children and Youth. *Journal of Literacy Research* 41 (4), 432–452. https://doi.org/10.1080/10862960903340165.

Babich, R.M. (1987) Dialects in the classroom: Their functions, some potential problems, and guidelines for teachers. *Journal of Thought* 22 (4), 89–94. Retrieved from https://www.jstor.org/stable/42589251?casa_token=3wpnvU5IW4UAAAAA:qNIkWAGlSqy3_8Rycz8K66Xk8-NkLUOl93v311Bvd97xMYnpKzMrgLoFmc0LOWoiQJjVayYGUkXEusj5YstE5ufgosqen3hqdLHjASXcMNWjUYhRf7IE&seq=1#metadata_info_tab_contents.

Bal, A., Afacam, K. and Cakir, H.I. (2018) Culturally responsive school discipline: Implementing learning lab at a high school for systemic transformation. *American Educational Research Journal* 55, 1007–1050.

Barrera, M. and Liu, K.K. (2006) Involving parents of English language learners with disabilities through instructional dialogues. *Journal of Special Education Leadership* 19 (1), 43-51. Retrieved from https://eric.ed.gov/?id=EJ804080.

Brown, A.L., Palincsar, A.S. and Armbruster, B.B. (1984) Instructing comprehension-fostering activities in interactive learning situations. In H. Mandl, N.L. Stein and T. Trabasso (eds) *Learning and Comprehension of Text* (pp. 255–286). Hillsdale, NJ: Lawrence Erlbaum.

Burr, E., Haas, E. and Ferriere, K. (2015) *Identifying and Supporting English Learner Students with Learning Disabilities: Key Issues in the Literature and State Practice*. Washington, DC: US Department of Education, Institute of Education Sciences, National Center for Education Evaluation and Regional Assistance, Regional Educational Laboratory West. Retrieved from https://files.eric.ed.gov/fulltext/ED558163.pdf.

Calhoon, M.B., Al Otaiba, S., Cihak, D., King, A. and Avalos, A. (2007) Effects of a peer-mediated program on reading skill acquisition for two-way bilingual first-grade classrooms. *Learning Disability Quarterly* 30 (3), 169–184. http://doi.org/10.2307/30035562.

Carta, J.J., Greenwood, C.R., Goldstein, H., McConnell, S.T., Kaminski, R., Bradfield, T.A. and Atwater, J. (2016) Advances in multi-tiered systems of support for prekindergarten children: Lessons learned from 5 years of research and development from the center for response to intervention in early childhood. In S.R. Jimerson, M.K. Burns and A.M. VanDerHeyden (eds) *Handbook of Response to Intervention: The Science and Practice of Multi-tiered Systems of Support* (pp. 587–606). New York, NY: Springer.

Cheatham, G.A. and Hart Barnett, J.E. (2017) Overcoming common misunderstandings about students with disabilities who are English language learners. *Intervention in School and Clinic* 53 (1), 58–63. doi: 1053451216644819.

Cheatham, G.A., Santos, R.M. and Kerkutluoglu, A. (2012) Review of comparison studies investigating bilingualism and bilingual instruction for students with disabilities. *Focus on Exceptional Children* 45 (3), 1–12. https://doi.org/10.17161/foec.v45i3.6681.

Cloud, N. (2002) Culturally and linguistically responsive Instructional planning. In A.J. Artiles and A.A. Ortiz (eds) *English Language Learners with Special Education Needs: Identification, Assessment, and Instruction* (pp. 107-131). Washington, DC and McHenry, IL: Center for Applied Linguistics and Delta Systems Co., Inc. Retrieved from https://files.eric.ed.gov/fulltext/ED482995.pdf.

Cole, M. (1996) *Cultural Psychology: A Once and Future Discipline.* Cambridge, MA: Harvard University Press.

Englert, C.S. and Mariage, T.V. (1996) A sociocultural perspective: Teaching ways-of-thinking and ways-of-talking in a literacy community. *Learning Disabilities Research and Practice* 11 (3), 157–67. Retrieved from https://eric.ed.gov/?id=EJ530721.

Fillmore, L.W. and Snow, C.E. (2000) *What Teachers Need to Know about Language.* Washington, DC: Center for Applied Linguistics. Retrieved from https://people.ucsc.edu/~ktellez/wongfill-snow.html.

Fuchs, D. and Fuchs, L.S. (2006) Introduction to response to intervention: What, why, and how valid is it? *Reading Research Quarterly* 41 (1), 93–99. https://ila.onlinelibrary.wiley.com/doi/pdf/10.1598/RRQ.41.1.4.

García, S.B. and Ortiz, A. (2008) A framework for culturally and linguistically responsive design of response-to-intervention models. *Multiple Voices for Ethnically Diverse Exceptional Learners* 11 (1), 24–41. Retrieved from https://multiplevoicesjournal.org/doi/abs/10.5555/muvo.11.1.gu04327p723217t0.

Gay, G. (2002). Culturally responsive teaching in special education for ethnically diverse students: Setting the stage. *International Journal of Qualitative Studies in Education*, 15 (6), 613–629. Retrieved from http://culturallyresponsiveteaching.weebly.com/uploads/1/8/1/5/18153535/__crt_in_sped.pdf.

González, T. and Artiles, A.J. (2015) Reframing venerable standpoints about language and learning differences: The need for research on the literate lives of Latina/o language minority students. *Journal of Multilingual Education Research* 6 (1), 3. Retrieved from https://fordham.bepress.com/jmer/vol6/iss1/3.

González, T., Tefera, A. and Artiles, A.J. (2015) The intersections of language differences and learning disabilities: Narratives in action. In M. Bigelow and J. Ennser-Kananen (eds) *The Handbook of Educational Linguistics* (pp. 145–157). New York, NY: Routledge.

Greeno, J.G. and Engeström, Y. (2014) Learning in activity. In R.K. Sawyer (ed.) *The Cambridge Handbook of the Learning Sciences* (pp. 128–147). Cambridge: Cambridge University Press.

Hoffman-Kipp, P., Artiles, A.J. and Lopez-Torres, L. (2003) Beyond reflection: Teacher learning as praxis. *Theory into Practice* 42 (3), 248–254. https://doi.org/10.1207/s15430421tip4203_12.

Hoover, J. and Collier, C. (2004) Methods and materials for bilingual special education. In L.M. Baca and H.T. Cervantes (eds) *The Bilingual Special Education Interface* (pp. 274–297). Upper Saddle River, NJ: Pearson Education.

Hoover, J.J., Klingner, J., Baca, L.M. and Patton, J.M. (2008) *Methods for Teaching Culturally and Linguistically Diverse Exceptional Learners.* Upper Saddle River, NJ: Pearson.

Huerta, T.M. (2011) Humanizing pedagogy: Beliefs and practices on the teaching of Latino children. *Bilingual Research Journal* 34 (1), 38–57. https://doi.org/10.1080/15235882.2011.568826.

Jimerson, S.R., Burns, M.K. and VanDerHeyden A.M. (2016) From response to intervention to multi-tiered systems of support: Advances in the science and practice of assessment and intervention. In M.T. Tejero Hughes and E. Talbott (eds) *The Wiley Handbook of Diversity in Special Education* (pp. 1–6). Malden, MA: Wiley.

Kangas, S.E. (2018) Breaking one law to uphold another: How schools provide services to English learners with disabilities. *TESOL Quarterly* 52 (4), 877–910. https://doi.org/10.1002/tesq.431.

Kea, C.D. and Trent, S.C. (2013) Providing culturally responsive teaching in field-based and student teaching experiences: A case study. *Interdisciplinary Journal of Teaching and Learning* 3 (2), 82–101. Retrieved from https://eric.ed.gov/?id=EJ1063229.

King Thorius, K.K. and Sullivan, A.L. (2013) Interrogating instruction and intervention in RTI research with students identified as English language learners. *Reading & Writing Quarterly* 29 (1), 64–88. https://doi.org/10.1080/10573569.2013.741953.

King Thorius, K. and Santamaría Graff, C. (2018) Extending peer-assisted learning strategies for racially, linguistically, and ability diverse learners. *Intervention in School and Clinic* 53 (3), 163–170. https://doi.org/10.1177/1053451217702113.

King Thorius, K., Artiles, A.J. and Sullivan, A.L. (2013) Effective reading interventions for English language learners. In R.A. McWilliam, B.G. Cook and M. Tankersley (eds) *Research-based Strategies for Improving Outcomes for Targeted Groups or Learners* (pp. 44–60). Upper Saddle River, NJ: Pearson Education.

Klingner, J.K. and Edwards, P.A. (2006) Cultural considerations with response to intervention models. *Reading Research Quarterly* 41 (1), 108–117. https://doi.org/10.1598/RRQ.41.1.6.

Klingner, J.K., Vaughn, S. and Boardman, A. (2015) *Teaching Reading Comprehension to Students with Learning Difficulties*. New York, NY: Guilford Press.

Klingner, J.K., Boelé, A., Linan-Thompson, S. and Rodriguez, D. (2014) Essential components of special education for English language learners with learning disabilities: Position statement of the Division for Learning Disabilities of the Council for Exceptional Children. *Learning Disabilities Research & Practice* 29 (3), 93–96. Retrieved from http://drdrodriguez.net/articles/Essential_Components.pdf.

Krashen, S. (1982) *Principles and Practices in Second Language Acquisition*. Oxford: Pergamon.

Ladson-Billings, G. (1991) Beyond multicultural illiteracy. *The Journal of Negro Education* 60 (2), 147–157. doi:10.2307/229506.

Ladson-Billings, G. (2014) Culturally relevant pedagogy 2.0: Aka the remix. *Harvard Educational Review* 84 (1), 74–84. https://doi-org.ezproxy1.lib.asu.edu/10.17763/haer.84.1.p2rj131485484751.

Lambert, R. and Tan, P. (2017) Conceptualizations of students with and without disabilities as mathematical problem solvers in educational research: A critical review. *Education Sciences* 7 (2), 51. https://doi.org/10.3390/educsci7020051.

Lesaux, N.K. and Harris, J.R. (2013) Linguistically diverse students' reading difficulties: Implications for models of learning disabilities identification and effective instruction. In K.L. Swanson, K.R. Harris and S. Graham (eds) *Handbook of Learning Disabilities* (pp. 69–84). New York, NY: Guilford Press.

Linan-Thompson, S. and Cavazos, H. (2017) Reading instruction for diverse students with learning disabilities. In M.T. Tejero Hughes and E. Talbott (eds) *The Wiley Handbook of Diversity in Special Education* (pp. 253–275). Malden, MA: Wiley.

Lindholm-Leary, K. and Howard, E.R. (2008) Language development and academic achievement in two-way immersion programs. In T.W. Fortune and D.J. Tedick (eds) *Pathways to Multilingualism: Evolving Perspectives on Immersion Education* (pp. 177–200). Tonawanda, NY: Multilingual Matters.

Liu, K.K., Ward, J.M., Thurlow, M.L. and Christensen, L.L. (2017) Large-scale assessment and English language learners with disabilities. *Educational Policy* 31 (5), 551–583. https://doi.org/10.1177/0895904815613443.

Lucas, T., Villegas, A.M. and Freedson-Gonzalez, M. (2008) Linguistically responsive teacher education: Preparing classroom teachers to teach English language learners. *Journal of Teacher Education* 59 (4), 361–373. https://doi.org/10.1177/0022487108322110.

McCray, A.D. and García, S.B. (2002) The stories we must tell: Developing a research agenda for multicultural and bilingual special education. *International Journal of Qualitative Studies in Education* 15 (6), 599–612. https://doi.org/10.1080/0951839022000014330.

McKeown, M.G., Beck, I.L. and Blake, R.G. (2009) Rethinking reading comprehension instruction: A comparison of instruction for strategies and content approaches. *Reading Research Quarterly* 44 (3), 218–253. doi: 10.1598/RRQ.44.3.1.

National Academies of Sciences, Engineering, and Medicine (2017) *Promoting the Educational Sccess of Children and Youth Learning English: Promising Futures*. Washington, DC: National Academies Press. doi: 10.17226/24677.

Nieto, S. (2015) *The Light in their Eyes: Creating Multicultural Learning Communities*. New York, NY: Teachers College Press.

Orosco, M.J. and Klingner, J. (2010) One school's implementation of RTI with English language learners: "Referring into RTI". *Journal of Learning Disabilities* 43 (3), 269–288. https://doi.org/10.1177/0022219409355474.

Ortiz, A.A. and Yates, J.R. (2001) A framework for serving English language learners with disabilities. *Journal of Special Education Leadership* 14 (2), 72–80. Retrieved from http://case.readyhosting.com/documents/jsel/jsel_14.2.pdf#page=26.

Ortiz, A. and Artiles, A.J. (2010) Meeting the needs of ELLs with disabilities: A linguistically and culturally responsive model. In G. Li and P. Edwards (eds) *Best Practices in ELL Instruction* (pp. 247–272). New York, NY: Guilford Press.

Ortiz, A.A. and Robertson, P.M. (2018) Preparing teachers to serve English learners with language- and/or literacy-related difficulties and disabilities. *Teacher Education and Special Education* 41 (3) 176–187. https://doi.org/10.1177/0888406418757035.

Paris, D. (2012) Culturally sustaining pedagogy: A needed change in stance, terminology, and practice. *Educational Researcher* 41 (3), 93–97. https://doi.org/10.3102/0013189X12441244.

Pew Research Center (2018) 6 facts about English language learners in US public schools. *Fact Tank* (October 25). Retrieved from https://www.pewresearch.org/fact-tank/2018/10/25/6-facts-about-english-language-learners-in-u-s-public-schools/.

Pullen, P.C., van Dijk, W., Gonsalves, V.E., Lane, H.B. and Ashworth, K.E. (2019) Response to intervention and multi-tiered systems of support: How do they differ and how are they the same, if at all? In P.C. Pullen and M.J. Kennedy (eds) *Handbook of Response to Intervention and Multi-tiered Systems of Support* (pp. 5–10). New York, NY: Routledge.

Rivera, M.O., Moughamian, A.C., Lesaux, N.K. and Francis, D.J. (2009) *Language and Reading Interventions for English Language Learners and English Language Learners with Disabilities*. Portsmouth, NH: RMC Research Corporation, Center on Instruction. Retrieved from https://files.eric.ed.gov/fulltext/ED521569.pdf.

Ruiz, N. (1991) Effective instruction for language minority children with mild disabilities. ERIC Digest #E499. Reston, VA: ERIC Clearinghouse on Disabilities and Gifted Education VA. Retrieved from https://files.eric.ed.gov/fulltext/ED416696.pdf#page=74.

Saenz, L.M., Fuchs, L.S. and Fuchs, D. (2005) Peer-assisted learning strategies for English language learners with learning disabilities. *Exceptional Children* 71 (3), 231–247. https://doi.org/10.1177/001440290507100302.

Santamaría, L.J., Fletcher, T.V. and Bos, C.S. (2002) Effective pedagogy for English language learners in inclusive classrooms. In A.J. Artiles and A.A. Ortiz (eds) *English Language Learners with Special Education Needs: Identification, Assessment, and Instruction* (pp. 133–157). Washington, DC and McHenry, IL: Center for Applied Linguistics and Delta Systems Co., Inc.

Solano-Flores, G. (2006) Language, dialect, and register: Sociolinguistics and the estimation of measurement error in the testing of English language learners. *Teachers College Record* 108 (11), 2354. Retrieved from http://www.linguisticsnetwork.com/wp-content/uploads/TCR-2006-Lang-dialect-and-register.compressed.pdf.

Soto, G. and Yu, B. (2014) Considerations for the provisions of services to bilingual children who use augmentative and alternative communication. *Augmentative and Alternative Communication* 30 (1), 83–92. https://doi.org/10.3109/07434618.2013.878751.

Staples, K.E. and Diliberto, J.A. (2010) Guidelines for successful parent involvement: Working with parents of students with disabilities. *Teaching Exceptional Children* 42 (6), 58–63. Retrieved from https://education.fcps.org/specialeducation/sites/specialeducation/files/guidelines_for_successful_parent_involvement.pdf.

Stone, C.A. (1998) The metaphor of scaffolding: Its utility for the field of learning disabilities. *Journal of Learning Disabilities* 31, 344–364. https://doi.org/10.1177/002222194803100404.

Terry, N.P., Connor, C.M., Petscher, Y. and Conlin, C.R. (2012) Dialect variation and reading: Is change in nonmainstream American English use related to reading achievement in first and second grades? *Journal of Speech, Language, and Hearing Research* 55 (1), 55–69. doi:10.1044/1092-4388(2011/09-0257).

Trent, S.C., Artiles, A.J. and Englert, C.S. (1998) From deficit thinking to social constructivism: A review of theory, research, and practice in special education. *Review of Research in Education* 23 (1), 277–307. doi: 10.2307/1167293.

Turnbull, A., Turnbull, R., Wehmeyer, M.L. and Shogren, K.A. (2015) *Exceptional Lives: Special Education in Today's Schools* (8th edition). Columbus, OH: Pearson.

van de Pol, J., Volman, M. and Beishuizen, J. (2010) Scaffolding in teacher–student interaction: A decade of research. *Educational Psychology Review* 22 (3), 271–296. Retrieved from https://link.springer.com/article/10.1007/s10648-010-9127-6.

Vaughn, S. and Fuchs, L.S. (2006) A response to "Competing views: A dialogue on response to intervention": Why response to intervention is necessary but not sufficient for identifying students with learning disabilities. *Assessment for Effective Intervention* 32 (1), 58–61. https://doi.org/10.1177/15345084060320010801.

Vygotsky, L. (1978) Interaction between learning and development. In M. Cole, V. John-Steiner, S. Scribner and E. Souberman (eds) *Mind in Society: The Development of Higher Psychological Orocesses* (pp. 79–91). Cambridge, MA: Harvard University Press.

Waitoller, F.R. and King Thorius, K.A. (2016) Cross-pollinating culturally sustaining pedagogy and universal design for learning: Toward an inclusive pedagogy that accounts for dis/ability. *Harvard Educational Review* 86 (3), 366–389. https://doi.org/10.17763/1943-5045-86.3.366.

6 Language Learning and Language Disability: Equity Issues in the Assessment of Young Bilingual Learners

Maria Adelaida Restrepo and Anny P. Castilla-Earls

This chapter discusses how the need to differentiate language learning from language disability is still a challenge for early interventionists and special educators. The limited availability of valid and reliable assessment instruments for bilingual children, and assessment policies and procedures that do not take into account students' bilingual development characteristics, results in the inaccurate identification or under-identification of these children for early intervention and special education services. These challenges apply also to assessments conducted for progress monitoring and intervention planning purposes. This chapter gives an overview of these issues and outlines emerging findings that promise to advance this area of inquiry. In addition, we discuss some educational policy issues that further affect language development, and consequently compound the difficulties in assessment and intervention.

Defining Language Learning Disabilities and Bilingualism

Language learning disabilities are those difficulties that children present in the understanding or using of language and in learning through language, affecting both receptive and expressive skills and written and oral modalities. It is estimated that approximately 7% of the population present with language learning difficulties that are not explained by cognitive, hearing, or neurological problems (Tomblin et al., 1997). Language learning disabilities affect both monolingual and bilingual children in similar ways. Bilingual children with language learning disabilities show language learning difficulties in both languages. If language difficulties are only present in one of the two languages, then it is not considered the result of language learning difficulties but, rather, the result of limited exposure to language, such as when the child is learning a second language.

Bilingualism in the context of this chapter refers to the child's ability to use at least two languages. The range of skills, however, ranges from use only of receptive language skills in one of the languages to full proficiency in oral and written language for both languages, and from beginner in a second language to advanced knowledge in two or more languages. Included in this definition are children who are bicultural but not bilingual, but whose language is also considered a minority language because of its cultural and dialectal characteristics. Although issues related to assessment in language minority populations can vary greatly, the language assessment problem of differentiating language difference from disorder is similar across different language minority groups (Castilla-Earls et al., 2020).

Unfortunately, there is considerable evidence that bilingual children are disproportionately represented in special education programs. In some instances, we observe a pattern of over-representation (e.g., Artiles et al., 1998; Artiles et al., 2002), which is potentially originated by cases of mistaken identity (Paradis, 2005). In this situation, typically developing bilingual children are incorrectly identified as having language learning disabilities. We also observe patterns of under-representation. For example, Spanish-speaking children are disproportionately under-represented in special education programs, particularly in the early grades, and are less likely to be identified as having speech and language impairments than other children (Morgan et al., 2015; Samson & Lesaux, 2009). This is often a result of cases of missed identity (Paradis, 2005). In cases of missed identity, bilingual children with language learning disabilities are not identified, which has important consequences for later academic performance.

The following two case studies illustrate cases of missed identity and mistaken identity with bilingual children. The first case study, an example of missed identity, is of Andres, a 6-year-old boy who is attending kindergarten in an English-only school. At home, Andres speaks Spanish, and his parents are not proficient in English. Both of Andres's parents work on a chicken farm, and neither of them was able to complete high school. Andres qualified for an English-only Head Start program based on his parents' low income, so he has been exposed to English for approximately two years. However, he has shown limited progress in learning English in comparison to his peers. His kindergarten teacher was concerned about Andres's English skills and requested a speech and language evaluation, but there were no trained bilingual speech-language pathologists in his school district at the time. Because the school is aware that learning a second language takes time, they decided to use the "wait-and-see approach." The "wait-and-see approach" helped to evidence continued language learning difficulties but negatively affected Andres. He missed the early support he needed for academic success, which would have prevented greater difficulties in learning to read and tell stories. Andres is a classic example of missed identity that may result in patterns of under-identification of children with language learning disabilities. A combination of the lack of availability of trained bilingual personnel, insufficient understanding/knowledge of bilingual language acquisition processes, and the potential confounding effect of low socioeconomic status, low parental education, and education in only English on the identification of language learning disabilities made the diagnostic process for Andres complicated. Furthermore, language loss occurring in this child complicates the process, as some of the characteristics of language loss also resemble language impairment.

The second case study, an example of mistaken identity, is of Liliana, a 7-year-old girl who was raised speaking Spanish at home. Her family moved from Honduras to a rural area of the United States two years ago and enrolled her in kindergarten in an English-only school. She seems to enjoy socializing in the classroom with other children. However, her school has very limited experience with second language learners, and they are worried about how long it has taken Liliana to learn English. They don't have qualified personnel to conduct bilingual language evaluations, so the English-speaking speech-language pathologist who covers the school district evaluated Liliana. The speech-language pathologist conducted a language evaluation in English and administered the *Clinical Evaluation of Language Fundamentals: CELF-4* (Semel et al., 2003) in English. The results of the English CELF testing indicated that Liliana's English skills were two standard deviations below the mean. In addition, an English language sample was collected, and the results indicated that Liliana makes grammatical errors, code switches to Spanish often, produces simple sentences, and has limited vocabulary in comparison to English-speaking children. The speech-language pathologist concluded that Liliana's language skills were below expectations after two years of English exposure and recommended that she receive speech and language intervention. The information that the school, teacher, and speech-language pathologist missed is that Liliana has normal Spanish language development. She is a typical second language learner of English, who makes grammatical errors and has limited English vocabulary and syntactic complexity, because she has not had enough exposure to English. Two years is not enough time for a child to perform in a comparable way to monolingual English-speaking children (Greenberg et al., 2016). This case of mistaken identity is the result of limited speech-language pathologists' training on bilingual language acquisition and bilingual assessment, limited availability of trained personnel, and the misuse of testing tools developed for monolingual English-speaking children to identify bilingual children with language learning disabilities.

In sum, the identification of bilingual children with language learning disabilities is challenging. The difficulties stem from various sources, including the limitations in our current knowledge of bilingual language acquisition, the difficulty in developing appropriate language assessments that are valid for bilingual children, and the great variability across the many different language and culture combinations. In addition, difficulties come from variability in the children's experiences in general, the scarce availability of bilingual trained personnel to do such assessments, and the language and special education policies in states and programs that are not conducive to equitable assessments. In many cases, the confounding effects of low socioeconomic status and low parental education for minority children living and going to school in subtractive language environments also make the identification of bilingual children with language impairments difficult.

Why is Language Assessment in Bilingual Children Difficult?

There are multiple and compounding factors that make it difficult to differentiate language difference from disorder. No one single issue explains the problem, and thus, depending on the population and combination of languages and cultures, the interaction of factors complicates the problem. Given that language and culture are dynamic systems that interact with each other, understanding of these issues from a descriptive perspective does not accurately explain the complex phenomena. In the next sections, we review some of the more salient issues that we face in language assessment in general and then provide some suggestions on how to approach some of these issues.

Language variation in the bilingual child

Language is a dynamic system that is dependent on a variety of external factors and factors internal to the child, which affect the multiple components of grammar, semantics, pragmatics, and phonology in predictable ways in monolingual children. Internal factors that affect language development include the child's general language ability and cognitive skills, such as memory, attention, and executive function. External factors are those related to the sociocultural aspects and contextual factors that affect language development. Such factors include maternal input, which can affect rate of vocabulary growth in early years; and teacher language complexity, which can affect the child's syntactic complexity and vocabulary development (Bowers & Vasilyeva, 2011; Huttenlocher et al., 2002; Wasik et al., 2006). When a child speaks more than one language, the variability in development increases because there are different sources of input; the age of exposure and time of exposure to the second language affect the development not only of the second language but also of the native language. For example, Restrepo et al. (2010) demonstrated that native language growth in preschool continued in mean length of utterance and sentence complexity when children received Spanish instruction supplemental to the regular English preschool instruction for 30 minutes a day. In contrast, children who did not receive the supplemental instruction demonstrated limited growth in sentence length and complexity in the native language. Further, second language acquisition is variable. Chondrogianni and Marinis (2012) demonstrated great variability in the acquisition of grammatical morphemes in English as a second language. These are often problematic for children with language disabilities as well. However, this variability is considered normal in second language acquisition and does not indicate atypical language development. Moreover, Paradis (2011) found that children who speak a non-inflected language like Mandarin take longer to acquire English morphemes than children who speak more inflected languages like Spanish.

Another important source of variation in bilingual language acquisition is the pattern of language use in the child's family. A well-known approach to raising bilingual children is one-parent-one language. In this approach, each of the parents of the bilingual child uses one language "exclusively" to communicate with the child, with the aim of providing bilingual exposure from birth. However, there is limited empirical support for this approach. For example, De Houwer (2007) found that families in which both parents spoke the minority language were more successful at raising bilingual children than families who use the one-parent-one-language approach. It is possible that the one-parent one-language approach is more successful in contexts where bilingualism is the norm but not in contexts with a minority/majority language. The language spoken by siblings also affects the patterns of language acquisition in bilingual children. Bridges and Hoff (2014) investigated the role of older siblings in the language development of bilingual toddlers. They found that toddlers who had an older sibling were more advanced in their English as a second language skills than children without siblings. In addition, they found that older siblings used more English than Spanish at home, and that the mothers also tended to speak more English when there was a school-age child in the household. Additionally, Place and Hoff (2011) found that the language spoken by the mother had a strong impact in the vocabulary development of toddlers. In their study, children raised in families with a native Spanish-speaking mother showed more balanced vocabularies in Spanish and English, in comparison to families with English-speaking mothers, in which children showed richer vocabularies in English than in Spanish. In conclusion, the language spoken by the various family members has a direct impact on the language proficiency of the child.

Age of exposure to the second language can also affect how well each language develops, but this relationship is not necessarily linear. That is, there is a correlation between the quantity of input and language proficiency; however, the quality of the input, and the interaction with other factors, such as similarity between languages, and educational factors all account for variability in the child's development. Therefore, developing measures that can capture normal variation in bilingual children in each language is not only difficult but also costly.

In addition to factors internal and external to the child, language contact leads to effects in language development that complicate assessment. For example, when a child receives education strictly in the second language, the acquisition of the second language can resemble language impairment if only that language is evaluated (Paradis, 2005). In addition, intensive input in the second language, with limited input in the native language, can slow down the development of the native language and, in some cases, lead to language attrition or incomplete acquisition of the native language (Anderson, 2012; Castilla-Earls *et al.*, 2019; Montrul, 2008; Morgan *et al.*, 2013; Restrepo & Kruth, 2000). These bilingual effects are a normal variation in bilingual language development and do not reflect a disorder, but they can be confused with language impairment. Therefore, quality and quantity of input at home, and educational policies and practices, can affect how well a child develops the native language and whether the child becomes biliterate, which would help in the native language development, and how much academic language the child develops in each language.

Cultural variability in language socialization practices

In addition to language variation across languages in bilingual children, culture affects how children are socialized through language. Socialization practices vary from culture to culture and help us learn to express concepts; therefore, we vary in how we communicate through language. For example, story structure in Navajo is not linear. Therefore, stories do not follow a sequential order of events, and their sense of plot may not be considered an important factor in telling a story. Rather, the use of descriptive terms in the environment and character characteristics may be considered more important to the story than the problem or plot of the story. The consequences of a circular story structure that surrounds a theme but does not always present a problem with a resolution may be evaluated or perceived as a disorganized story, a characteristic in stories of children with language impairment in mainstream cultures. The circular story may, in fact, be a good story in Navajo because of its teaching model and richness of descriptions. Moreover, Navajo children are not expected to retell stories and, thus, the practice of retelling a story that they have heard over and over is not appropriate in their culture. Therefore, Navajo children may be reluctant to retell stories and, when they do, they do not come to school with skills and practice in telling the linear stories expected in the majority culture.

Socialization can also affect performance on vocabulary measures. For example, many Latino cultures do not talk about the obvious (Peña et al., 2001) and, therefore, many children are not socialized to label objects that they know. Labeling pictures and objects is a frequent practice in English-speaking mainstream cultures in the United States, and parents often rehearse routines with their children labeling objects (Peña et al., 2001). When Latino children are asked to label objects during vocabulary measures, they often respond with the object function, but this does not necessarily indicate that they do not know the word or the object (Peña et al., 2001). Peña and colleagues examined what the effects of a dynamic assessment protocol were, in which they taught language minority children, including Latino children, how to label objects, and they found that the children with training learned the task, which in turn helped identify which children presented with language disorders and differentiated them from those with typical development.

Language assessment in itself is a practice that reflects cultural values and socialization practices. Thus, when practitioners use standardized measures, they need to determine whether these measures' normative samples and assessment practices match those of the child they are assessing. For example, preschool achievement, IQ measures, and language measures often ask children for their address, to name colors and shapes, or to use language to answer obvious questions. These skills are not necessarily emphasized in Latino homes. Similarly, measures assessing ability to follow directions often use concepts, such as before touching the X, touch the Y. In Navajo language, directions out of sequence are not appropriate, and therefore, missing these items does not indicate disorder.

Measurement development and norming

Given the variability in monolingual and bilingual language development, assessments specifically designed for bilingual children are difficult to find, and even though there are some available, many of these have inherent problems in their validity for the different groups of children. For example, a frequently used measure, the Clinical Evaluation of Language Fundamentals (CELF), is designed for mainstream English-speaking children. In one administration, it included 11% of children from "other" ethnic groups, matching the US Census distribution (African American or Hispanic are accounted separately) that included Native American children. Therefore, when we examined Navajo children's performance on this measure, they scored one standard deviation below the mean as a group (Henderson & Restrepo, 2014). Further, when we performed an item analysis, we found that several items in grammatical structures and in following directions were problematic for Navajo children, contributing to their low scores that can lead to over-identification of a language disorder when there is none.

Similar to the English version, the Spanish version of CELF-4 (Semel et al., 2006), also proved problematic. This measure is designed for Spanish-speaking children in the United States who are bilingual and in English-contact situations. The measure's sample seems adequate for the population of bilingual children in the United States, given their sampling procedures. However, the norms are not stratified by any group other than age. When we give the measure to monolingual Spanish-speaking children, they score one full standard deviation above the mean, and thus, the recommended cut score would under-identify children with a language disorder (Morgan et al., 2009). On the other hand, when we gave this measure to more than 700 bilingual Spanish-proficient children from low-income homes attending English-only education, the sample mean was below one standard deviation from the mean. Therefore, using the test's recommended cut score of 85 ($x = 100$), we would have identified 55% of the sample as having a language disorder (Barragan et al., 2018). These results indicate that, at least for our sample of children, with no instruction in the native language, living in poverty, and with 60% of the parents with less than a high school education, the norms do not reflect their true ability. Moreover, even when we adjust the cut score, the test accuracy does not improve significantly.

There is a variety of possibilities that can explain this. The measure uses an English model of language development and disorders, despite its development in Spanish. The items sections and areas assessed are the same as those on the English measure. There are no separate norms for the different exposure groups. Although the authors discuss in the manual that it is not necessary, our evidence indicates otherwise. Although there is a variety of measures being developed for Latinos in the United States, often the tests' theoretical and developmental frameworks are problematic. Some measures are not designed to capture language disorders in the Spanish-speaking population; therefore, the items and content developed do not reflect current understanding of these characteristics. Instead, they use an English developmental model or a disorders model for English, which is not applicable to Spanish.

For example, the Spanish edition of the Preschool Language Scale 3 was originally translated into Spanish from English. Restrepo and Silverman (2001) found that it over-identified children as presenting language disorders. Items were not appropriate for Spanish speakers. Subsequent versions, however, use a very similar model, although the items are not now translated. Even when the measures are adapted and developed from the beginning in Spanish, the target skills should be specific to the population. For example, a measure focused on test items that evaluate past tense in Spanish will not be sensitive to the difficulties in gender agreement in the noun phrase seen in Spanish speakers with language disorders. On the other hand, when the focus is academic skills in Spanish, but the children receive all instruction in English, low performance in Spanish academic skills – such as defining words or story retelling skills – do not reflect a disorder but, rather, performance reflects limited experience with Spanish for academic purposes. For example, knowledge of colors in Spanish is often low in preschool and kindergarten Spanish speakers, who start schooling in preschool in English, even though their home backgrounds are Spanish. Often these are not skills that Latino families emphasize, and preschools teach these skills in English.

Availability of trained bilingual personnel

One of the big challenges in special education, early intervention, speech-language pathology, and related fields is the availability of appropriately trained personnel. Finding bilingual speech-language pathologists, for example, is not easy, even in more frequently used languages in the United States, such as Spanish. For example, in 2014 the American Speech-Language-Hearing Association had 161,163 members and, of those, only 7,214 or 5.8% were bilingual; only half of those were Spanish-English bilingual. Moreover, in language combinations such as Arabic-English or Mandarin-English, the numbers are much lower, and thus the number of speech-language pathologists who speak those languages and are trained on bilingual assessment and intervention is significantly below what would be expected in the population (American Speech-Language-Hearing Association, 2014).

One of the main concerns in the assessment of bilingual children is that even when we find bilingual personnel, being bilingual is not sufficient to perform adequate assessment and intervention. Interventionists need to be trained specifically in appropriate practices in assessing culturally and linguistically diverse children, in identifying the linguistic and cultural characteristics that impact performance on language assessment, and in using evidence-based practices that are fair and equitable. While the interventionist is looking for converging evidence to determine if the child presents with a language difference or disorder, they must also demonstrate understanding of bilingualism and its effects on the different components of language and how culture affects socialization practices (Castilla-Earls *et al.*, 2020). Moreover, when the child's languages and culture are less familiar to the practitioner, there is a need to research the linguistic characteristics of the language, such as the phonology or sound system, syntax or word order, that could possibly transfer to English, and cultural characteristics and socialization practices. Then, the clinician must analyze which aspects in each language indicate typical bilingual development and which aspects indicate atypical language development. Further, the clinician must account for the quantity and quality of input in each language and look for converging evidence for the presence or absence of a language impairment. Therefore, speaking the language is not sufficient, and there continues to be a need for programs that graduate culturally and linguistically competent clinicians.

Finally, there are times when bilingual personnel are not available, and monolingual clinicians must provide assessments in bilingual populations. These providers also need to be trained in culturally sensitive and appropriate techniques, on the use of interpreters, and on understanding bilingualism and cultural factors. It is not sufficient to say that they cannot speak the language and cannot provide at least adequate assessment through alternative means or get help through the community or the family. For example, according to the American Speech-Language-Hearing Association, it is unethical to deny services on the basis of language and culture. But, first, attempts should be made to find bilingual personnel who are trained to do so (American Speech-Language-Hearing Association, 2016).

The impact of school and program policies on language assessment

Federal laws regarding appropriate assessments, as in the Individuals with Disabilities Education Act (2004), require that children be evaluated so they are not over-identified with disabilities due to their racial or ethnic backgrounds. This includes that their language and cultural differences be appropriately considered in their assessment and that their true abilities be examined. In addition, it requires that children be evaluated in their native language and by personnel qualified to makes those determinations. However, the practice and implementation of these policies is often not up to standard, as described above.

Assessment policies in districts and early intervention programs often do not match federal law. These local districts and programs often set arbitrary rules on what cut scores to use for a child to qualify for services. In addition, districts also may require that teachers and speech-language pathologists give standardized tests even when evaluating language minority children, for whom there are no valid measures.

Arbitrary cut scores are rarely based on evidence and are not specific to the measures' recommended cut scores and research on what the optimal cut score is. These practices can result in under- or over-identification of children with language disabilities.

Language policies in schools are also having effects on a variety of factors. English-only schools and programs, due to their focus on English, often do not hire bilingual personnel; thus, the availability of bilingual services and qualified assessors is reduced, and the quality of the assessment is compromised. For example, when a child speaks Spanish as the native language and is learning English as a second language, the schools should have a bilingual speech-language pathologist evaluate the child. When such is not available, often interpreters of bilingual speech-language assistants can help provide the assessment, if available. When they are not available, the monolingual speech-language pathologist performs an assessment that is not appropriate and may provide services that do not match the child's actual needs. On the other hand, they may delay assessment until the child speaks more English, further delaying appropriate intervention if the child actually presents with a language learning disability.

English-only programs also present a confounding factor in both assessment and intervention. These programs have curricula that teachers deliver in only the second language; thus, the native language does not grow. Besides the complicating factors discussed in assessment, in terms of intervention these programs tend to discourage the use of the native language and thus result in greater protracted development and language loss. Even if the speech-language pathologist can provide input, one or two half-hour sessions a week most likely are not sufficient to accelerate growth. This issue can be further compounded when teachers do not allow the children to speak with each other in the native language and scold them for doing so. Moreover, when parents are discouraged from communicating with the children in their native language, this brings a disconnect between the family and their children with disabilities (Yu, 2013), as they cannot support their native language and feel that focusing on the second language is the way to help their children, which is a myth.

Socioeconomic status as a confounding factor in bilingual homes

Socioeconomic status (SES) seems to be an important confounding factor for the language abilities of bilingual children. Low SES can impact a wide variety of developmental outcomes due to reduced access to resources, parental attitudes, and environmental stressors (Horton-Ikard & Weismer, 2007). Children from low SES families tend to receive reduced language input in comparison to children from higher SES families, which affects their vocabulary development

(Hart & Risley, 1995). Regarding language assessment, children from low SES backgrounds typically perform worse than expected on standardized tests measuring language abilities (Gilliam & de Mesquita, 2000; Qi *et al.*, 2003; Washington & Craig, 1999) and spontaneous language measures, such as the number of different words used to retell a story (Campbell *et al.*, 1997). The low performance on these measures might be explained by the fact that these measures are experience-dependent and based on mainstream vocabulary. Mothers with low SES backgrounds tend to also present with low levels of education and may not be able to provide enriching experiences for their children (Campbell *et al.*, 1997; Horton-Ikard & Weismer, 2007). Unfortunately, bilingualism in the United States is often associated with minority groups that live in poverty. For example, Hispanic children are twice more likely to live in poverty than non-Hispanic children (Gamboa, 2015). In Arizona 86% of Latino children qualify for free and reduced lunch. In addition, children from recent immigrant families are typically from low SES families and are more likely to use the minority language at home (Bohman *et al.*, 2010). Therefore, during the assessment process, it is difficult to determine whether low language skills are the result of limitations in the quantity and quality of language input or are due to language learning difficulties, which makes the diagnosis of bilingual children more complicated. Bilingualism *per se* provides enriching experiences and has many benefits for children's potential academic and employment status. Language and educational policies could work with this strength, especially with at-risk children.

In summary, the evaluation of bilingual children requires bilingual personnel who are well trained in bilingual assessment, such as taking into consideration bilingual language development and cultural characteristics. Children who live in subtractive language environments tend to have slower native language development, incomplete acquisition, and language loss. In addition, school district assessment and educational policies can have an impact not only the children's language development but also on the availability of trained personnel who can provide fair and equitable assessments. Moreover, schools can have identification and assessment policies that are in line with federal law, but often their policies lead to over-identification of bilingual children into special education when the clinicians are required to use invalid assessment instruments. On the other hand, policies that involve waiting for the child to acquire English can lead to under-identification, when early intervention can prevent more significant difficulties. Factors such as SES, quality and quantity of input, language of education, and characteristics of the languages that the children speak, need to be considered in the assessment. Often the difficulties we see are the result of these at-risk factors, not bilingualism or language disorders. However, it is possible that the language disorders are compounded with the risk factors. Clinicians with experience and training in bilingual assessment are important in the valid and fair process of identifying and treating bilingual children with language disabilities.

How Can Children Be Assessed in a Fair, Appropriate, and Equitable Manner?

Current research on language assessment of language minority children indicates some gains in the development of measures and procedures. There is a worldwide concern for better assessment in bilingual children. For example, The European Union had a COST (Cooperation in Science and Technology, 2009) action specifically dedicated to improving assessment of bilingual children from 2009 to 2013. In the United States, in the early 2000s, the National Institutes of Health had a special request for proposals for the development of language assessment tools for bilingual children. Similarly, the US Department of Education has continuously encouraged grant submission for this purpose. Therefore, there has been an increase in research and measures oriented towards bilingual children.

Current research indicates that there are potential techniques/approaches for accurate assessment of bilingual children in general, and specifically for Spanish-speaking bilingual children. For Spanish-English bilingual children, for example, we have identified grammatical areas that are vulnerable in language disorders (Bedore & Leonard, 2001; Gutierrez-Clellen *et al.*, 2006; Morgan *et al.*, 2013; Restrepo, 1998). We also have made recommendations regarding the use of alternative assessment procedures, such as language sample analysis to examine sentence length and grammaticality (Castilla-Earls *et al.*, 2020). In addition, researchers have found that dynamic assessment procedures, which are designed to assess language learning abilities instead of current language skills, can reduce bias in the assessment process and possibly reduce over-representation of language minority children in special education (Kapantzoglou *et al.*, 2012; Peña, Gillam *et al.*, 2014).

The advantage of these alternative assessment procedures is that they do not require prior experience or background knowledge. For example, language sample analyses are based on the child's spontaneous language skills. Using these assessment approaches, children have a better chance of demonstrating true ability and learning skills and are less likely to indicate the presence of a disorder. However, many of these procedures need further validation and continue to have the same kind of problems seen in standardized assessments: they are missing norms that help identify the population and the standardized procedures so that assessors know what typical and atypical language performance is in the different tasks. Our approach is that of obtaining converging evidence across standardized, observational, parent questionnaires, and alternative approaches. That is, no one single measure is the defining factor but the converging evidence across the different measures (Castilla-Earls *et al.*, 2020).

The addition of promising measures, such as sentence repetition, with a variety of language contact groups such as Russian, Hebrew, English, French, and multiple other languages, may facilitate norming development and evidence as to when and under what circumstances some of these tasks are more appropriate (Meir *et al.*, 2015; Ziethe *et al.*, 2013). Similarly, non-word repetition measures have been found to differentiate ability groups (e.g., Archibald & Joanisse, 2009; Girbau & Schwartz, 2008). Language processing measures, therefore, seem to provide a measure of language ability that is somewhat independent of language experience, although clinically these measures are not widely used, because they have no norms.

Standardized testing

The availability of tests designed for and normed on bilingual populations is scarce. One of the few tests available is the Bilingual English Spanish Assessment (BESA) (Peña *et al.*, 2018). Unlike other bilingual tests available in the United States, the BESA was developed to target the specific language characteristics of Spanish-English bilingual children, and it is not an adaptation or translation of an English test. This test examines phonological, morphosyntactic, and semantic skills in both Spanish and English and was normed on bilingual children between the ages of four and six. An important characteristic of the BESA is that it uses the standard score of both languages (Spanish or English) to identify children with language impairments, which seems to account for the variability of bilingual profiles.

Other tests developed for Spanish-speaking children are available commercially but might not have enough research evidence to support their use. For example, our current research indicates that the Spanish Clinical Evaluation of Language Fundamentals (CELF), 4th edition, might over-identify children from low socioeconomic status as language impaired. In our study, CELF identified 50% of the children from low SES families as language impaired (Barragan *et al.*, 2018). Recall that there is a confound effect of low SES on language ability. Ideally, standardized tests should account for the effect of low SES and identify children with poor language learning skills and not only those with limited language skills at a given point in time. In addition, part of the problem is that the constructs used are not sensitive to language disorders. Rather, constructs are used that are affected by language experience, such as vocabulary or academic skills.

In-depth parent questionnaires

Parent questionnaires examining the development of the home language have been shown to help make accurate decisions during the diagnostic process. Seminal work by Restrepo (1998) showed that a parent questionnaire significantly increased the diagnostic accuracy of bilingual children with language impairment. Other researchers have adapted, modified, and expanded Restrepo's (1998) work and advanced the usefulness of questionnaires during the assessment process. For example, Paradis *et al.* (2010) designed the Alberta Language and Development Questionnaire (ALDeQ) to be used with bilingual families from a variety of linguistic and cultural backgrounds. The ALDeQ includes 18 questions addressing early language milestones, current home language abilities, behaviors and activities related to language, and family history of speech and language problems. This questionnaire has been shown to be helpful in identifying children: it is accurate at identifying only the children who have language impairment (good specificity), although it misses some children with language impairment (poor sensitivity) when the questionnaire is used by itself (Paradis *et al.*, 2010). The ALDeQ has improved diagnostic accuracy when used in conjunction with English-standardized measures (Paradis *et al.*, 2014). Other parent questionnaires for bilingual children are also available.

Although the increase in research is encouraging, some principles are still necessary to ensure that appropriate practices lead to the best assessment possible, assessment that is fair and equitable, not only in identifying the presence or not of a disorder but also in accurately identifying the child's strengths and weakness and the needs in each language to set up appropriate interventions. The need for converging evidence is still critical in appropriate evaluations (Castilla-Earls *et al.*, 2020). Given the variability in language performance in the different language contact groups and given within-group variability, it is unlikely that we will have the perfect measure, and assessors need to continue to rely on finding converging evidence from multiple sources to determine whether the child presents with a language disorder in both languages. Further, to make this determination, there is always the need for an in-depth parent questionnaire that addresses language use and contact history in addition to the typical case history. In addition, understanding the child's language proficiency in each language, the linguistic characteristics in terms of syntax, phonology, the rules of language use and morphology, and the cultural and socialization practices that inform the evidence, is critical. See Figure 6.1 for considerations in the assessment of a bilingual child and Figure 6.2 for information needed to obtain converging evidence that the child presents with a language disorder.

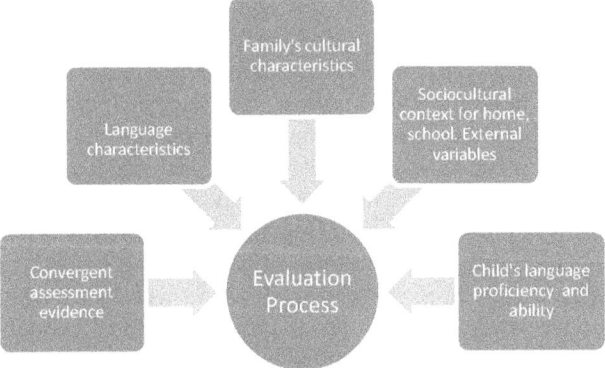

Figure 6.1 Factors to consider when reviewing a child's language proficiency

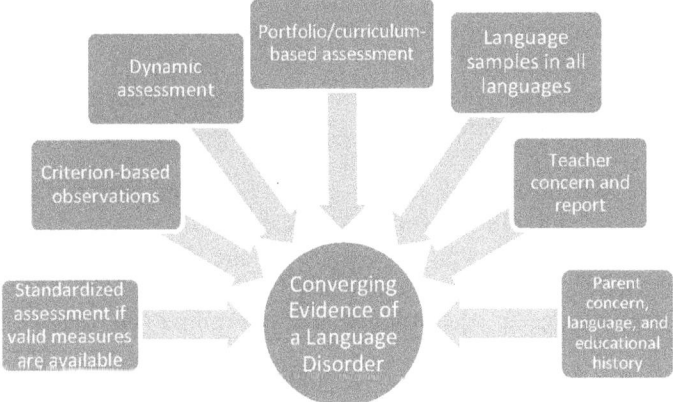

Figure 6.2 Information needed to determine if a child has a language disorder

Using resources in the community, including interpreters

The use of interpreters has long been recommended for evaluation and intervention with multilingual children when there are no trained personnel to do so (Langdon, 2002). Although this method is promising, the validity evidence of such a process is not available. However, Langdon recommended a 3-phase process: BID – briefing, interaction, and debriefing. In the briefing phase, the clinician previews the process and goals of the assessment and provides training for the interpreter on speech and language development and how to organize time, and discusses the importance of getting an accurate description of the child. If the interpreter and clinician work on multiple assignments, it will save time and become more efficient. In the interaction phase, the interpreter helps evaluate the child directly through parent interviews and direct assessments. In this part, the interpreter interacts with the parent or the child and translates verbatim what the clinician or child/parent says. The clinician should use simple terminology and shorter sentences and pause frequently for the interpreter. During the debriefing phase, the clinician and interpreter meet to discuss the results and the actual process. In addition, based on the information obtained with the interpreter, the clinician makes a decision regarding the child's actual ability in the native language and differentiates cultural and linguistic difference from disorder. This process seems to work well when the clinician and interpreter work together for a period of time through multiple assignments, where they can learn from each other and work on making the process more efficient. Having to train a different interpreter each time is difficult. There are recommendations for the process beyond the three phases. For example, the clinician should always address the parent or the child, rather than the interpreter. The interpreter should always stay within the context of the assessment and not provide additional or interpretative information.

According to the American Speech-Language-Hearing Association, the interpreter should have:

(a) Native-like proficiency in the child's language and the ability to provide accurate interpretation/translations
(b) Familiarity with and positive regard for the child's particular culture and speech community or communicative environments
(c) Understanding of the role of the interpreter on the team (not including their own opinion)
(d) Knowledge of interview techniques, including ethnographic interviewing
(e) Professional ethics and client/patient confidentiality
(f) Professional terminology
(g) Basic principles of assessment and/or intervention principles to provide context for understanding objectives. (American Speech-Language-Hearing Association, n.d.)

As we can see, this is no small task, and the skills that are needed require advanced training and preparation. This relationship can be very productive – but it takes time.

To illustrate a successful collaboration between a clinician and an interpreter, we describe Abdul's story. Abdul is a 9-year-old Somali child who has been in the United States for two years. His mother speaks Somali to him, although volunteers in the refugee camp in Yemen also used Arabic with the children. In the United States, he started third grade due to his age. Although formal schooling was not available in the refugee camp in Yemen, his family and refugee volunteers worked with him on some basic academic skills. When he came to school in the United States, however, he was very behind. The school's teacher and the refugee agency assumed that the lack of schooling, spending two years in a refugee camp, and having parents with limited education, warranted a wait-and-see approach. After two years in school, he has learned some English, but he still sounds telegraphic. His reading and writing are still at kindergarten level, and the teacher is unsure whether or not the child presents with a disability but feels that he has not made significant gains in the two years at school. The special education director approved the use of an interpreter to work with the mother and the child in the native language, Somali. The mother is more comfortable in Somali, although she is learning English. Through the interpreter, the clinician found out that the mother has been concerned about Abdul's development for a long time. She said that he never spoke like other children in the village and that his uncle spoke "funny" like Abdul. She was very appreciative of the clinician trying to help her child. The assessment through the interpreter also revealed that Abdul, for his age, used really short sentences in Somali. His sentence length was three to words on average. The mother felt that Abdul did not understand the main point of a story and could not recall who the characters were in a story. The mother reported that she often had to repeat her directions and questions to ensure that Abdul follows through. She has a younger child who seems to do better. The clinician did a dynamic assessment of word learning in English using grade three vocabulary, and the interpreter used dynamic assessment of stories. Results of both assessments indicated that the child needed a lot of repetition and examiner effort to learn some of the skills. There was no transfer or generalization. If we pull this information, we seem to have converging evidence from the teacher, the parent, the language sample, and the dynamic assessment. The use of standardized assessments would not be appropriate in this case. We may conclude that Abdul has a language learning disorder that is affecting his second language acquisition and learning to read and write in English, and that his problems are not due to second language difficulties but they are due to an actual language learning disability that manifests in difficulties in the two languages.

Conclusion

In conclusion, the speech and language assessment of bilingual children requires trained personnel to determine whether the child presents with a language difference or a disorder. Training requires the understanding of bilingual language development, second language acquisition, and the impact of language input, such as English-only education, in the children's overall development. Translating measures or asking someone to translate a test on the spur of the moment is not appropriate. Although some measures are available in some languages, the validity of many of these measures has not been established. Moreover, the impact of other risk factors such as poverty and low parental education must be considered in the assessment results, given that often the differences are not due to bilingual skills but to additional risk factors or a combination of factors.

Evaluating the two languages and identifying the strengths and weaknesses in the two languages are important in not only determining whether a child has a disability but also in establishing appropriate programming for the child that addresses the nature of the difficulty and the needs in each language. Best practices suggest using converging evidence to determine the presence of disability. Sources of evidence include parent reports, teacher concerns, dynamic assessment in both languages, language sample analyses, and observation of the child in the different contexts.

References

American Speech-Language-Hearing Association (2014) *Demographic Profile of ASHA Members Providing Bilingual Services*. Retrieved from www.asha.org/uploadedFiles/Demographic-Profile-Bilingual-Spanish-Service-Members.pdf.

American Speech-Language-Hearing Association (2016) Code of Ethics. Retrieved from http://www.asha.org.ezproxy1.lib.asu.edu/Code-of-Ethics/.

American Speech-Language-Hearing Association (n.d.). Bilingual Service Delivery (Practice Portal). Retrieved March, 4, 2021, from www.asha.org/Practice-Portal/Professional-Issues/Bilingual-Service-Delivery/.

Anderson, R.T. (2012) First language loss in Spanish-speaking children. In B.A. Goldstein (ed.) *Bilingual Language Development and Disorders in Spanish-English Speakers* (pp. 193–213). Baltimore, MD: Brookes Publishing.

Archibald, L.M. and Joanisse, M.F. (2009) On the sensitivity and specificity of nonword repetition and sentence recall to language and memory impairments in children. *Journal of Speech, Language, and Hearing Research* 52 (4), 899–914.

Artiles, A.J., Aguirre-Muñoz, Z. and Abedi, J. (1998) Predicting placement in learning disabilities programs: Do predictors vary by ethnic group? *Exceptional Children* 64 (4), 543–559.

Artiles, A.J., Rueda, R., Salazar, J.J. and Higareda, I. (2002) English-language learner representation in special education in California urban school districts. In D.J. Losen and G. Orfield (eds) *Racial Inequity in Special Education* (pp. 117–136). Cambridge, MA: Harvard Education Press.

Barragan, B., Martinez-Nieto, M.L., Castilla, A., Restrepo, M.A. and Gray, S. (2018) Performance of low income Spanish-English bilingual children in English-only schools on the CELF-4 edition Spanish. *Language Speech and Hearing Services in the Schools* 49 (2), 292–305. https://doi.org/10.1044/2017_LSHSS-17-0013.

Bedore, L. and Leonard, L. (2001) Grammatical morphology deficits in Spanish-speaking children with specific language impairment. *Journal of Speech, Language, and Hearing Research* 44 (4), 905–924. http://doi.org/10.1044/1092-4388(2001/072).

Bohman, T.M., Bedore, L.M., Peña, E.D., Mendez-Perez, A. and Gillam, R.B. (2010) What you hear and what you say: Language performance in Spanish–English bilinguals. *International Journal of Bilingual Education and Bilingualism* 13 (3), 325–344.

Bowers, E.P. and Vasilyeva, M. (2011) The relation between teacher input and lexical growth of preschoolers. *Applied Psycholinguistics* 32 (1), 221–241.

Bridges, K. and Hoff, E. (2014) Older sibling influences on the language environment and language development of toddlers in bilingual homes. *Applied Psycholinguistics* 35 (2), 225–241. http://doi.org/10.1017/S0142716412000379.

Campbell, T., Dollaghan, C., Needleman, H. and Janosky, J. (1997) Reducing bias in language assessment: Processing dependent measures. *Journal of Speech, Language, and Hearing Research* 40 (3), 519–525.

Castilla-Earls, A., Francis, D., Iglesias, A. and Davidson, K. (2019) The impact of the Spanish to English proficiency shift on the grammaticality of English learners. *Journal of Speech, Language and Hearing Research* 62 (6), 1739–1754.

Castilla-Earls, A., Bedore, L., Rojas, R., Fabiano-Smith, L., Pruitt-Lord, S., Restrepo, M.A. and Peña, E. (2020) Beyond scores: Using converging evidence to determine speech and language services eligibility for dual language learners. *American Journal of Speech-Language Pathology* 29 (3), 116–132. http://doi.org/10.1044/2020_AJSLP-19-00179.

Chondrogianni, V. and Marinis, T. (2012) Production and processing asymmetries in the acquisition of tense morphology by sequential bilingual children. *Bilingualism: Language and Cognition* 15 (1), 5–21.

Cooperation in Science and Technology (COST) (2009) Language impairment in a multilingual society: Linguistic patterns and the road to assessment. Cost Action IS0804. http://www.cost.eu/COST_Actions/isch/IS0804.

De Houwer, A. (2007) Parental language input patterns and children's bilingual use. *Applied Psycholinguistics* 28 (3), 411–424. http://doi.org/10.1017/S0142716407070221.

Gamboa, S. (2015) More Latino-kids in low income but more financially stable households. NBC News, December 8, 2015. Retrieved from http://www.nbcnews.com/news/latino/more-latino-kids-financially-stable-low-income-households-n476146.

Gilliam, W.S. and de Mesquita, P.B. (2000) The relationship between language and cognitive development and emotional-behavioral problems in financially-disadvantaged pre-schoolers: A longitudinal investigation. *Early Child Development and Care* 162 (1), 9–24.

Girbau, D. and Schwartz, R.G. (2008) Phonological working memory in Spanish-English bilingual children with and without specific language impairment. *Journal of Communication Disorders* 41 (2), 124–145.

Greenberg Motamedi, J., Singh, M. and Thompson, K.D. (2016) English learner student characteristics and time to reclassification: An example from Washington state (REL 2016 – 128). Washington, DC: US Department of Education, Institute of Education Sciences, National Center for Education Evaluation and Regional Assistance, Regional Educational Laboratory Northwest. Retrieved from http://ies.ed.gov/ncee/edlabs.

Gutiérrez-Clellen, V.F., Restrepo, M.A. and Simón-Cereijido, G. (2006) Evaluating the discriminant accuracy of a grammatical measure with Spanish-speaking children. *Journal of Speech, Language, and Hearing Research* 49 (6), 1209–1223.

Hart, B. and Risley, T.R. (1995) *Meaningful Differences in the Everyday Experience of Young American Children*. Baltimore, MD: Brookes Publishing.

Henderson, D. and Restrepo, M.A. (2014) Culture and anguage considerations among Navajo assessments and interventions. Paper presented at the Annual American Speech-Language-Hearing Association Convention, November 20–22, Orlando, Florida.

Horton-Ikard, R, and Weismer, S.E. (2007) A preliminary examination of vocabulary and word learning in African American toddlers from middle and low socioeconomic status homes. *American Journal of Speech-Language Pathology* 16 (4), 381–392.

Huttenlocher, J., Vasilyeva, M., Cymerman, E. and Levine, S. (2002) Language input and child syntax. *Cognitive Psychology* 45 (3), 337–374.

IDEA. (2004) Individuals with Disabilities Education Act, 20 U.S.C. § 1400 (2004).

Kapantzoglou, M., Restrepo, M.A. and Thompson, M.S. (2012) Dynamic assessment of word learning skills: Identifying language impairment in bilingual children. *Language, Speech, and Hearing Services in Schools* 43 (1), 81–96.

Langdon, H.W. (2002) Language interpreters and translator. Bridging communication with clients and families. *The ASHA Leader* 7 (6), 14–15.

Meir, N., Walters, J. and Armon-Lotem, S. (2015) Disentangling SLI and bilingualism using sentence repetition tasks: The impact of L1 and L2 properties. *International Journal of Bilingualism* 20 (4), 421–452.

Montrul, S. (2008) *Incomplete Acquisition in Bilingualism. Re-examining the Age Factor*. Amsterdam: John Benjamins.

Morgan, G., Restrepo, M.A. and Auza, A. (2009) Variability in the grammatical profiles of Spanish-speaking children with specific language impairment. In J. Grinstead (ed.) *Hispanic Child Languages: Typical and Impaired Development*. Amsterdam: John Benjamins.

Morgan, G., Restrepo, M.A. and Auza, A. (2013) Comparison of Spanish morphology in monolingual and Spanish-English bilingual children with and without language impairment. *Bilingualism: Language and Cognition* 16 (3), 578–596. http://doi.org/10.1017/S1366728912000697.

Morgan, P., Farkas, G., Hillemeier, M., Matisson, R., Maczuga, S., Li, H. and Cook, M. (2015) Minorities are disproportionately underrepresented in special education: Longitudinal evidence across five disabilities conditions. *Educational Researcher* 20, 1–15.

Paradis, J. (2005) Grammatical morphology in children learning English as a second language: Implications of similarities with specific language impairment. *Language, Speech, and Hearing Services in Schools* 36 (3), 172–187.

Paradis, J. (2011) Individual differences in child English second language acquisition. Comparing child-internal and child-external factors. *Linguistic Approaches to Bilingualism* 1 (3) 213–237.

Paradis, J., Emmerzael, K. and Sorenson Duncan, T. (2010) Assessment of English language learners: Using parent report on first language development. *Journal of Communication Disorders* 43 (6), 474–497.

Paradis, J., Schneider, P. and Sorenson Duncan, T. (2014) Discriminating children with language impairment among English-language learners from diverse first-language backgrounds. *Journal of Speech, Language and Hearing Research* 56 (3), 971–981.

Peña, E., Iglesias, A. and Lidz, C.S. (2001) Reducing test bias through dynamic assessment of children's word learning ability. *American Journal of Speech-Language Pathology* 10 (2), 138–154

Peña, E.D., Gillam, R.B. and Bedore, L.M. (2014) Dynamic assessment of narrative ability in English accurately identifies language impairment in English language learners. *Journal of Speech, Language, and Hearing Research* 57(6), 2208–2220.

Peña, E.D., Gutiérrez-Clellen, V.F., Iglesias, A., Goldstein, B. and Bedore, L.M. (2018) *Bilingual English-Spanish Assessment*. Baltimore, MD: Brookes Publishing.

Place, S. and Hoff, E. (2011) Properties of dual language exposure that influence 2-year-olds' bilingual proficiency. *Child Development* 82 (6), 1834–1849.

Qi, C.H., Kaiser, A.P., Milan, S.E., Yzquierdo, Z. and Hancock, T.B. (2003) The performance of low-income, African American children on the Preschool Language Scale – 3. *Journal of Speech, Language, and Hearing Research* 46 (3), 576–590.

Restrepo, M.A. (1998) Identifiers of predominantly Spanish-speaking children with language impairment. *Journal of Speech, Language, and Hearing Research* 41, 1398–1441.

Restrepo, A. and Kruth, K. (2000) Grammatical characteristics of a Spanish-English bilingual child with specific language impairment. *Communication Disorders Quarterly* 21 (2), 66–76. http://doi.org/10.1177/152574010002100201.

Restrepo, M.A. and Silverman, S. (2001) Validity of the Spanish Preschool Language Scale-3 for use with bilingual children. *American Journal of Speech-Language Pathology* 10, 382–393.

Restrepo, M.A., Castilla, A.P., Schwanenflugel, P.J., Neuharth-Pritchett, S., Hamilton, C.E. and Arboleda, A. (2010) Effects of a supplemental Spanish oral language program on sentence length, complexity, and grammaticality in Spanish-speaking children attending English-only preschools. *Language, Speech, and Hearing Services in Schools* 41 (1), 3–13.

Samson, J. and Lesaux, N.K. (2009) Language minority learners in special education: Rates and predictors of identification for services. *Journal of Learning Disabilities* 42 (2), 148–162.

Semel, E., Wiig, E.H. and Secord, W.A. (2003) *Clinical Evaluation of Language Fundamentals, 4th edition (CELF-4)*. Toronto, Canada: The Psychological Corporation/A Harcourt Assessment Company.

Semel, E., Wiig, E.H. and Secord, W. (2006) *The Clinical Evaluation of Language Fundamentals 4th edition Spanish Version (CELF-4 Spanish)*. San Antonio, TX: Pearson Education Inc.

Tomblin, J.B., Records, N.L., Buckwalter, P., Zhang, X., Smith, E. and O'Brien, M. (1997) Prevalence of specific language impairment in kindergarten children. *Journal of Speech, Language, and Hearing Research* 40 (6), 1245–1260.

Washington, J.A. and Craig, H.K. (1999) Performances of at-risk, African American preschoolers on the peabody picture vocabulary test-III. *Language, Speech, and Hearing Services in Schools* 30 (1), 75–82.

Wasik, B.A., Bond, M.A. and Hindman, A. (2006) The effects of a language and literacy intervention on Head Start children and teachers. *Journal of Educational Psychology* 98 (1), 63.

Yu, B. (2013) Issues in bilingualism and heritage language maintenance: Perspectives of minority-language mothers of children with autism spectrum disorders. *American Journal of Speech-Language Pathology* 22 (1), 10–24.

Ziethe, A., Eysholdt, U. and Doellinger, M. (2013) Sentence repetition and digit span: Potential markers of bilingual children with suspected SLI? *Logopedics Phoniatrics Vocology* 38 (1), 1–10.

7 Learning from Sociocultural Contexts: Partnering with Families of Young Bilingual Children with Disabilities

Cristina Gillanders and Sylvia Y. Sánchez

Parents want the best for their children. In the task of raising children, including those with disabilities, families orchestrate the experiences that will ensure that their children can be active participants in their communities. As children are involved in these experiences, they develop and learn the cultural tools that they will use in their home and community environments. As a cultural process, human development is defined by children's participation in their sociocultural contexts (Rogoff, 2003). Accordingly, development cannot be explained without understanding the demands of the cultural contexts in which humans are going to participate (Rogoff, 2003). In this chapter we examine how families of young bilinguals with special needs arrange these experiences and the ways professionals can support them.

The family's orchestration of experiences may or may not be explicit lessons for children about the cultural practices of the community. However, children's active participation is always an opportunity to learn about interaction with others in their communities. Parents' goals and child-raising practices have been commonly explained as "being part of their culture." Yet, this explanation is general, static in nature, and too simplistic. Several researchers have helped us go beyond these general categorizations to identify specific aspects that constitute the sociocultural contexts in which children and families conduct their everyday activities. Researchers such as Whiting and Whiting (1975) stress that the situations in which people develop include aspects such as: the physical environment; the history of migrations, borrowings, and inventions; means of production; social structure; law and social control; the settings in the child's environment; the mother's workload; and the tasks assigned, among others. Bronfenbrenner's (1977) ecological system model underscores the relationship among the micro-, meso-, exo- and macrosystems, and reminds us not only of the child's immediate experiences but also of those more removed or distal, such as the ideology and organization of the pervasive social institutions of the culture. In the case of children from an ethnically and linguistically diverse minority background, García *et al.* (1996) underscore the importance of considering racism, prejudice, oppression, and segregation as part of the sociocultural context of these families. Finally, Rogoff (2003) adds to these theories, formulating that rather than all these contextual factors being an "influence" in children's individual development, "people contribute to the creation of cultural processes and cultural processes contribute to the creation of people" (Rogoff, 2003: 51).

Consideration of these developmental frameworks is of particular importance when working with culturally diverse families of young bilingual learners, including those with disabilities. Traditional frameworks for studying child development are not informative for early educators. Much of the research on children's development has been framed in paradigms that are influenced by the cultural contexts of monolingual middle-class Anglo Americans. Consequently, when these paradigms are applied to children from marginalized and bilingual environments, findings reveal a deficit perspective toward children's development and learning. For example, early studies on the consequences of bilingualism on the IQ of bilingual and monolingual children revealed lower scores for bilinguals as compared to those of monolinguals (Barac *et al.*, 2014). These outcomes were then explained as "deficits" in the child rearing and family contexts and as a "mental confusion" caused by bilingualism (Barac *et al.*, 2014).

In the last few years, there has been a call from developmental psychologists to view children's development from a sociocultural perspective (Rogoff, 2003). This view emphasizes that routines in everyday practices in each family or cultural community can explain the differences in children's performance on tasks used by researchers to observe their development and learning (Rogoff *et al.*, 2018). Children's functioning has to be understood within the contexts of their participation in these family routines and the practices of their communities. For example, Tamis-LeMonda *et al.* (2012) examined gestural and verbal interactions in 226 mother-infant pairs from Mexican, Dominican, and African American backgrounds when infants were 14 months and 2 years old and related these interactions to infants' emerging skills. Dyads were videotaped as they shared a wordless number book, a wordless emotion book, and beads and strings. At 2 years old, children were assessed on receptive and expressive language and on sequencing and imitation of actions. Mothers differed in their gesturing, distributions of the two types of language, and coupling of language and gestures. Mexican mothers gestured most and tended to expand language with gestures more than African American and Dominican mothers. Mexican and Dominican mothers tended to talk more during the bead stringing tasks than during the book reading compared to African American mothers. These differences were reflected in children's outcomes. Mexican and Dominican infants had larger gestural vocabularies than African American infants but showed lower scores in expressive language.

It is important to note that language is not divorced from all other forms of cultural practice. Within the cultural practices in which all children are engaged, language is "inextricably integrated with ways of talking, thinking, believing, knowing, acting, interacting, valuing, and feeling associated with specific, socially situated identities" (Gee, 2003: 31). Therefore, to understand bilingual children's development, we need to take a close look at families' ways with language and making meaning of the world within their sociocultural practices.

Through their participation in these cultural practices, children not only acquire knowledge, skills, and dispositions but also are agents of transformation of their cultural communities (Rogoff, 2003). For example, Gillanders and Jimenez (2004) observed that Mexican mothers of kindergarteners began reading aloud to their children as a result of a request from their children's teacher. An uncommon practice for these families, it became a daily routine as a consequence of children's participation in US schools. This notion is of particular significance to immigrant families, since they both acquire and transform the cultural practices of the host country. Therefore, static views of the "culture" of particular groups misrepresent the dynamic nature of human development in the cultural context (Gutierrez & Rogoff, 2003). In the examples we provide below, the reader will be able to see that although the family's culture of origin plays a significant role in the beliefs and practices of raising children, families also make decisions based on their reactions against or in favor of the cultural practices of the host community. For instance, to preserve their children's connection to their cultural roots, many parents place more emphasis on involving their children in cultural events from their culture of origin than they would if they were living in their own country. This could be a reaction to families' perceptions of the cultural practices in the more influential host society, cultural practices that are different from their own.

Since children will participate not only in their own ethnic and cultural communities but also in the mainstream culture present in the schools, teachers who are working with families of young bilingual learners with disabilities need to develop the knowledge, skills, and dispositions to create culturally sustaining classrooms. Culturally sustaining pedagogy promotes and sustains children's skills and knowledge learned in their community contexts *and* gives children opportunities to acquire the knowledge and skills needed to succeed in school (Paris, 2012). To create such environments, teachers need to learn directly from the children and families about their lives, sociocultural beliefs, and practices. This understanding will contribute to teachers being more effective in implementing responsive teaching practices. Equally significant, teachers working with culturally and linguistically diverse families need to gain insight about the hopes and dreams for the children. As their children's natural long-term advocates, families' decisions related to special education services and practices are often misunderstood, especially as professional early childhood special education jargon is translated into languages other than English and can be a cause of family-professional conflict. Teachers can be a powerful source of support for families if they know them outside the classroom walls and have a trusting and reciprocal relationship with them. It requires constructing a partnership with families in which there is a balance of power and a genuine exchange of ideas. Such a partnership will entail an authentic and positive relationship between the families and special education practitioners.

We believe that, for early childhood special educators to develop such a partnership, they must first learn directly from families about their familial history, which demonstrates their strengths, beliefs, struggles, and resilience, and the sociocultural forces that have influenced their lives. Second, this information about their life, needs to be gathered in a context that deepens the positive and authentic relationship between the early childhood educator and the families. Finally, the educator must be committed to using this information to implement culturally sustaining classroom practices that maximize the children's strengths, interests, and preferences, and link their lives to the new knowledge and skills presented in the formal educational setting.

This process is critical when working with young bilingual learners with disabilities. First, as discussed in this volume, young bilingual learners represent a disproportionately large percentage of children identified with disabilities (Artiles *et al.*, 2002). Second, a history of marginalization and discrimination is reinforced when young bilingual learners are identified as disabled (Harry, 2008). Finally, there is a strong potential for miscommunication between early childhood special educators and the families of young bilingual learners (Harry, 2008). An authentic and deep understanding of families' beliefs and practices can allow early childhood educators to create true partnerships with families engaged in the difficult task of raising children and, at the same time, can facilitate the process of inclusion of young bilingual learners with special needs. After all, the main tenets of the Individuals with Disabilities Education Act (IDEA, 2004) include a strong commitment to providing family-centered rather than provider-centered services.

In this chapter we illustrate this process, first describing examples of families' beliefs and practices that are particularly relevant to families of young bilingual learners with special needs. We refer mostly to immigrant families, which families comprise the majority of families of young bilingual learners. Although Native American families cannot be considered immigrants, many of the same issues we discuss can also be applied to Native Americans, since many use a non-majority language, live in poverty, and experience challenges that are similar to those of immigrant families.

In the following section, we discuss families' beliefs and child rearing practices regarding supporting home language and bilingualism, and their views about children with disabilities. We then describe the processes involved in establishing positive, respectful, and authentic partnerships with families in the context of meaningful relationships. We end our discussion with examples of ways in which early childhood special educators incorporate the information gained about families' sociocultural beliefs and practices in the curriculum and teaching of young bilingual learners with special needs.

Parents' Ideas about Home Language and Bilingualism

A critical feature that distinguishes children from bilingual families from other ethnically and culturally diverse groups is their use of two or more languages for everyday routines and activities. From a macro-analysis perspective, a typical pattern of language shift in the United States is that the first generation learns enough English to survive economically and continues using the home language for all other aspects of life, the second generation speaks the home language with the family but uses English for school and work, and by the third generation, the home language shifts to English only (Portes & Schauffler, 1994). Although this is a common trend, it is certainly not the experience for *all* bilingual families. Examining how different families approach issues of language learning and bilingualism might be of more importance for early childhood educators. Rather than doing a thorough review of the different studies that reflect what "most" bilingual families believe and do in terms of language maintenance and learning (which would be beyond the purpose of this chapter), we include here a series of exemplar studies that illustrate the types of beliefs and practices that early childhood educators might encounter while working with bilingual families.

Several studies have examined immigrant parents' motivations to ensure that their children grow up as bilinguals. In the studies reviewed, most parents demonstrated a positive attitude toward maintaining the home language while at the same time ensuring that their children learned English. Parents reported that maintaining the home language was important for children's development of self-identity (Farruggio,

2010; Lao, 2004; Park & Sarkar, 2007). For some parents, bilingualism allowed children to appreciate their parents' culture of origin and heritage (Farruggio, 2010). They also believed that their children had better career opportunities if they were bilingual (Lao, 2004) and had a greater possibility of going to college in the country of origin (Hashimoto & Lee, 2011). A few parents recognized that having a strong home language could facilitate the acquisition of a second language (Park & Sarkar, 2007). Parents' language goals were that their children be competent to communicate with their grandparents and relatives in their home countries (Park & Sarkar, 2007) and that they be biliterate (Hashimoto & Lee, 2011).

Parents also imposed a series of rules for ensuring home language maintenance. For example, Hashimoto and Lee (2011) found that parents implemented a "Japanese-only at home" rule. Other parents asked their children to only address them in their home language, even though the children used English with their siblings. In some cases, parents' low English proficiency facilitated their children using only the home language when interacting with parents (Velázquez, 2013). Velázquez (2014) found, in a group of Latino mothers, that they believed that the home and family had the principal responsibility for promoting Spanish language development, while the school and community were mainly responsible for developing English. As main agents for children's acquisition of the home language, parents organized a series of tasks and experiences for children in order to give them the opportunity to acquire the home language. Some parents bought grammar, vocabulary, and picture books from their country of origin to read to their children (Farruggio, 2010; Park & Sarkar, 2007); organized visits to the home country for extended periods of time (Farruggio, 2010; Hashimoto & Lee, 2011); enlisted their children to participate in cultural clubs and dance troupes; encouraged the children to speak on the phone to relatives living in the country of origin (Farruggio, 2010); enrolled them in religious educational programs in the home language; had family meals in which only the home language was allowed; and told them that speaking the home language is important (Velázquez, 2014).

Families' social networks create opportunities for children to listen and use the home language. Velázquez (2014) found that social networks shaped Latino mothers' views about the benefits and downsides of supporting home language development. Interaction with other Latino mothers who had longer histories of residency in the United States provided important information to first-generation mothers about parenting in a minority-language setting. Another source of information for immigrant mothers with young bilingual learners with special needs was special education teachers and therapists.

Many parents of young bilingual learners with disabilities worry about making it more difficult for their children if they expect them to learn another language. These parents are concerned that adding an additional language might be beyond the child's capabilities. This view is often a reflection of what they hear from some teachers and therapists who believe that learning two languages is an added challenge for children with disabilities. However, recent research has found no indication that bilingualism can cause an additional burden for children with autism, language impairments, or Down Syndrome (e.g., Bedore & Peña, 2008; Bird *et al.*, 2016; Hambly & Fombonne, 2012). Furthermore, the American Speech-Language-Hearing Association (ASHA, 2004) recommends as best practice to respect and support the family's language and cultural preferences.

In part, these concerns might emerge in parents and specialists from the difficulties of finding providers who can implement interventions in both languages and opportunities for children with disabilities to receive bilingual education (Marinova-Todd *et al.*, 2016). Yu (2013) interviewed a group of Mandarin-Chinese-speaking mothers with children with a documented diagnosis of autism spectrum disorder (ASD) about their beliefs and practices regarding home language maintenance and bilingualism. Findings revealed that most of the mothers were highly committed to supporting the children in learning English, as this was the dominant language. However, as described above with parents of typically developing children, these mothers also valued that their children be able to learn Chinese. Yet, these parents also indicated that it was a challenge to find providers who could work with their children in Chinese. Accordingly, they believed that receiving the recommended intervention took precedence over learning to speak Chinese. Because of this situation, mothers decided to speak to children only in English, even if it was not their stronger language, to ensure they could benefit from the interventions in English.

Similar to the Velázquez study (2013), in which the mothers were influenced in their support of the home language, these mothers followed the advice of speech therapists, psychologists, and teachers, to speak English to their children as early as they could and to stop speaking Chinese. The decision to speak only English was not viewed without challenges. Although the parents in this study self-described as relatively proficient in English, they felt that it was unnatural to speak to their spouses, closest friends, and children in English. They tried to follow the recommendations of the specialists with regards to language but, when they were able to use their language of preference, they conducted the intervention strategies more frequently (Yu, 2013).

Parents' Ideas about Young Bilingual Learners' Special Needs

In addition to considering parents' beliefs about the importance of promoting bilingualism, it is important to take into account their knowledge and ideas about their children's special needs. The use at home of a language other than English might have repercussions on parents' knowledge of particular disabilities. For example, Colbert *et al.* (2017) reported disproportionately lower rates of Latino children being diagnosed with ASD as compared to other ethnic and racial groups. The researchers discussed the possibility that parents with lower English proficiency might have fewer opportunities to receive information about the different types of disability or to find available free diagnosis services.

It is also possible that parents might have a different conceptualization of disability and, therefore, might not feel it necessary to have their child diagnosed. Skinner and Weisner (2007) describe:

> Disabilities, in addition to their cognitive or physical manifestations or genetic etiologies, are sociocultural phenomena. How disability is defined and labeled, families respond and adapt, barriers and opportunities are created, differences in abilities are linked to other societal differences, and professional practices and institutions develop are all social and cultural constructions that have evolved over time at multiple levels within particular historical and political contexts (Skinner & Weisner, 2007: 302).

Bilingual parents might attribute different meanings and values to the conventional terms of a diagnosis of disability based on their view of child rearing as deemed appropriate in their particular cultural and community setting. As is the case with families' beliefs about language learning and bilingualism, families will make decisions and engage in practices to raise their children according to these beliefs. They will also interact with individuals, agencies, and institutions beyond their homes, in ways that not only reflect these beliefs but also the allowances and constraints of their everyday lives.

Some bilingual families may interpret their child's special needs from a religious point of view. Skinner *et al.* (2001) found that their sample of Mexican and Puerto Rican parents in the United States interpreted their child's disability from three different models. In one model, the child's disability was considered a punishment sent by God for one's sins. This model was only expressed by 3% of the sample. In a second model, parents viewed the child's disability as a gift of God to reward the parents' worthiness. The majority of parents (68%) adhered to this model. Finally, in a third model, parents believed that God had provided this child as a test or a challenge to overcome in their lives. Eleven percent of the parents embraced this model. Religion was also viewed as a source of strength to overcome the challenges in raising a child with special needs.

Cultural variations have also been found in the interpretations of having and raising a child with special needs. In a study examining the different perceptions of child rearing of Latina and Anglo mothers of children with intellectual disability, Blacher *et al.* (2013) found that

Latina mothers viewed raising a child with intellectual disability more positively than did Anglo mothers. This positive view persisted as the child became older. According to these authors, Latina mothers might embrace the role of motherhood with an attitude of self-sacrifice or *marianismo* (Withrow, 2008). In their view, raising a child with an intellectual disability requires resignation and acceptance. Similarly, a resilient view of life might also help them perceive adversity in a positive light.

These positive beliefs toward their children can also be observed in parents' attributions to children's problem behaviors. Chavira *et al.* (2000) examined the relationship between Latina mothers' attributions of responsibility and their emotional and behavioral reactions to problem behaviors of their children with disabilities. Study findings indicated that Latina mothers of children with developmental disabilities tended to view their child as not responsible for their problem behavior. However, some mothers ascribed high responsibility when the problem behavior was related to behavioral excesses (e.g., temper tantrums) rather than behavior deficits (e.g., lack of speech). As a consequence, mothers who attributed high responsibility to their child's behavior tended to have negative emotions, which translated into harsh criticism or aggressive behaviors. More research is needed to examine how bilingual families might vary in their conceptualization of disability as well as their attributions to children's challenging behaviors.

Learning from Families with Young Bilingual Learners with Special Needs

In the previous section we discuss families' beliefs and practices regarding home language and bilingualism, and disability. The studies reviewed above can provide some insight for early childhood educators about the types of belief and practices that they might encounter as they work with culturally and linguistically diverse families. Notice that our discussion about bilingual families highlights the interconnectedness between families' language, beliefs, and practices, since bilingualism cannot be understood without taking these into consideration. In addition, we emphasize that the list of beliefs and practices described is certainly not exhaustive or applicable to all families, and that in order for early childhood educators to learn *from* instead of *about* families, it is critical that they establish positive relationships with bilingual families. Learning *from* families, especially those from bilingual contexts, is not easily gained through traditional methods such as questionnaires and surveys (Harry, 2008). Histories of discrimination and racism have made some of these families wary of providing information about their lives. Therefore, developing a positive and authentic relationship with each family is essential when working with families of young bilingual learners with special needs.

Building relationships with families

To better understand a child, teachers need to first gain an understanding of who the child is in the context of their family. Families know their children best. As we describe in previous sections, to know the family means to gain insight into their sociocultural beliefs, values, history, and child rearing practices, as well as their hopes, dreams, and possibilities for their children. An authentic reciprocal relationship between families and educators will help the family and teacher gain each other's trust to begin the process that leads to this understanding. This kind of relationship also encourages the sharing of stories and information about the family and their child. The educator links what they learn from the family about their child's interests, preferences, and life, to their classroom interactions and practices. Because of this partnership with the family, the teacher creates a supportive learning environment with meaningful experiences where the child has a greater potential to flourish (Sánchez & Thorp, 2008; Thorp *et al.*, 2018).

In their teacher preparation program, most early special educators learn about the legislation (IDEA, 2004) that fosters family-centered practices. All too often at the school level, it is interpreted as the mandate to invite the family or primary caregiver to a meeting to discuss the needs of the child. The discussion with the family often centers around disabilities and weaknesses, rather than strengths. The support for developing reciprocal authentic relationships between teachers and families is a fairly recent practice.

For most early educators, their teacher education program exposed them to the work of such early theorists as Dewey (1902, 1938), Piaget (1932, 1952), Bronfenbrenner (1977), and Vygotsky (1978, 1986). These theorists contribute to teachers' understanding that knowing about children's prior experiences, their preferences and interests, and their understanding of the world around them has a powerful impact on how children respond to and benefit cognitively from new learning experiences. However, none of these known theorists specifically addresses issues of bilingualism and diversity.

Nonetheless, more recent researchers from the field of special education and teacher preparation have contributed to a greater understanding about culturally and linguistically diverse families and their role in the lives of their children with disabilities. More importantly, they have challenged the more traditional deficit perspective related to poverty, race, and linguistic diversity. They have emphasized that special educators need to learn from families about the children they work with and to develop strong partnerships with diverse families that can lead to the development and implementation of culturally sustaining practices in their work with young bilingual learners. These views are counter to a deficit model where the educator is the expert and the family has little to offer and has no significant role to play in the formal educational process. More researchers continue to expand research on the intersection of families, language and culture, disability, socioeconomic status, and the preparation of culturally responsive early childhood special educators (Kalyanpur & Harry, 2012; Kidd *et al.*, 2008; Puig, 2012; Recchia & Lee, 2013; Rossetti *et al.*, 2017; Saurer & Rossetti, 2019). An emphasis on relationship building is inherent in this intersection of working with bilingual children and their families.

Sociocultural dimensions of relationship building

As a special education researcher, Beth Harry's (1992) work significantly influenced the early childhood special education field. She has asked the controversial and difficult question: "Why are so many racial minority students in special education?" (Harry & Klingner, 2006). Her research supports the need to assume a more culturally approachable posture when working with young bilingual learners with disabilities and their families, has explored the centrality of culture in the lives of children, families, and professionals, and has questioned the practices of a special education system that often functions to the detriment of family voices and their potential role as advocates for their children. For example, in her seminal ethnographic study of the experiences and views of 12 Puerto Rican families of children with disabilities in their dealings with the special education system, Harry (1992) explored the intersectionality of being poor, of color, culturally and linguistically diverse, and having a child with a disability. She reports that special education systematically marginalized culturally and linguistically diverse families by using a legalistic approach that consistently offered parents the sole role of consent-giver. Families were not expected to engage in a dialogue with the professionals, collaborate in the assessment or placement process, be knowledgeable about what would be best for their child, nor share their cultural experiences and views to enhance their child's learning experience.

According to Kalyanpur and Harry (1997, 2012), what is needed is for educators to assume a posture of reciprocity. This would involve an attitude or stance that moves the educator forward to connect with families different from them. It is assumed that when the cultural views of the family are similar to those of the provider, the educator will feel more comfortable with the family and a positive connection will result that bridges home and school. However, if a cultural and linguistic difference exists between the family and educator, the communication may not be positive, and the school-home connection fails to materialize. According to Harry and her colleagues, a posture of reciprocity needs to exist so the educator takes the initiative to reach out to diverse families for the purpose of finding mutual ground that can foster positive communication and information-sharing between home and school. This two-way process is also termed "cultural reciprocity" (Harry *et al.*, 1999). It involves the educator working to build bridges across cultural and linguistic boundaries. These bridges will ultimately create the type of reciprocal family-professional relationship that will lead to greater understanding of, and connection between, schools and the diverse families of children with disabilities.

Barrera and Corso (2003) use a skilled dialogue framework to describe the respect, reciprocity and responsiveness that are integral to the formation of authentic partnerships across cultural and linguistic boundaries in early childhood settings. The framework emphasizes the importance of suspending judgment, taking time for reflection, and staying engaged to allow for varied worldviews to be shared when building relationships with culturally diverse families. There are two components at the core of the skilled dialogue framework: anchored understanding and third space. The authentic partnership across cultural boundaries has the potential to give rise to a cultural hybridity or transformation that emerges from the process of negotiation of meaning and representation shared across cultural and linguistic boundaries. According to Barrera and Corso (2003), the cultural hybridity or transformed worldview or meaning is broader than before the transformation. New meanings and greater understanding of the complexity of the issues evolve from the differing views and stories shared by the diverse partners involved in the skilled dialogue. This broader anchored understanding is a result of skilled dialogue by a professional who respects and appreciates the actions, intentions, and beliefs of a particular family, even in situations where the professional might have acted or thought differently.

Brown and Barrera (1999) use the concept of third space to identify the junction or border crossing that occurs when the process of cultural hybridity gives rise to a new or differing worldview that has been influenced or blurred in the process of passing through cultural barriers. According to Barrera and her colleagues, it is the formation of authentic relationships that permits the transformation and broader understanding to occur and permits family and professionals to each reach a new point of view without abandoning their individual perspectives.

Researchers who challenged the traditional parent involvement paradigm that typically marginalized linguistically and culturally diverse families and communities living in poverty also contributed to helping the early childhood special education field examine and address the need for a more equity-based view of relationship building with families. For example, Delpit (1995), Moll *et al.* (1992) and Olivos (2006) challenged general educators to develop practices that reached children and families outside the comfort of their classroom walls, to question their assumptions about diverse families, and to consider the social, economic, and sociohistorical influences, including issues of race, class and language, that impact educators' relationship with families, students, and communities. Home visits are a recommended practice to help teachers observe and learn about the children in their natural home environment.

Building reciprocal relationships and culturally sustaining practices

Most early childhood educators know about and feel comfortable with the need to develop a strong relationship with the children in their classrooms. All too often, however, early childhood educators think about relationship building with young children as occurring within the classroom walls. Even when teachers include the families in relationship building activities, teachers often focus on activities or interactions to be done by the teacher within the educational setting, not outside the classroom in the families' natural home environment. For example, teachers wanting to know more about the diverse cultural and linguistic communities represented in their classroom may intuitively turn to the academic readings used in many teacher preparation programs to learn more about the diverse families they work with. Some early childhood teachers who have traveled to a country represented in their classroom have experiences that brought them in contact with a segment of that particular community. These experiences create a sense that they know where this particular group came from prior to emigrating to the United States. Those who have even a basic level of proficiency of the home language represented in their classroom often feel more confident when they interact with the families and their children.

Without a doubt, these are significant strengths that can certainly support a teacher in their initial relationship building efforts. What may be overlooked by teachers is that assumptions and stereotypes made about an immigrant group's language and culture based on limited contact as a tourist or through reading overviews found in textbooks can be just as limiting as not knowing anything about that particular group. The well known adage that each person is an island has some bearing on our work with immigrant families. There are unique individual and family/community experiences and social factors that affect the lives of each individual, family, and immigrant group in different ways. No immigrant group is monolithic: rather, it is composed of people differentially affected by various relevant issues faced in their lives – race, class, gender, disability, immigration status, and national and/or ethnic history. Making assumptions about a group based on limited experiences as a tourist in a foreign country, or knowing a few families from that country through work, ignores the reality that there is diversity within each immigrant group that needs to be considered when teachers are committed to developing their skills as a culturally responsive educator.

Sometimes biases and stereotypes about immigrant families are willingly and openly shared by others. For example, a teacher intern shared (Thorp *et al.*, 2018) that before conducting a home visit she had been told by other teachers that Alejandro's parents were recent immigrants, spoke no English, were not interested in their child's education, were too busy working to care for their child, and that it was very likely that they were illiterate. Nonetheless, she asked a classmate to help her write a note in Spanish asking if she could visit their home on a Saturday. Alejandro's family responded the next day and accepted her request for a home visit. The intern went on the home visit and found out that the father was a teacher in his home country, and that the parents were very concerned about Alejandro's progress. They had many Spanish language books at home that the father used when he taught in his country. They held back from using them with Alejandro because they did not want to interfere with the role of the teacher by teaching him at home. They were afraid they would teach him the wrong way or hurt his progress in English. The teacher intern assured them that Alejandro would benefit by them using the Spanish language books to help foster his language and literacy development, and that learning English would follow easily if he had a strong foundation in his first language. The intern learned directly from the family, and it helped both the teacher and the family gain a deeper understanding of their views about the role of the home language and how it influences overall learning. Importantly, for the student intern it broke stereotypes about immigrant families.

To develop as a culturally sustaining teacher for young bilingual learners, it is essential that teachers first be committed to entering the lives of the children through their families. This involves building an authentic and reciprocal relationship with the families of young bilingual children to learn *from* families, not *about* families.

Learning from families, not about families

There is a difference between learning from families and learning about families (Thorp *et al.*, 2018). Learning from, rather than about, a family assumes that the family is the expert. They are the experts about their children and their lives, and the teacher is the learner. The power dynamics between family and educator are somewhat equalized when the family becomes the expert. This is different from the typical first encounter that occurs between family and educator in the school building or classroom, in which the educator is the expert who is there to teach the child and inform the family. Assuming a posture as a learner committed to learning about the child and the child's family directly from the family, requires a commitment that can lead to a partnership. Teachers do not assume the role of an expert when they encounter families. They do not come to the family with an interview form that needs to be completed or other compliance forms that need to be signed or read to the family. Assigning the teacher to the role of an expert is based on a traditional parent involvement model that hinders equity among partners. It structures the family-professional relationship into one where the family is assigned the role of consent-giver and the teacher to the role with the power. A shared partnership does not undergird this type of relationship.

Learning directly from families about the hopes and dreams they have for their children; their family's unique story; and the children's strengths, interests, and preferences, can lead to implementing culturally sustaining environments for the children (Gillanders *et al.*, 2012; Kidd *et al.*, 2002a, 2002b, 2004a, 2004b, 2005; Moll *et al.*, 1992). This can only be done when early childhood educators embrace the principle that an important first step in knowing the child is developing an authentic and reciprocal relationship with families who can help them learn from the family. It is particularly essential for educators to learn directly from families different from their own if they are to avoid basing their practices on assumptions or stereotypes from superficial or cursory interactions with culturally and linguistically diverse communities.

An intern reported about working with Emily, a child with a physical disability (Kidd *et al.*, 2008). Because of her gross motor coordination, the child would fall frequently and hurt herself. The intern's first and natural instinct was to run to Emily's rescue. She assumed that the family shared her view of how to work with Emily. From her interactions with the family during home visits, she learned that their hope and dream for Emily was that she should grow up to be independent and strong. Their view was that if Emily fell, she needed to learn to get back up all on her own. Independence and self-care were primary goals for the family. The intern would not have been able to gain this insight were she not prepared to build authentic and reciprocal relationships with linguistically diverse families and visit the child and the family in their home.

Most of the students enrolled in early childhood special teacher education are young white females who are monolingual and come from middle class backgrounds. Their personal experiences with culturally and linguistically diverse communities, especially with those living in poverty, are nonexistent or limited. Some school districts are beginning to acknowledge this limitation and are requiring that early childhood teachers visit the children in their homes prior to the beginning of the school year. This small, but potentially powerful, step encourages teachers to make the initial contact with children in their families' natural environment rather than in the formal school setting. Any time that teachers go outside their classroom walls and into the homes and communities, it is a positive step that will likely lead to a better understanding of the sociocultural context, including the interests, preferences, history, and challenges that influence the children's development and learning. This understanding has the potential to help teachers increase their use of culturally sustaining practices in the classroom (Kidd *et al.*, 2005; Moll *et al.*, 1992).

The Individuals with Disabilities Education Act (IDEA, 2004), the federal law that ensures services for young children and youth with disabilities and which governs the way that states and public agencies provide these services, addresses some key aspects of the family-professional collaboration that is legislatively required. However, for the collaboration to meet the intention of the law and reap optimal benefits for children, it is essential for the families and professionals to understand and trust each other. But it is often a challenge and this challenge is further compounded when the teacher's home language and culture are different from those of the children and families they are working with (Cheatham & Lim-Mulllins, 2018). Interacting through interpreters in any situation is not easy. Cross-linguistic interactions in two or more languages can lead to both conceptual and cultural misunderstandings between families and professionals. Equally challenging to the collaborative process is the professional jargon used in the field of special education. It is conceptually difficult to understand in any language, even when the interaction occurs among monolingual English speakers (Cheatham & Lim-Mullins, 2018). For families from diverse cultural and linguistic communities, their young children entering the special education system can cause tremendous stress to the family. Establishing an authentic and reciprocal relationship may necessitate that families learn from the teacher and the school context as well as that the teacher learn from the families and the home context. This type of relationship between families and professionals can lead to a respectful and trusting collaboration that reduces misunderstandings, distrust, and stress, even if teachers and families speak different languages.

Teachers who understand and are committed to building authentic and reciprocal relationships with families can minimize the potential challenges of mistrust and inappropriate practices by actualizing the view that learning from families is an endeavor that supports children's overall development and learning, both inside and outside the classroom, and is critical when working with diverse families and their children with disabilities. They can also be aware that both the teacher and families can speak different languages, and a focus on clear communication must be planned prior to approaching families (see Cheatham & Lim-Mullins, 2018, for a list of recommendations for communication strategies).

Families as allies and advocates for bilingualism

Establishing an authentic relationship with the families of young bilingual learners with disabilities is a principle that is inherently central to the practices of all effective teachers working with young children. It is understood that young children do not come to school on their own: they come with their families. Young children need their families, and their families are at the center of their lives. Hence, in congruence with their role as early education teachers, there is the corollary principle that involves the practice of intentionally sustaining the strong socio-emotional bond between families and their children. For teachers working with young bilingual children with disabilities, it not only includes building on families' understanding and knowledge about their children's strengths, interests, and preferences but also providing the parents with information about the services and accommodations that will help them advocate for their children. It also means that teachers must specifically acknowledge the important role and contribution of the home language in the life of children and support the ongoing use of the home language by the family. The concept and practice of culturally sustaining pedagogy (Paris, 2012) applies in this case. This approach has as an explicit goal for educators to perpetuate, foster, or sustain the linguistic, literate, and cultural practices of the family and heritage community. Paris (2012) proposes that this stance and practice are congruent with the cultural pluralism and multilingualism that are part of the democratic project of schools and are a needed response to the demographic and social changes occurring in the United States.

By supporting the use of the home language (or languages), teachers will further enhance the sense of belonging and meaningful interactions between the child and the family; thus, socio-emotional bonds are intentionally strengthened and sustained. Families should never be asked to switch from their home language to English. A switch could cause loss of the home language as well as a weakening of the emotional bonds between the child and the family. The sustained interactions will further help to affirm the child's membership in the family, the larger extended family, and the cultural community. Not to be minimized in importance is the positive impact that a strong home language has on overall learning and development. It can help a child to access better the new learning environment and to successfully continue to build on their prior knowledge.

All too often, educators have the misconception that the home language is an educational barrier: it is viewed similar to a language disability such as language delay. Puig (2010) describes how, often, early intervention services are provided by English-only providers who unintentionally may be placing the child's home language and culture "at risk". As was illustrated in Yu's (2013) research, described above, because families want the best for their children, and teachers play a powerful and influential role in the lives of children with disabilities, it is important that educators do not inadvertently stress the acquisition of the second language over the home language. Ultimately, it is this significant socio-emotional bond, and the ongoing meaningful interactions in their home language, that families carry with them as they assume their active role as the primary advocate and ally on behalf of their children. Hence, families can serve as a role model for their children later, when the children need to develop self-advocacy skills as adults.

Young bilingual children with disabilities and their families often face challenges that intersect with issues of poverty, language, race, gender, culture, immigration status, and ethnicity. If children are to develop the resilience needed to face the societal challenges prevalent in diverse language and cultural communities, they need their family to be fully committed to their role as advocates and allies from the very beginning of their formal education. For most culturally and linguistically diverse young children (García & Gonzáles, 2006; National Task Force on Early Education for Hispanics, 2007), especially those from immigrant families, participation in school-based early intervention programs is the first time they are away from the care of a family member. For the majority of immigrants, life is stressful, especially if they are living in poverty and have to work long hours in multiple jobs. If teachers are aware of the multiple societal forces affecting the lives of families, they can better understand that the issues of housing, access to medical treatment, employment, and isolation, can have a debilitating effect on adults and children. By embracing the principle of sustaining the strong bond between children and families, teachers can also strengthen the role of families as advocates and allies on behalf of their children with disabilities. Teachers can build on the hopes and dreams that families have for their children by sharing and highlighting their observations of the children's valuable assets or abilities. At the same time, teachers can use a family-friendly approach to find ways to increase the use of strength-based and culturally and linguistically sustaining opportunities for children and families to interact and enjoy each other.

Implementing culturally sustaining interactions focused on strengthening family bonds is not just for engaging parents but for including all significant family members as well. For many young bilingual children, the concept of family extends beyond parents and siblings and includes grandparents, aunts and uncles, even cousins and close family friends. It is this socio-emotional base that can influence and motivate families to develop the knowledge and skills needed to advocate on behalf of their young children with disabilities and to potentially be lifelong advocates as extended family members.

Integrating What Has Been Learned from Families into the Classroom

In previous sections we discussed the importance of establishing positive relationships with families in order to learn about their sociocultural beliefs and practices. The knowledge we gain through this process is of limited value if we do not use this information for creating culturally sustaining classroom practices and environments that maximize the families' and children's strengths. The work of Moll *et al.* (1992), and others who have followed (Gillanders *et al.*, 2012; Kidd *et al.*, 2002a, 2002b, 2004a, 2004b, 2005), reminded the field of education that the homes of linguistically and culturally diverse children are a rich and complex social and cultural context that supports their overall learning and cognitive development, even if the home differs from that of the educators who school them. To the detriment of the children, educators typically take no notice of the wealth of learning or funds of knowledge present even in the poorest of homes. They ignore the potential of these homes to enhance student learning both in and out of school. As early educators, we may understand the importance of continuity in development but we often fail to understand how continuity as a construct applies when considering issues of race, class, and language and are more apt to create discontinuity between home and school (Thorp & Sánchez, 1998).

It is more likely that parents will engage and share with early childhood educators if there is a trusting relationship and if the recommendations and practices for supporting children's development are based on the everyday repertoire of families' activities and routines, which also includes the use of the home language. As described above, Yu (2013) found that although parents followed the advice of the specialists regarding using English when speaking to their children, they were more likely to implement the intervention strategies when they were able to use their home language, Chinese.

In early intervention settings with very young bilingual learners, early interventionists can use the natural community and home settings to learn how to best support development. Together with the parent and the child, the early childhood educator can use what has been learned about the community setting to support development by drawing on the available equipment, materials, signage in the home language, or relationships with community members. The community context, together with the family's strengths, interests, and preferences serve as the backdrop for the best culturally sustaining practices modeled by the early interventionist. Community sites can include the nearest playground, fire or police station, grocery store, eateries, and other family-favorite neighborhood sites and people. In the home setting, the early childhood educator can join in the family's authentic routines such as cooking, cleaning or setting the table, washing dishes, picking up or playing with favorite toys, and playing with siblings or other family members, to demonstrate how significant everyday life events are to the development of a young child with disabilities. To support language and literacy development, the service provider can learn about the family's literacy traditions and communication styles in their home language.

For example, lullabies, rhymes, sayings, folktales, family stories or children's songs can be used to co-create picture books or puppets. This type of activity can both foster and sustain language and literacy in families. Families can experience the value of their cultural literacy practices and also recognize the important role that their culture and home language play in their child's language and socio-emotional development (Sánchez, 1999).

In early childhood special education settings, teachers can also use what they learn from families to build on and support family practices. Inviting families into the classroom to be the experts and lead learning activities also acknowledges that families are the children's first teachers. Families can be invited to lead cooking activities; share cultural traditions and history; demonstrate crafts or technical skills such as crocheting, bread or tortilla making, or the use of building and other occupational tools; and teach traditional songs or dance.

In one classroom (Dombrink-Green, 2010; Moran *et al.*, 2010), an early childhood preschool teacher responded to a concern shared by several families that their young children were not behaving appropriately when visiting family friends, and that this behavior was affecting their family's social life. He created a project in his classroom and called it "La Sala," (the living room). His idea was to create a home-like atmosphere in the classroom (with the use of living room furniture, reading materials, and curios) to welcome families as natural partners in the classroom and to help all the children have more practice interacting appropriately with adults. The children established their own rules about the use of the living room, including a particularly interesting rule of "no spitting," to ensure that the living room was always inviting. The project benefited the children and the families. It was so successful in bringing families into the classroom to be partners in the teaching and learning process that the teacher was encouraged to continue it the next year.

In one study (Kidd *et al.*, 2004a), preservice teachers interning in early intervention settings were asked to gather a family story from a family whose cultural background was different from their own. This was part of a semester-long assignment. The interns reported learning much from the families, including how they learned that their child had a disability, and about the joys and frustrations of raising a child with a mild or severe disability. Many of the preservice teachers' comments addressed how what they learned from the family helped them work with the child. For example, an intern commented: "Understanding Mom's view on her child and her goals and needs helped me to see strengths of family and tailor my interactions with the child." They also reported gaining greater "understanding that an educator should support the home language and that research shows that children can acquire English in later years of development." Because of this intensive semester-long experience gathering a family story, they felt more competent in implementing culturally sustaining practices. The interns felt that they could now recommend home activities that were based on the individual family's goals, beliefs, and values.

In another study (Kidd *et al.*, 2002b), kindergarten through third grade preservice teachers interning in inclusive classrooms with culturally, linguistically, and ability-diverse young children implemented a family story project. The main goal was to engage the children with their family members and learn from them. Another goal was to help the preservice teachers learn more from the families represented in the classroom. The project-based learning included such themes as compiling a family and class cookbook, collecting meaningful family cultural artifacts and photographs for a class museum, learning about family trades and tools, gathering a story about when parents or grand parents were children, and creating a class book about each student's family. The projects addressed all areas of the curriculum, including mathematics, science, art, and literacy. The teachers reported how much the children enjoyed learning from their own family, how proud they were to tell stories or share information about their families, and how excited they were to see their families come as experts into the classrooms. The teachers also felt more competent as culturally sustaining teachers.

Conclusion

A sociocultural perspective is a useful framework with which to understand the unique contexts in which young bilingual learners with special needs live and develop. Families organize their children's lives around their cultural beliefs about child rearing and their everyday routines and practices. Beliefs about language learning and disability are also critical when raising young bilingual learners with disabilities. In order for early childhood educators to implement a strength-based, family-centered approach when working with bilingual families, it is crucial to understand the sociocultural context, including the historical, sociopolitical, and economic forces that affect diverse families' lives and, ultimately, the decisions they make as family members of young bilingual learners with disabilities.

Families are ultimately the decision makers in identifying the educational services and plans to support their children's overall development. Throughout their children's schooling, the families will play a key role in identifying best classroom practices and services for their often-vulnerable children. Developing authentic reciprocal relationships with the families of bilingual young children with disabilities can lead to greater insight into the decisions made by the families and reduce misunderstandings between educators and families.

References

American Speech-Language-Hearing Association (2004) *Knowledge and Skills Needed by Speech-language Pathologists and Audiologists to Provide Culturally and Linguistically Appropriate Service* [Knowledge and skills]. Available from www.asha.org/policy.

Artiles, A.J., Harry, B., Reschly, D.J. and Chinn, P.C. (2002) Over-identification of students of color in special education: A critical overview. *Multicultural Perspectives* 4 (1), 3–10.

Barac, R., Bialystok, E., Castro, D.C. and Sanchez, M. (2014) The cognitive development of young dual language learners: A critical review. *Early Childhood Research Quarterly* 29 (4), 699–714.

Barrera, I. and Corso, R.M. (2003) *Skilled Dialogue: Strategies for Responding to Cultural Diversity in Early Childhood*. Baltimore, MD: Brookes Publishing.

Bedore, L.M. and Peña, E.D. (2008) Assessment of bilingual children for identification of language impairment: Current findings and implications for practice. *International Journal of Bilingual Education and Bilingualism* 11 (1), 1–29.

Bird, E.K.R., Genesee, F. and Verhoeven, L. (2016) Bilingualism in children with developmental disorders: A narrative review. *Journal of Communication Disorders*, 63, 1–14.

Blacher, J., Begum, G.F., Marcoulides, G.A. and Baker, B.L. (2013) Longitudinal perspectives of child positive impact on families: Relationship to disability and culture. *American Journal on Intellectual and Developmental Disabilities* 118 (2), 141–155.

Bronfenbrenner, U. (1977) Toward an experimental ecology of human development. *American Psychologist* 32 (7), 513.

Brown, W. and Barrera, I. (1999) Enduring problems with assessment: The persistent challenges of cultural dynamics and family issues. *Infants and Young Children* 12 (1), 34–42.

Chavira, V., López, S.R., Blacher, J. and Shapiro, J. (2000) Latina mothers' attributions, emotions, and reactions to the problem behaviors of their children with developmental disabilities. *Journal of Child Psychology and Psychiatry* 41 (2), 245–252.

Cheatham, G.A. and Lim-Mullins, S. (2018) Immigrant, bilingual parents of students with disabilities: Positive perceptions and supportive dialogue. *Intervention in School and Clinic* 54 (1), 40–46.

Colbert, A.M., Webber, J. and Graham, R. (2017) Factors that influence autism knowledge in Hispanic cultures: A pilot study. *Journal of Racial and Ethnic Health Disparities* 4 (2), 156–164.

Delpit, L. (1995) *Other People's Children: Cultural Conflict in the Classroom*. New York, NY: The New Press.

Dewey, J. (1902) *The Child and the Curriculum*. Chicago, IL: University of Chicago Press.

Dewey, J. (1938) *Experience and Education*. New York, NY: Kappa Delta Pi.

Dombrink-Green, M. (2010) The NAEYC Annual Conference and Expo: A time for preschool teachers to explore, grow, and network. *Teaching Young Children* 3 (3), 26–28.

Farruggio, P. (2010) Latino immigrant parents' views of bilingual education as a vehicle for heritage preservation. *Journal of Latinos and Education* 9 (1), 3–21.

García, E.E. and Gonzáles, D. (2006) *Pre-K and Latinos: The Foundation for America's Future*. Washington, DC: Pre-K Now.

García Coll, C., Lamberty, G., Jenkins, R., McAdoo, H.P., Crnic, K., Wasik, B.H. and Vázquez García, H. (1996) An integrative model for the study of developmental competencies in minority children. *Child Development* 67 (5), 1891–1914.

Gee, J.P. (2003) A sociocultural perspective on early literacy development. In S.B. Neuman and D.K. Dickinson (eds) *Handbook of Early Literacy Research Volume 1* (pp. 30–42). New York, NY: Guilford Press.

Gillanders, C. and Jiménez, R.T. (2004) Reaching for success: A close-up of Mexican immigrant parents in the USA who foster literacy success for their kindergarten children. *Journal of Early Childhood Literacy* 4 (3), 243–269.

Gillanders, C., McKinney, M. and Ritchie, S. (2012) What kind of school would you like for your children? Exploring minority mothers' beliefs to promote home-school partnerships. *Early Childhood Education Journal* 40 (5), 285–294.

Gutierrez, K.D. and Rogoff, B. (2003) Cultural ways of learning: Individual traits or repertoires of practice. *Educational Researcher* 32 (5), 19–25.

Hambly, C. and Fombonne, E. (2012) The impact of bilingual environments on language development in children with autism spectrum disorders. *Journal of Autism and Developmental Disorders* 42 (7), 1342–1352.

Harry, B. (1992) *Cultural Diversity, Families, and the Special Education System: Communication and Empowerment.* New York, NY: Teachers College Press.

Harry, B. (2008) Collaboration with culturally and linguistically diverse families: Ideal versus reality. *Exceptional Children* 74 (3), 372–388.

Harry, B. and Klingner, J. (2006) *Why Are So Many Minority Students in Special Education?* New York, NY: Teachers College Press.

Harry, B., Kalyanpur, M. and Day, M. (1999) *Building Cultural Reciprocity with Families: Case Studies in Special Education.* Baltimore, MD: Brookes Publishing.

Hashimoto, K. and Lee, J.S. (2011) Heritage-language literacy practices: A case study of three Japanese American families. *Bilingual Research Journal* 34 (2), 161–184.

IDEA (2004) Individuals with Disabilities Education Act, 20 U.S.C. § 1400 (2004).

Kalyanpur, M. and Harry, B. (1997) A posture of reciprocity: A practical approach to collaboration between professionals and parents of culturally diverse backgrounds. *Journal of Child and Family Studies* 6 (4), 487–509.

Kalyanpur, M. and Harry, B. (2012) *Culture in Special Education: Building Reciprocal Family-Professional Relationships.* Baltimore, MD: Brookes Publishing.

Kidd, J.K., Sánchez, S.Y. and Thorp, E.K. (2002a) A focus on family stories: Enhancing preservice teachers' cultural awareness. In D.L. Shallert, C.M. Fairbanks, J. Worthy, B. Maloch and J.V. Hoffman (eds) *51st Yearbook of the National Reading Conference* (pp. 242–252). Chicago, IL: National Reading Conference.

Kidd, J.K., Thorp, E.K. and Sánchez, S.Y. (2002b) Family stories in K-3 classrooms: Promoting culturally responsive instruction. In P.E. Linder, M.B. Sampson, J.R. Dugan and B. Brancato (eds) *Celebrating the Faces of Literacy. 23rd Yearbook of the College Reading Association* (pp. 247–261). Commerce, TX: College Reading Association.

Kidd, J.K., Sánchez, S.Y. and Thorp, E.K. (2004a) Gathering family stories: Facilitating preservice teachers' cultural awareness and responsiveness. *Action in Teacher Education* 26 (1), 64–73.

Kidd, J.K., Sánchez, S.Y. and Thorp, E.K. (2004b) Listening to the stories families tell: Promoting culturally responsive language and literacy experiences. In C.M. Fairbanks, J. Worthy, B. Maloch, J.V. Hoffman and D.L. Shallert (eds) *53rd Yearbook of the National Reading Conference* (pp. 246–263). Chicago, IL: National Reading Conference.

Kidd, J.K., Sánchez, S.Y. and Thorp, E.K. (2005) Cracking the challenge of changing dispositions: Changing hearts and minds through stories, narratives, and direct cultural interactions. *Journal of Early Childhood Teacher Education* 26 (4), 347–359.

Kidd, J.K., Sánchez, S.Y. and Thorp, E.K. (2008) Defining moments: Developing culturally responsive dispositions and teaching practices in early childhood preservice teachers. *Teaching and Teacher Education* 24 (2), 316–329.

Lao, C. (2004) Parents' attitudes toward Chinese–English bilingual education and Chinese-language use. *Bilingual Research Journal* 28 (1), 99–121.

Marinova-Todd, S.H., Colozzo, P., Mirenda, P., Stahl, H., Bird, E.K.R., Parkington, K. and Genesee, F. (2016) Professional practices and opinions about services available to bilingual children with developmental disabilities: An international study. *Journal of Communication Disorders* 63, 47–62.

Moll, L.C., Amanti, C., Neff, D. and Gonzalez, N. (1992) Funds of knowledge for teaching: Using a qualitative approach to connect homes and classrooms. *Theory into Practice* 31 (2), 132–141.

Moran, S., Calderon, S., Sánchez, S.Y. and Thorp, E. (2010) Coming together in la sala: How adding a living room inside a preschool special education classroom promoted appropriate behaviors, literacy skills and more. Session presented at the National Association for the Education of Young Children Annual Conference and Expo, October 2010, Washington DC.

National Task Force on Early Childhood Education for Hispanics (2007) *Nuestros N iños: Expanding and Improving Early Education for Hispanics*. Available online at http://fcd-us.org/sites/default/files/MainReport.pdf.

Olivos, E.M. (2006) *The Power of Parents*. New York, NY: Peter Lang.

Paris, D. (2012) Culturally sustaining pedagogy: A needed change in stance, terminology, and practice. *Educational Researcher* 41 (3), 93–97.

Park, S.M. and Sarkar, M. (2007) Parents' attitudes toward heritage language maintenance for their children and their efforts to help their children maintain the heritage language: A case study of Korean-Canadian immigrants. *Language, Culture and Curriculum* 20 (3), 223–235.

Piaget. J. (1932) *The Moral Judgment of the Child*. Glencoe, Il: Free Press.

Piaget. J. (1952) *The Origins of Intelligence of Children*. New York, NY: International Universities Press.

Portes, A. and Schauffler, R. (1994) Language and the second generation: Bilingualism yesterday and today. *International Migration Review* 28 (4), Special Issue: The New Second Generation, 640–661.

Puig, V. (2010) Are early intervention services placing home languages and cultures "At risk"? *Early Childhood Research and Practice* 12 (1), 1–19.

Puig, V.I. (2012) Cultural and linguistic alchemy: Mining the resources of Spanish-speaking children and families receiving early intervention services. *Journal of Research in Childhood Education* 26 (3), 325–345.

Recchia, S.L. and Lee, Y. (2013) *Inclusion in the Early Classroom: What Makes a Difference?* New York, NY: Teachers College Press.

Rogoff, B. (2003) *The Cultural Nature of Human Development*. Oxford: Oxford University Press.

Rogoff, B., Dahl, A. and Callanan, M. (2018) The importance of understanding children's lived experience. *Developmental Review*, 50, 5–15.

Rossetti, Z, Saurer, J.S., Bui, O. and Ou, S. (2017) Developing collaborative partnerships with culturally and linguistically diverse families during the IEP process. *TEACHING Exceptional Children* 49, 328–338.

Sánchez, S.Y. (1999) Learning from the stories of culturally and linguistically diverse families and communities: A sociohistorical lens. *Remedial and Special Education* 20 (6), 351–359.

Sánchez, S.Y. and Thorp, E.K. (1998) Discovering meanings of continuity: Implications for the infant/family field. *Zero to Three Journal* 18 (6), 1–6.

Sánchez, S.Y. and Thorp, E.K. (2008) Teaching to transform: Infusing cultural and linguistic diversity. In P.J. Winton, J.A. McCollum and C. Catlett (eds) *Practical Approaches to Early Childhood Professional Development: Evidence, Strategies, and Resources* (pp. 81–97). Baltimore, MD: Paul H. Brookes.

Saurer, J.S. and Rossetti, Z. (2019) *Affirming Disability: Strengths-based Portraits of Culturally Diverse Families*. New York, NY: Teachers College Press.

Skinner, D. and Weisner, T.S. (2007) Sociocultural studies of families of children with intellectual disabilities. *Mental Retardation and Developmental Disabilities Research Reviews* 13 (4), 302–312.

Skinner, D.G., Correa, V., Skinner, M. and Bailey Jr, D.B. (2001) Role of religion in the lives of Latino families of young children with developmental delays. *American Journal on Mental Retardation* 106 (4), 297–313.

Tamis-LeMonda, C.S., Song, L., Leavell, A.S., Kahana-Kalman, R. and Yoshikawa, H. (2012) Ethnic differences in mother–infant language and gestural communications are associated with specific skills in infants. *Developmental Science* 15 (3), 384–397.

Thorp, E.K. and Sánchez, S.Y. (1998) The use of discontinuity in preparing early educators of culturally, linguistically, and ability-diverse young children and their families. *Zero to Three Journal* 18 (6), 27–33.

Thorp, E.K., Sánchez, S.Y. and Gosnell, E.S. (2018) Embracing cultural dilemmas: A framework for teachers working with immigrant students and their families. In S. Wong, E. Sánchez Gosnell, A. M. Foerster Luu, L. Dodson and A. Chomsky (eds) *Teachers as Allies: Transformative Practices for Teaching DREAMers and Undocumented Students* (pp. 17–34). New York, NY: Teachers College Press.

Velázquez, I. (2013) Mother's social network and family language maintenance. *Journal of Multilingual and Multicultural Development* 34 (2), 189–202.

Velázquez, I. (2014) Maternal perceptions of agency in intergenerational transmission of Spanish: The case of Latinos in the US Midwest. *Journal of Language, Identity & Education* 13 (3), 135–152.

Vygotsky, L.S. (1978) *Mind in Society: The Development of Higher Psychological Processes*. Cambridge, MA: Harvard University Press.

Vygotsky, L. (1986) *Thought and Language*. Cambridge, MA: MIT Press.

Whiting, B.B. and Whiting, J.W.M. (1975) *Children of Six Cultures: A Psycho-Cultural Analysis*. Cambridge, MA: Harvard University Press.

Withrow, R.L. (2008) Early intervention with Latino families: Implications for practice. *Journal of Multicultural Counseling and Development* 36 (4), 245–256.

Yu, B. (2013) Issues in bilingualism and heritage language maintenance: Perspectives of minority-language mothers of children with autism spectrum disorders. *American Journal of Speech-Language Pathology* 22 (1), 10–24.

8 Preparing Teachers of Young Bilingual Children with Disabilities

Norma A. López-Reyna, Cindy L. Collado, Mary Bay, and Wu-Ying Hsieh

The changing demographic profile in the United States has called for our nation to attend to the diverse needs of children and their families, including children with disabilities and those from culturally and linguistically diverse backgrounds. Young children with disabilities and their families are full members of the community and need to be able to participate in a broad range of learning activities, settings, and educational environments (Division for Early Childhood (DEC)/ National Association for the Education of Young Children (NAEYC), 2009). In 2016, approximately 67% of children ages 3 through 5 served under IDEA, Part B, attended a regular early childhood program and received their special education and related services from some amount of the time in such programs, where at least 50% of children without disabilities attended (US Department of Education, 2018). With the increasing number of children with disabilities included in regular early childhood settings, early childhood educators need to have the knowledge, skills, and dispositions to teach all children, with and without disabilities.

Another dramatic change is the number of children from culturally and linguistically diverse backgrounds. As noted in other chapters in this book, almost 44% of our nation's children are from culturally and linguistically diverse backgrounds. In 2016, 49% of all children were not White, and it is projected that by 2020, the majority of children will be children of color (Children's Defense Fund, 2017). The data suggest that children from culturally and linguistically diverse backgrounds are at higher risk of being recommended to receive special education services and that, as they grow older, they struggle in schools. For example, among fourth grade public school students, approximately 80% of Black and Hispanic students performed below grade level in reading (Black: 82%; Hispanic: 79%) and math (Black: 81%; Hispanic: 74%) in 2015 (Children's Defense Fund, 2017). Unsuccessful early experiences in school result in subsequent failures, such as dropping out, behavioral issues, and other negative outcomes. Hence, receiving a quality education is the best route to preventing such risk, by providing opportunities to improve children's educational outcomes.

While the number of culturally and linguistically diverse students in the United States continues to increase, the teaching force has remained largely white, female, and middle class (Aud et al., 2010; Bireda & Chait, 2011; Howard & Banks, 2020; Lowenstein, 2009). This represents opportunities and challenges for teachers with regard to meeting the children's needs, most of whom have not had formal preparation for teaching culturally diverse or English language learners (Lucas et al., 2008). In fact, a majority of teachers reports feeling unprepared for the realities of teaching both students with disabilities and those who are English language learners (Levine, 2006). Over a decade ago, Zehler and Fleishman (2003) estimated that nearly 25% of all US public school special education teachers taught at least one English language learner during the 2001–2002 school year. This number has certainly increased, while only 30% of teachers teaching English language learners have received any training for this population and less than 3% have a degree in English as a second language or bilingual education (Aud et al., 2010).

Teacher preparation programs need to improve if they are to prepare qualified teachers (American Association of Colleges for Teacher Education, AACTE, 2010). With historically high numbers of special education teachers leaving the profession (Aud et al., 2010), particularly within the first five years of teaching, and especially in high-poverty areas (Darling-Hammond, 2010), it is important to focus on increasing the quality of our teachers through supportive, cohesive teacher preparation programs that incorporate effective clinical experiences. This is especially true for teachers of culturally and linguistically diverse children with disabilities (Hoover et al., 2007; Klingner & Bianco, 2006; Samson & Collins, 2012).

In several ways, the education community has responded to the importance of offering high quality preparation to individuals who plan to teach. For example, extensive research available to teacher education reformers reveals the effectiveness of a pedagogy that responds to the learning styles of children of various racial and linguistic groups and with varying abilities (e.g., Artiles & McClafferty, 1998; Baca & Cervantes, 1989; Darling-Hammond, 2006a; Gay, 2010; Hoover et al., 2007; Nieto & Bode, 2011). Indeed, many culturally and linguistically diverse students enter classrooms with teachers who do not have shared backgrounds or communities and with experiences that are quite different from those expected in today's classrooms (Ford, 2012; Harry & Klingner, 2006).

More recently (2012), the Council for Exceptional Children (CEC) revised and developed its Initial and Advanced Standards to provide guidance in support of faculty in Institutes of Higher Education (IHEs) and professional development programs, to prepare individuals who are in pursuit of a special education license/credential or a special education specialist. The Council of the Accreditation of Educator Preparation (CAEP, formerly known as NCATE) has approved these standards in accreditation of personnel preparation programs in special education. DEC, one of CEC's 12 divisions, had a set of carefully constructed, comprehensive personnel preparation standards (see Division for Early Childhood, DEC, 1993) and later published a volume on personnel preparation in early childhood special education, highlighting exemplary programs that implemented the DEC-recommended practices in programs' learning activities and field experiences (Stayton et al., 2003). On the premise of preparing highly qualified professionals to work with children birth through 8 years of age with disabilities and their families, DEC has revised and developed corresponding Initial and Advanced Special Education Early Childhood Specialty Sets (see Chandler et al., 2012 for a comprehensive discussion). Although it can be challenging to provide preservice teachers with experiences for developing insights and understanding of cultures different from their own (Kidd et al., 2008), these refined and newly developed standards aligned with CEC standards are aimed at preparing professionals with the knowledge, skills, and dispositions in areas such as individualization, development, and learning for the child, family-centered practices, natural or inclusive environments, collaboration in culturally responsive ways, evidence-based instructional strategies, continuum of services and supports, and advocacy for the child and family (see Division for Early Childhood (2014) for details).

Finally, scholars have provided useful frameworks through which we can conceptualize programs as we design and improve them. For example, Darling-Hammond and her colleagues suggest that teacher educators provide teachers with authentic learning tasks that allow them to be adaptive teachers. Authentic learning tasks include immediate connections to the classroom through authentic pedagogical materials: examples of such vehicles for teaching teachers include field experiences, analysis of teaching events, case studies, autobiographies, professional inquiry, and action research (Darling-Hammond et al., 2005).

Shulman (1987) was one of the first to argue for the professionalization of teaching as teachers develop complex sets of knowledge about: (a) the learners; (b) the content, including context-specific understandings and curricula as tools for teaching the information; (c) general pedagogical strategies and content-specific pedagogy as ways of being and acting as a teacher; and (d) the educational system including the school, district, and community as well as historical approaches and social contexts. Similarly, Darling-Hammond and Bransford (2005) identified three sources of knowledge that teachers draw on, including knowledge about students, knowledge about the curriculum and social aspects of education, and pedagogical knowledge. They argued further for the importance of teachers understanding social influences on students as a way to develop a critical lens for understanding diverse student populations. To further elaborate on teaching in a diverse society, Han and Thomas (2010) described three themes of becoming a multicultural educator: (a) awareness including self-reflection about one's own culture and the influence of culture on an individual; (b) knowledge about others' cultures; and (c) skills to teach diverse students, including practices that are multicultural and culturally responsive.

Essential Program Topics

Recognizing that an entire book could be devoted to the preparation of individuals to teach young bilingual children with disabilities, in the first part of this chapter, we decided to use the limited space to focus on aspects of a program that we think are essential. Hence, we chose to focus on the following: the importance of learning about and from families; the use of a critical pedagogical approach that is culturally and linguistically responsive to the needs of the children and promotes learning; and specifically, the need to use and adapt formative assessment practices that draw the teacher into collaborative relationships with their families and which yield data that inform instructional content.

Essential curricular content area: The importance of families

The Division for Early Childhood of the Council for Exceptional Children (Division for Early Childhood, 2014) identified families as important contributors to the learning and assessment process for students with disabilities. Early childhood teachers can learn to connect with families and empower them and provide education opportunities that are well coordinated and agreed upon by both parents and teachers, as a way of providing appropriate and effective education for their children. In fact, teacher preparation programs that provide preservice teachers with direct experiences with families have demonstrated positive results, including "increased levels of confidence and self-awareness for preservice candidates, increased knowledge of diverse families and their role in education, and the ability to use knowledge about families and communities to improve instruction" (Evans, 2013: 126). Often, teachers struggle to see positive ways to involve families beyond communicating during Individualized Education Program (IEP) meetings and parent-teacher conferences (Collado, 2015). It can be even more challenging when families and educators do not speak the same language, come from different cultures, and have varying beliefs about child development (Ntuli *et al.*, 2014). Indeed, two main barriers to building positive relationships with families of culturally and linguistically diverse students is the perception that these families do not support their child's learning or that they do not value education (Turner, 2007). By engaging teacher candidates with families, their beliefs about culturally different children and families can be enriched.

Through work with preservice teachers on a semester-long project collecting family stories, Sánchez (1999) found that key to preservice teachers' transformation toward culturally competent work with families were seven dispositions. These seven dispositions pushed teachers to be okay with feeling uncomfortable talking about racial and economic disparities, challenging dominant views of culture and education, seeing the school as only one source of learning, and taking the perspective of families and recognizing their strengths and their resiliency. Collecting and analyzing family stories was also a powerful strategy used by Miller and Fuller (2006) in a larger project toward increased cultural understanding and connections with families. In their teacher preparation project, they used a modified version of the ABCs of Cultural Understanding and Communication Model (Schmidt, 1998), including requiring students to write an autobiography, a biography of a diverse family, an analysis of cross-cultural similarities and differences, communication strategies for connecting with the home, and reflection on the experience. As a result of this project, Miller and Fuller (2006) found that preservice teachers were more confident in working and building relationships with families, prepared to engage with families, and were aware of the broader role that educators play in working with culturally and linguistically diverse families and children.

Preservice teachers can learn to see family involvement beyond the minimal reaching out to families via notes home and see collaboration as developing relationships with families that allow them to recognize the diversity within families and challenge their own preconceived judgments about certain cultures (Evans, 2013). Wager *et al.* (2015) recommend shifting how families' participation with regard to the assessment and learning processes is viewed toward an awareness and consideration of their *funds of knowledge* (Moll *et al.*, 1992): families can provide insight on their child's knowledge and abilities, their preferences, and their social skills, and so forth. Preservice teachers can also learn from the families about a family's immigration history, their favorite activities, and family composition (Villegas & Lucas, 2007) through parent questionnaires (see discussion in Chapter 6) and interviews. These understandings can inform teachers' instruction and the types of recommendations they make to families for enhancing their children's development, so that they are more in line with their cultural contexts and their current perceptions and expectations for the child, given their disability.

Particularly for families of children with disabilities, it is important for preservice teachers to learn about the challenges they face, the information they seek, and how to advocate for and with the families. In doing so, teachers can move away from a deficit view of families (Harry, 2008) toward a strengths-based view. Shadowing families of bilingual children with disabilities during daily activities, interviewing them, or conducting home visits could provide preservice teachers with valuable insight into what life is like outside school (Bernheimer & Koegh, 1995; Hansuvadha, 2009). This knowledge about, and ability to seek, such information about future families with whom they work could have a positive impact on the development of caring and empathetic dispositions that lead to collaborative relationships with families. Villegas and Lucas (2002) also recommend tapping into families via family questionnaires and interviews. Teacher preparation programs can model ways of understanding and getting to know families by engaging students in informally created qualitative interviews and questionnaires that ask families about their activities, values, expertise, and experiences. Then teachers need to learn how to incorporate this information into classroom practices and perspectives as they develop a classroom community, address cultural differences, and build on each other's strengths. Simply learning techniques to understand families, however, may not change teachers' beliefs and judgments about families, especially when deficits-based views of families and stereotypes persist (Harry, 2008). It is important that experiences involving understanding families be paired with reflective practices, supportive professional learning communities, service learning experiences, and discussions that support teachers in shifting toward developing a strengths-based lens when working with families.

Some other strategies for teaching preservice teachers about ways to appreciate and involve families in the education of their child, otherwise known as family-centered practices, focus on increasing the involvement of families at the preservice level (Pretti-Frontczak *et al.*, 2002). High- and moderate-level family involvement experiences include: hiring family members as co-teachers for courses, particularly for providing feedback and facilitating group work; semester-long partnerships with families of bilingual children with disabilities; family panels; engagement in assessment and planning experiences such as Individualized Education Program (IEP) meetings and play-based assessments; gathering information for families on services and experiences available in the community; and involving family members in simulated meetings that challenge students' professionalism (Evans, 2013; Pretti-Frontczack *et al.*, 2002).

An essential curricular content area: Culturally and linguistically responsive pedagogy

When teaching students who are both culturally and linguistically diverse as well as ability diverse, culturally responsive teaching focuses on the strengths and experiences of the students, effectively moving away from a deficit focus (Seidl & Pugach, 2009). Gay (2000) defined culturally responsive teaching as:

> using the cultural knowledge, prior experiences, frames of reference, and performance styles of ethnically diverse students to make learning encounters more relevant to and effective for them. It teaches *to and through* the strengths of these students. It is culturally *validating and affirming.* (Gay, 2000: 29)

Some individuals view the teaching practices of culturally responsive teachers as "just good teaching"; however, it is more purposeful and addresses multiple levels of social consciousness.

A key tenet of culturally responsive teaching is for teachers to know their students' cultures. Teachers' knowledge about other cultures as well as their own can provide a foundation by which teachers see their students as individuals representing a rich and valid culture rather than seeing their actions as simply a set of behaviors (Han & Thomas, 2010). This may be particularly challenging for teachers from a European American background, especially if they have grown up in a community and attended school in settings that were not very diverse. With US school curricula that do not typically include adequately deep or varied treatment of a variety of perspectives, it is no wonder that most teacher candidates will not have learned or even noticed that there are different ways of knowing and learning. Banks (2001) notes that becoming culturally responsive is an ongoing process, which begins with increased awareness of other cultures as well as one's own and that this builds toward an appreciation of the strengths and needs of individuals across cultural groups.

To increase preservice teachers' knowledge about different cultures, one program implemented a multicultural literacy project (Howrey & Whelan-Kim, 2009). This project required students to choose a culture from a list of those representing the cultures of students in the local school district; research the culture, particularly focusing on the immigration experiences of families; read seven children's books representing that culture; prepare a poster presentation; and reflect on the experience. As a result of this project, the teacher candidates learned about other cultures, increased their awareness of similarities and differences between other cultures and their own, and developed a social justice perspective by which they aimed to develop similar increased understandings within the communities of their future students (Howrey & Whelan-Kim, 2009).

Beyond learning about other cultures and histories, teacher candidates must also develop an understanding of how such differences can influence how children learn. Teacher preparation programs can model this awareness and understanding through their practices (see

Baumgartner *et al.*, 2015). There are many ways to engage teacher candidates through assignments and projects to promote understanding. These might include ethnographies of the school, student and family interviews, reflective writing and discussions, autobiographies, simulations and games, exploring personal histories and microcultures, case studies, inquiry projects, learning about the history and current experiences of diverse groups, service learning, guest speakers, and field experiences with diverse learners (Kea *et al.*, 2006; McHatton *et al.*, 2006; Villegas & Lucas, 2002).

The impact of student-teacher relationships is critical to the academic, social, and emotional success of young children. In studies examining the impact of preschool on diverse populations of students (Camilli *et al.*, 2010; Peisner-Feinberg *et al.*, 2001), researchers found that while classroom structures and practices were strongly correlated with higher cognitive and language skills, it was the closeness of the preschool teachers' relationships with the children that was more predictive of children's later positive behaviors and social skills (Peisner Feinberg *et al.*, 2001). Ladson-Billings (1995) argued that to develop cultural responsiveness, teachers needed to develop a "sociocultural consciousness" or awareness that culture is the lens through which individuals see the world. Building strong, positive relationships with students, particularly those who come from different cultural experiences than your own, begins with developing a caring disposition (Talbert-Johnson, 2006). Talbert-Johnson defines a caring disposition as a combined focus on addressing the learning needs of each student, developing a classroom community, and developing relationships based on trust and understanding. By focusing on developing dispositions in preservice teachers in tandem with pedagogical approaches to working with culturally and linguistically diverse students, teacher preparation programs increase the chances of teachers working from a culturally responsive stance.

Often overlooked in teacher education programs that are not specifically preparing teachers to serve English language learners (e.g., bilingual and English as a Second Language teaching certification) is the teaching of language development as it pertains to second language acquisition. Culture and language are intricately linked, so that it is very difficult to understand one without the other. Zepeda *et al.* (2011) assert that language develops within the home culture and that the culture's beliefs and patterns have a direct bearing on how and when language is used. They go on to remind us that English language learners are tasked with learning oral and written skills in the new language while also learning about a culture that may be very different from what they are accustomed to at home (Zepeda *et al.*, 2011). It is important for teacher candidates to understand how language and literacy develop in young English language learners, and this includes knowing about language development (in the language of their families) and second language development (see Tabors, 2008).

With gradual professional scaffolding, preservice teachers develop their teaching practice based on deep understandings of the interplay of children's language, cognitive development, and social development within various contexts across school and home. Inquiry learning can provide teacher candidates with the necessary tools and learning environments to develop their own understanding of what it means to be a teacher, and to develop in the essential tasks common to all teachers. Teacher candidates need multiple and sustained opportunities to experience their new knowledge and understandings in the context of classrooms. Inquiry learning through a constructivist approach (Villegas & Lucas, 2002) needs to be threaded throughout teacher preparation programs. Such learning sets the stage for teacher candidates to be immediately immersed in the classroom, beginning with observations that permit them to find instances of learning and exploration, language use and problem solving, social engagement, and differences among children's enactments according to their linguistic ability and cultural individualities.

Finally, an essential component of the preparation of candidates in critically analyzing the learning context is participation in a community discussion. Preparing teachers involves going beyond both pedagogical and practical knowledge to guide teachers in inquiry communities that aid in developing them into agents of change in their schools (Cochran-Smith & Lytle, 1999). To set the stage, Zeichner (2010) suggests using the concept of a "third space" to socialize prospective teachers into the discourse of the teaching community (Hollins, 2011). Teacher candidates should be provided with new ways of interacting with practicing teachers in ways that allow for the development of a shared critical lens in the diverse school contexts. The focus is not on instilling knowledge and ways of teaching but on engaging in a community of equal colleagues who examine the complicated nature of schools, families, and policies.

An essential curricular content area: Formative assessment practices

A critical aspect of teaching is the process of assessing students' progress and collecting data that are useful to informing instructional planning. In the past ten years, requirements to demonstrate student learning through test data have been on the rise, presumably as if collecting more evidence of student learning would subsequently lead to improved learning conditions. In fact, summative evaluations of student academic abilities, measured at only one point in time (i.e., high-stakes tests, standardized measures) can narrow instruction, demotivate students experiencing school failure, be more likely to be culturally biased, and negatively influence teacher attrition (Amrein & Berlinner, 2003; Saeki et al., 2018; Sahlberg, 2007). In contrast to summative measures that are not designed to improve learning, qualitatively measuring student understanding in the midst of instruction and learning, called formative assessment or *ongoing assessment* in early childhood (Akers et al., 2016; Dichtelmiller, 2011), provides both teachers and students with the valuable information or data to generate ways to build on those ideas and build learning experiences that match students' cultural expectations for learning (Moss & Brookhart, 2019). Additionally, positive learning experiences for all students can be possible when classrooms shift from learning basic skills to deeper learning of fewer concepts, so that students engage in dialogue around authentic learning tasks (Morocco, 2001). In this sense, measures of the quality of learning and understanding can empower teachers and students.

Teachers can cultivate a whole understanding of each student's unique learning needs within developmentally appropriate practice by utilizing daily assessment tools to inform the development of more personalized learning experiences for all students (Grisham-Brown & Pretti-Frontczak, 2011; Helm et al., 1997; McFarland, 2008). They would need to understand assessment as the systematic collection of evidence from students, analysis of the information, and application of the information for a variety of purposes (Akers et al., 2016; Salvia et al., 2017). In particular, they need an understanding of the balance between using assessments for *summative* purposes (e.g., norm-referenced and criterion-referenced) to evaluate student performance according to a developmental norm or criterion, and for *formative* purposes (e.g., anecdotal records, student interviews, discussions) to describe student understanding that informs instruction and improves learning (Moss & Brookhart, 2019; Chappuis et al., 2011).

Ongoing assessment (Akers et al., 2016; Dichtelmiller, 2011) is a process of observing student learning to reveal their understandings and misunderstandings, and then using those data to inform scaffolding practices that are uniquely responsive to individual students' learning styles, abilities, experiences, and linguistic competence. Teachers often describe a familiarity with collecting informal data about students using written or mental notes as they observe during lessons and play activities (Elicker & McMullen, 2013; Grisham-Brown & Pretti-Frontczak, 2011); however, in the absence of a systematic approach to collecting, interpreting, and applying those data, the potential impact is often lost (Akers et al., 2016; Collado, 2015). Indeed, teachers are often not fully cognizant of the role of in-the-moment and daily types of assessment, and it has been noted that "too often assessment results are seen as an end product rather than as knowledge that opens the door to learning about each child and to planning a meaningful curriculum" (Dodge et al., 2004: 21). Teacher preparation programs need to emphasize the importance of formatively assessing children, as this approach is more likely to guide culturally responsive practices.

A critical purpose for assessing in the early childhood classroom is to develop and sustain meaningful collaborative relationships with families and students built on trust that can lead to a greater realization (and accuracy) of who the student is as a complete individual (Elicker & McMullen, 2013; Grisham-Brown & Pretti-Frontczak, 2011; Jablon *et al.*, 2007; McFarland, 2008; Peisner-Feinberg *et al.*, 2001; Rhodes & Nathenson-Mejia, 1992). To this end, teacher education programs need to educate teachers on the use of formative assessments in classrooms and to move beyond the classroom and involve families, with the goal of building their understandings about what the children know, how they learn, what their everyday lives are like and what goals and aspirations their families have for them. One common approach to creating culturally relevant education programs for older students with disabilities can also be used effectively with younger children. Person-centered planning or Making Action Plans (MAPs) involves the family, the child, and the school team in a discussion about the family's hopes, dreams, and goals for the child's future (Hansuvadha, 2009; Wells & Sheehey, 2012). In this approach, MAPs are created and used to guide the development of personalized programs that integrate the goals of the families and can be sensitive to what they value as important for their child. This, in turn, provides valuable information that can be infused into curriculum and instructional planning.

Another assessment strategy that teachers can use to engage families is *Learning Stories*, a narrative dialogue between families, teachers, and students about learning strengths and individual progress (Bourke *et al.*, 2011; Carr, 2001; Pak, 2016; Wager *et al.*, 2015). Learning stories serve as both an individualized and collaborative assessment approach. Narrative assessment moves away from a developmental perspective to a sociocultural perspective, where the environment, peers, teachers, and parents are integral to the assessment process, and where assessment is premised on the belief that context makes a difference to student learning and assessment results, and that there is not a linear progression to child development. "For learners with high and very high needs, this approach is critical, given that developmental stages are unpredictable, and often irrelevant to their learning needs" (Bourke *et al.*, 2011: 408). In contrast to descriptions about meeting predetermined performance criteria, learning stories are a process of telling a personalized story about the child's approach to learning at the child's individual level of ability and interest.

Preservice teachers working with diverse students must also learn about the process of collecting information about students through interactions such as questioning and scaffolding, as this too provides detailed information about student learning. Shepard described these interactions as scaffolding or "supports that teachers provide to the learner during problem solving – in the form of reminders, hints, and encouragement – to ensure successful completion of a task" (Shepard, 2005: 66). As is the goal in dynamic assessments (Grigorenko & Sternberg, 1998; Lerma & Stewart, 2012; Lidz & Peña, 1996) and scaffolding procedures (Shepard, 2005), the goal for teachers is to discover each child's learning potential by challenging the child at his or her individual level of ability and interest. In such moments, teachers can employ a response-prompting approach similar to a *least-to-most strategy*, whereby they begin scaffolding by providing the least amount of support and increase the level of prompting until the student engages in or completes the task (Boat *et al.*, 2010; Grisham-Brown & Hemmeter, 2017). These mini formative assessment cycles are like "a mini-experiment in intervention, with the child's performance serving to confirm or dispute the assessor's hypotheses about what might work to improve the child's functioning" (Lidz & Peña, 1996: 368).

In the discussion above, we present key curricular areas that we highly recommend for inclusion in teacher preparation programs, with examples of how that content can be incorporated into a program's coursework and experiences. In this next section, we provide a description of the initiatives that a group of teacher educators undertook as they worked to improve their early childhood programs to better prepare individuals to teach all young children. Our intent here is to initiate a discussion about the rewards and challenges of designing high-quality, accredited, early childhood teacher preparation programs.

Reforming Teacher Preparation Programs

Many early childhood and special education preparation program faculty in universities and colleges have been engaging in efforts to revise and improve early childhood programs to address the diverse needs of children and their families. In particular, faculty members from different disciplines have collaborated and communicated to create and sustain successful blended programs that incorporate knowledge and skills from early childhood special education, early childhood education (Division for Early Childhood/National Association for the Education of Young Children, 2009), and bilingual education. More often than not, it is the vision and commitment of faculty that creates the path toward such a program. Providing preservice teachers with practical experiences through the embedding of theories and concepts into field-based learning activities is critical. Additionally, creating positive experiences with children in field experiences or coursework for preservice teachers results in more positive attitudes later in classroom settings. For example, research shows that practicing teachers' attitudes toward inclusion appear to be influenced by their previous positive experiences in inclusive classrooms (e.g., interacted with a child with a disability, engaged in a hands-on activity in coursework) (Hsieh & Hsieh, 2012; Leatherman

& Niemeyer, 2005). The efforts of higher education faculty in blended program revisions aim to prepare preservice teachers to fulfill multiple roles in a variety of contexts in today's early childhood inclusive practices (Stayton, 2003). Change, however, does not come easily and is a highly complex process that involves persistence, attention to various dimensions of contexts, and knowledge of teacher education and early childhood educational research, as well as embedded understandings of how the dimensions of learning and teaching are affected by the need to effectively serve young children who do not yet speak fluent English (Bay et al., 2017).

Preparation of early childhood educators requires constant attention to the variety of contexts that affect teacher education programs. National-level priorities and funding opportunities can influence a program's course. Research findings must be regularly incorporated into a program's curriculum and field experiences. States periodically develop new sets of standards and mandate program alignment. For example, in 2013, the Education Commission of States identified 38 bills from 25 states specifically targeting early education policies (Workman, 2013). Among these, two states specifically introduced legislation that would increase the requirements for P-3 teachers. Accreditation agencies issue new requirements in an effort to ensure high-quality preparation and consistency across programs. Campus-level changes in administration often result in a new vision for the unit, and fluctuating local school district needs also affect the ways in which teachers are prepared. Most critically, the need to respond to the changing demographics of the children who the graduating teachers will serve needs to be at the center of all program design efforts.

Program Reform with the Monarch Center

In 2011, a group of faculty teams from various universities jointly engaged in a year-long project with the Monarch Center (at the University of Illinois at Chicago) with the common goal of collaborating across programs to improve their programs and/or to create blended programs involving early childhood and special education. The participants were faculty members who were involved in the complexity of transforming teacher education and early childhood scholarship, federal and state mandates, and certification standards and procedures, into programs of study that effectively respond to the needs of young children with disabilities and their families. The approaches and actions that the teams chose toward the goal of creating blended programs were based on the DEC-recommended practices (2014) for personnel preparation and took a variety of forms in response to unique departmental structures, state standards, availability of personnel and student resources, and levels of shared leadership. The center's particular emphasis was to support faculty members' efforts toward creating programs that graduated teachers who are prepared to engage in culturally responsive practice with students with disabilities.

Through an application process, 23 faculty teams (71 faculty members) were identified and, among these, 9 teams (26 faculty members from early childhood and special education) were focused on improving their programs to ensure that their graduates were well prepared to teach all young children, including those with cultural, linguistic, and ability differences. Their shared goal was to blend their early childhood education and early childhood special education programs or to infuse special education content into their general early childhood programs.

The teams met for a 2.5-day professional development (PD) work session that was structured around DEC's principles encompassed within five themes: (1) family as partners; (2) the use of a cross-disciplinary approach; (3) a focus on early childhood and early childhood special education; (4) collaboration; and (5) support for family-centered practices. DEC further elaborated on these themes through a set of recommended practices for personnel preparation (Stayton et al., 2003). Specifically included in the professional development were topics of culturally and linguistically responsive pedagogy, assessment of young children, collaboration with families, and the design of field experiences. The teams were provided with a wide variety of resources that could be used in university courses (e.g., video cases, dilemmas of practice, textbooks, and articles). Throughout the professional development, time was allocated for each team to develop a plan of action with specific objectives for implementation on their home campuses.

During the following year, the Monarch Center provided material and resource supports as well as mentor support from the professional development facilitators, periodic group conference calls to report on progress and, in some cases, more individualized support such as coaching regarding the development of an NCATE (National Council for Accreditation of Teacher Education, 2010) conceptual framework and teacher candidate assessment system. The teams remained connected via group phone conferencing and email, whereby they checked in on one another, provided feedback and insights to one another, and openly shared ideas. At the end of the 12 months of work, the teams reconvened for a 2-day session to report the extent to which they attained their action plan objectives.

Through thematic analysis of collected action plans, conference call notes, and final oral and written reports, commonly recurring ideas were identified and coded for analysis (Gibbs, 2007; Miles et al., 2019). The process of drawing meaning from the coded data was simultaneously guided by the DEC-recommended practices for personnel preparation (Sandall et al., 2005) and the principles of grounded theory approaches to data analysis (Lichtman, 2011). The analysis revealed some patterns in the content and approaches taken by the teams: the content was largely aligned with the content of the professional development work session, while the approaches emerged from the impetus to complete the goals stated in their plans of action within a timeframe and the unspoken commitment of the participants to other teams in their professional development work session.

With one exception, all the teams were successful in making significant improvements to their programs within the one-year timeframe. The themes noted through the analysis are presented in the following in the form of experience-based lessons. They are topics and approaches that were determined to be essential to successful reform and change in the programs.

Initial stages

Though not explicitly stated in the form of an objective toward program improvement by any of the teams, the content of progress and final reports was clear on the need to garner the support of faculty colleagues, gain departmental approval to proceed, and come to consensus with regard to needed changes in the current personnel preparation programs prior to engaging in any type of new program creation, course revisions, or the blending of existing programs. It was clear that all faculty team members, with the exception of two teams that had their entire program faculty at the professional development seminar (2-3 members each), were a part of a larger community with whom they coordinated efforts toward the preparation of early childhood educators. The teams were acutely aware of potential resistance (and, therefore, the need to garner support), especially given the overall shared sense of a climate of varied beliefs, scarce resources, budget cutbacks, and its subsequent effect on faculty who were all being asked to absorb additional responsibilities with no additional compensation. Several teams commented on unfilled vacancies, additional teaching loads, interim administrative responsibilities, and lowered enrollments due to scholarship funding cutbacks.

With the exception of one team, they all aimed to create or enhance blended early childhood/early childhood special education programs, resulting in dual certification. Having had the opportunity to meet to reach agreement about a vision for a program, the team members were focused on enacting the vision of a program that prepared candidates for racially, linguistically, and economically diverse children with attention to children with disabilities. They understood that beyond agreement on a vision, they needed to develop a sense of ownership of the work among members of the faculty. Faculty in both early childhood and special education departments had to jointly plan and merge program philosophies, form work groups across programs, convene focus groups among current students to ascertain their ideas and interests, seek approval from program chairs and deans; or, in the case of a non-existent base for a blended program, review federal and state standards and policies for creating a blended early childhood personnel preparation program. Coming to agreement about a vision for the program through studying and considering new relevant knowledge, building professional learning communities, and fostering a sense of ownership through distributed responsibility and leadership were critical steps in the initial "setting the stage" phase. According to Fullan (2005), learning from each other widens the pool of ideas, fosters "coherence making," and enhances a greater "we-we" identity. These types of activities were considered initial steps that would foster "buy in" and agreement about a vision for the program.

Reviewing and revising course syllabi and identifying inclusive practicum sites

All 9 teams had the preparation of their candidates to serve children from culturally and linguistically diverse backgrounds as a key goal in their program improvement plan. Most began the process by using the *Crosswalks Coursework, Practica, and Program Evaluation* (Crosswalks National Institute, 2005) and/or the DEC personnel preparation self-awareness checklist (Sandall *et al.*, 2005). Noting that teachers need to be prepared to serve children from an array of culturally and linguistically diverse backgrounds, team members reviewed various sources of video clips, vignettes, and demonstrations that could be used in their university classes. In addition to what was presented at the professional development, teams shared and discussed the use of various textbooks and articles that others had used. Embedded in this theme was the attention to family, with only one team involving families as instructional partners, while the others planned to create a family-focused curriculum and infuse more assignments and projects into the coursework to prepare teacher candidates with the knowledge and understandings needed to work with families. A few of the teams did not specifically address the need to increase preparation to serve culturally and linguistically diverse children and families; however, virtually all of their population of school children was from culturally and linguistically diverse families, and the programs' curricula were already saturated with these types of assignments and readings. This was clearly evident in the examples and descriptions shared during follow-on "check-ins" and in final reports.

Repeated use of such phrases as "culturally responsive practices," "cultural competence," "multicultural interventions," and "value families and cultures" were evident throughout the documents, reports, and presentations. The principal way through which these objectives were accomplished was through changes in course content and field assignment revisions.

The process began by reviewing the content of DEC's recommendations for personnel preparation standards and envisioning a program that would meet these guidelines in the context of their respective state standards, university structures, and existing programs, as well as the potential fit with the numbers of faculty and students at the undergraduate and graduate levels. A common theme among all 9 teams' action plans was to engage in a careful examination of the content of their coursework in both early childhood and special education for a variety of purposes, including the development of all new courses by one team for their newly developed blended program. The most widely cited purposes were to review the extent to which the course content was aligned with state and national competencies, to examine the effectiveness of assignments and projects toward knowledge and skills attainment for teaching in inclusive settings, and to ensure that teacher candidates would have ample opportunities to learn about the implications for teaching culturally and linguistically diverse populations. As they engaged in these activities, faculty used the opportunity to encourage their colleagues to infuse their course content with readings and assignments that would support teacher candidates in their preparation. Several teams then reviewed course syllabi for overlap and redundancy, to create courses and field experiences that would address a "cross-section" of early childhood and special education and incorporate the needs of diverse pupil populations. Follow-on phone conferences regularly included conversations about texts, assignments, and resources that had been successfully implemented by other teams. Team members often directed one another to online resources as well as new texts, and they referred to two program cases that had been provided at the professional development work session, as both were examples of programs that met all professional standards and included creative projects and practicum experiences. From a more mechanical perspective, some of the teams created matrices of knowledge and skills competencies and cross-checked all their existing course syllabi to identify gaps and overlapping content. Others began with a set of courses in early childhood and infused the content of other courses as a means of creating coherent programs that could be completed in a timely manner and would guide teacher candidates in understanding the interplay of academic, social, and cognitive needs of children and their families. When improvements of existing courses were not sufficient, new syllabi were created for new courses.

Most of the teams cited the need to locate exemplary inclusive practicum sites where teacher candidates could experience the education of an integrated group of young children with and without disabilities. All teams agreed that this was critical to a successful program. One team specifically planned and developed a rubric with detailed examples of levels of competency that could be used to assess candidate success in the field. Attention was given to the importance of students being able to experience and learn in inclusive settings in order to fully connect the program curriculum with the social and academic needs of young children in the schools.

Several of the teams noted that practicum and student teaching experiences were managed by external offices of field placement and that this added another layer of complexity for blended programs, as the majority of current early childhood settings were not inclusive of children with disabilities. This made the task of designing and coordinating fieldwork that supported the program curriculum more challenging. One team outlined plans to use and extend their community contacts to assess interest and enlist new practicum settings. (See Goeke et al., 2018, for a collection of cases pertaining to special education preparation program reform.)

Securing campus and state approval and external funding

It is worth noting that, in all cases, the level of program redesign, course modification, and in several cases, crafting of altogether new courses, required departmental, college, and campus-level approval for the respective degree program changes. Additionally, as the programs involved the granting of teaching certificates, the teams recognized that they would also require approval from their respective teacher licensure units, which needed to be obtained, both on campus and from their state office. These approvals added another layer of planned objectives for all teams. The sheer volume of work involved in securing approvals from multiple units at various levels was evident as teams described their initiatives. Regardless of the type of institution, the state in which the institution resided, the size of institution, or the level of program (e.g., BA, MEd), teams spent considerable time and energy addressing the myriad requirements mandated by agencies, such as program governing committees, departments, colleges, teacher education units, campus-level divisions of academic affairs, and state-level boards of education.

Finally, all teams also planned to write grant proposals to seek funding to support the program changes and/or to use for scholarships to attract more students to the new programs. Clearly, the need for external funding – to cover the costs for paying for adjunct instructors and field instructors to teach the new or additional courses, purchasing needed materials and resources, recruiting new students, and for other expenses of a new or revised program – was critical to a timely and high-quality program.

Consistent with the research on educational change and educational reform efforts, the experiences of the early childhood teams in the above initiatives indicate that there are multiple paths to teacher education program change but, regardless of the path taken, there is a need for faculty to pay careful attention to the beginning phase of the change initiative, a phase that is complex and demanding (e.g., Bryk *et al.*, 2010; Hargreaves & Fullan, 2009). In addition to vision building, some teams emphasized activities that allowed colleagues to develop a sense of ownership of the work. The field experience components of preparation programs (see Darling-Hammond, 2006b) are critical. Finding and partnering with exemplary schools/classrooms where teacher candidates can see quality culturally responsive pedagogy demonstrated in settings where all young children, including those with disabilities, are educated is key. Whereas finding such settings proved to be quite challenging for all teams, some decided to foster stronger partnerships with school districts to create such high-quality field sites. Establishing such partnerships with schools and creating exemplary field sites where teacher candidates can practice their professional skills under the tutelage of a mentor reveals yet another layer of program improvement effort in which many higher education faculty engage. Indeed, the work of transforming college textbook and journal articles into authentic, direct experiences in the actual contexts, with all their unique ethos, political backdrop, power structures, diverse student populations, and so forth, involves a type of scholarship that is rigorous, necessary and, ironically, undervalued (Bay *et al.*, under review). Furthermore, to approach program improvement initiatives in a sequential, step-by-step manner would have been counterproductive, given the fluidity of ideas across those faculty involved as well as the interplay of requirements across divisions and agencies. It was necessary simultaneously to work in the present, keep an eye on the political backdrop both locally and statewide, and be cognizant of movement toward intended as well as required outcomes (Bay *et al.*, 2017).

These findings reveal the multi-layered, complex, labor intensive process which higher education faculty undertake when they aim to improve the quality of their personnel preparation programs or create a new program. (For a discussion of the challenges involved in program reform, see Goeke *et al.*, 2018.)

Looking across the various themes that surfaced in this set of experiences, the nature of the work requires a range of understandings and abilities, from knowing the research on effective teaching and learning practices, to understanding the necessary components of a preparation program, to being able to work with colleagues to create a cohesive program that meets a long list of agency requirements, to shepherding the proposed program through the various approval processes, and finally, to securing the resources to undertake and complete this endeavor. While these teams indicated that program work is simultaneously daunting, extremely time consuming, and too often not rewarded in terms of tenure and promotion, they found it to be a rewarding aspect of their professional lives as they continue to prepare exemplary teachers for our nation's schools.

Questions to Contemplate and Issues to Consider

In this chapter, we recommend three areas of content that we assert it is vital to include in programs designed to prepare individuals to teach young bilingual children with disabilities. These areas are: the importance of involving families, the use of a culturally and linguistically responsive pedagogy, and the use of formative assessment systems that inform teaching. Additionally, we have described the work associated with the reform of programs to better prepare individuals for teaching today's young children. As part of the discussion about reform efforts, we suggest that the local, state, and national contexts create a situation that makes the design of such high-quality programs challenging. However, as our work at the Monarch Center demonstrated, programs can be created, and the work can be done (Lopez-Reyna et al., 2011).

The topic of this chapter raises important questions for the field of early childhood teacher preparation, many of which are presented in other chapters in this volume. Baumgartner et al. (2015) recently completed an extensive review of the literature on culturally responsive teaching, noting that research on the role of teacher educators in preparing culturally responsive teachers is nearly non-existent. They outline eight sets of recommended teaching practices for teacher educators that serve to model and demonstrate when they are teaching preservice teachers. They note that: "demonstrating culturally responsive practice in the university classroom is critical to encouraging teacher candidates to teach in a similar way" (Baumgartner et al., 2015: 45). This echoes the words of Freire (1998), who stated: "An educational practice in which there is no coherent relationship between what educators say and what they do is a disaster" (Freire, 1998: 55; cited in Baumgartner et al., 2015). For teacher educators who are charged with preparing early childhood teachers to serve bilingual learners with disabilities, this is certainly the greatest challenge.

It is unsettling to know, however, that programs in states with less concentration of Latino or English language learners are less likely to include specific coursework and practicum focused on language diversity (Lim et al., 2009). It also appears that the presence of non-white faculty makes it more likely that coursework on cultural diversity will be required. Lim et al. (2009) suggest that it may be that non-white faculty are more comfortable tackling diversity issues or that they are more likely to perceive the need for such content. Regardless, in addition to recruiting more diverse faculty, it is important to advocate for program reform that will include coursework, assignments, and practicum throughout the program so that cultural, linguistic, and ability diversity are understood and supported in school and the community.

References

Akers, L., Del Grosso, P., Snell, E.K., Atkins-Burnett, S., Wasik, B., Carta, J. and Monahan, S. (2016) Tailored teaching: Emerging themes from the literature on teachers' use of ongoing child assessment to individualize instruction. *NHSA Dialog* 18, 133–150.

American Association of Colleges for Teacher Education (AACTE) (2010) *The Clinical Preparation of Teachers: A Policy Brief*. Washington, DC: AACTE.

Amrein, A.L. and Berliner, D.C. (2003) The effects of high-stakes testing on student motivation and learning. *Educational Leadership* 60 (5), 32–38.

Artiles, A.J. and McClafferty, K. (1998) Learning to teach culturally diverse learners: Charting change in preservice teachers' thinking about effective teaching. *Elementary School Journal* 98 (3), 189–220.

Aud, S., Fox, M.A. and KewalRamani, A. (2010) *Status and Trends in the Education of Racial and Ethnic Groups. NCES 2010–2015*. Washington, DC: National Center for Education Statistics. Retrieved from http://files.eric.ed.gov/fulltext/ED510909.pdf.

Baca, L.M. and Cervantes, H.T. (eds) (1989) *The Bilingual Special Education Interface* (2nd edition). Columbus, OH: Merrill.

Banks, J.A. (2001) *Cultural Diversity and Education: Foundations, Curriculum, and Teaching*. Boston, MA: Allyn & Bacon.

Baumgartner, D., Bay, M., Lopez-Reyna, N.A., Snowden, P.A. and Maiorano, M.J. (2015) Culturally responsive practice for teacher educators: Eight recommendations. *Multiple Voices for Ethnically Diverse Exceptional Learners* 15 (1), 44–58.

Bay, M., Lopez-Reyna, N.A. and Ward, R. (2017) Special education teacher preparation reform in context: Lessons from a decade of program support. In E. Petchauer and L. Mawhinney (eds) *Teacher Education Across Minority Serving Institutions: Programs, Policies and Social Justice* (pp. 109–127). New Brunswick, NJ: Rutgers University Press.

Bay, M., Ward, R. and Lopez-Reyna, N.A. (under review) Learning about special education teacher preparation: Program reform from faculty at minority-serving institutions. *Teacher Education and Special Education*.

Bernheimer, L.P. and Koegh, B.K. (1995) Weaving interventions into the fabric of everyday life: An approach to family assessment. *Topics in Early Childhood Special Education* 15 (4), 415–433.

Bireda, S. and Chait, R. (2011) *Increasing Teacher Diversity: Strategies to Improve the Teacher Workforce*. Center for American Progress, Progress 2050: New Ideas for a Diverse America. Retrieved from https://www.americanprogress.org/issues/education/reports/2011/11/09/10636/increasing-teacher-diversity/.

Boat, M.B., Dinnebeil, L.A. and Bae, Y. (2010) Individualizing instruction in preschool classrooms. *Dimensions of Early Childhood* 38 (1), 3–11.

Bourke, R., Mentis, M. and Todd, L. (2011) Visibly learning: Teachers' assessment practices for students with high and very high needs. *International Journal of Inclusive Education* 15 (4), 405–419.

Bryk, A.S., Sebring, P.B., Allensworth, E., Luppescu, S. and Easton, J.Q. (2010) *Organizing Schools for Improvement: Lessons from Chicago*. Chicago, IL: University of Chicago Press.

Camilli, G., Vargas, S., Ryan, S. and Barnett, W.S. (2010) Meta-analysis of the effects of early education interventions on cognitive and social development. *Teachers College Record*, 112 (3), 579–620.

Carr, M. (2001) *Assessment in Early Childhood Settings: Learning Stories*. Thousand Oaks, CA: Sage Publishing.

Chandler, L.K., Cochran, D.C., Christensen, K.A., Dinnebeil, L.A., Gallagher, P.A., Lifter, K. and Spino, M. (2012) The alignment of CEC/DEC and NAEYC personnel preparation standards. *Topics in Early Childhood Special Education* 32 (1), 52–63.

Chappuis, J., Stiggins, R., Chappuis, S. and Arter, J. (2011) *Classroom Assessment for Student Learning: Doing It Right – Using It Well* (2nd edition). Boston, MA: Pearson.

Children's Defense Fund (2017) *The State of America's Children*, 2017, Retrieved from https://www.childrensdefense.org/reports/2017/the-state-of-americas-children-2017-report/.
Cochran-Smith, M. and Lytle, S.L. (1999) Relationships of knowledge and practice: Teacher learning in communities. *Review of Research in Education* 24, 249–305.
Collado, C.L. (2015) A Case Study of Formative Assessment Processes in Preschool Education Settings. Unpublished doctoral dissertation, University of Illinois at Chicago.
Crosswalks National Institute (2005) *Crosswalks Coursework, Practica, and Program Evaluation*. Retrieved from http://www.fpg.unc.edu/~scpp/crosswalks/pdfs/CCPPE-FINAL.pdf.
Darling-Hammond, L. (2006a) Constructing 21st century teacher education. *Journal of Teacher Education* 57 (3), 300–314.
Darling-Hammond, L. (2006b) *Powerful Teacher Education: Lessons from Exemplary Programs*. San Francisco, CA: Jossey-Bass.
Darling-Hammond, L. (2010) *The Flat World and Education: How America's Commitment to Equity Will Determine Our Future*. New York, NY: Teachers College Press.
Darling-Hammond, L. and Bransford, J. (eds) (2005) *Preparing Teachers for a Changing World: What Teachers Should Learn and Be Able to Do*. San Francisco, CA: Jossey-Bass.
Darling-Hammond, L., Hammerness, K., Grossman, P., Rust, F. and Shulman, L. (2005) The design of teacher education programs. In L. Darling-Hammond and J. Bransford (eds) *Preparing Teachers for a Changing World: What Teachers Should Learn and Be Able to Do* (pp. 390–441). San Francisco, CA: Jossey-Bass.
Dichtelmiller, M.L. (2011) *The Power of Assessment: Transforming Teaching and Learning*. Washington, DC: Teaching Strategies.
Division for Early Childhood (DEC) (1993) *Personnel Standards for Early Education and Early Intervention*. Retrieved from http://www.dec-sped.org/uploads/docs/about_dec/position_concept_papers/PositionStatement_PersStan.pdf.
Division for Early Childhood (2014) *DEC Recommended Practices in Early Intervention/Early Childhood Special Education 2014*. Retrieved from http://www.dec-sped.org/recommendedpractices.
Division for Early Childhood/National Association for the Education of Young Children (DEC /NAEYC) (2009) *Early Childhood Inclusion: A Joint Position Statement of the Division for Early Childhood (DEC) and the National Association for the Education of Young Children (NAEYC)*. Chapel Hill: University of North Carolina, FPG Child Development Institute.
Dodge, D.T., Heroman, C., Charles, J. and Maiorca, J. (2004) Beyond outcomes: How ongoing assessment supports children's learning and leads to meaningful curriculum. *Young Children* 59 (1), 20–28.
Elicker, J. and McMullen, M.B. (2013) Appropriate and meaningful assessment in family-centered programs. *Young Children* 68 (3), 22–27.
Evans, M.P. (2013) Educating preservice teachers for family, school, and community engagement. *Teaching Education* 24 (2), 123–133.
Ford, D.Y. (2012) Culturally different students in special education: Looking backward to move forward. *Exceptional Children* 78 (4), 391–405.
Freire, P. (1998) *Teachers as Cultural Workers: Letters to Those Who Dare to Teach*. Boulder, CO: Westview Press.
Fullan, M. (2005) *Leadership and Sustainability: Systems Thinkers in Action*. Thousand Oaks, CA: Corwin Press.
Gay, G. (2000) *Culturally Responsive Teaching: Theory, Research, and Practice*. New York, NY: Teachers College Press.
Gay, G. (2010) *Culturally Responsive Teaching: Theory, Research, and Practice* (2nd edn). New York, NY: Teachers College Press.
Gibbs, G.R. (2007) *Analyzing Qualitative Data*. Los Angeles, CA: Sage.

Goeke, J.L., Mitchem, K.J. and Kossar, K.R. (2018) *Redesigning Special Education Teacher Preparation: Challenges and Solutions*. New York, NY: Routledge.

Grigorenko, E.L. and Sternberg, R.J. (1998) Dynamic testing. *Psychological Bulletin* 124 (1), 75–111.

Grisham-Brown, J. and Pretti-Frontczak, K. (2011) *Assessing Young Children in Inclusive Settings: The Blended Practices Approach*. Baltimore, MD: Brookes Publishing.

Grisham-Brown, J. and Hemmeter, M.L. (2017) *Blended Practices in Teaching Young Children in Inclusive Settings* (2nd edition). Baltimore, MD: Brookes Publishing.

Han, H.S. and Thomas, M.S. (2010) No child misunderstood: Enhancing early childhood teachers' multicultural responsiveness to the social competence of diverse children. *Early Childhood Education Journal* 37 (6), 469–476.

Hansuvadha, N. (2009) Compromise in collaborating with families: Perspectives of beginning special education teachers. *Journal of Early Childhood Teacher Education* 30, 346–362.

Hargreaves, A. and Fullan, M. (2009) *The Change Wars*. Bloomington, IN: Solution Tree.

Harry, B. (2008) Collaboration with culturally and linguistically diverse families: Ideal versus reality. *Exceptional Children* 74 (3), 372–388.

Harry, B. and Klingner, J. (2006) *Why Are There So Many Minority Students in Special Education? Understanding Race and Disability in Schools*. New York, NY: Teachers College Press.

Helm, J.H., Beneke, S. and Steinheimer, K. (1997) Documenting children's learning. *Childhood Education* 73 (4), 200–205.

Hollins, E.R. (2011) Teacher preparation for quality teaching. *Journal of Teacher Education* 62 (4), 395–407.

Hoover, J., Klingner, J.K., Baca, L. and Patton, J. (2007) *Methods for Teaching Culturally and Linguistically Diverse Exceptional Learners*. Upper Saddle River, NJ: Merrill/Prentice Hall.

Howard, T.C. and Banks, J.A. (2020) *Why Race and Culture Matter in Schools: Closing the Achievement Gap in America's Classrooms* (Multicultural Education Series). New York, NY: Teachers College Press.

Howrey, S.T. and Whelan-Kim, K. (2009) Building cultural responsiveness in rural, preservice teachers using a multicultural children's literature project. *Journal of Early Childhood Teacher Education* 30 (2), 123–137.

Hsieh, W.Y. and Hsieh, C.M. (2012) Urban early childhood teachers' attitudes towards inclusive education. *Early Child Development and Care* 182 (9), 1167–1184.

IDEA. (2004) Individuals with Disabilities Education Act, 20 U.S.C. § 1400 (2004).

Jablon, J.R., Dombro, A.L. and Dichtelmiller, M.L. (2007) *The Power of Observation: Birth to Age 8* (2nd edition). Washington, DC: Teaching Strategies.

Kea, C., Campbell-Whatley, G.D. and Richards, H.V. (2006) *Becoming Culturally Responsive Educators: Rethinking Teacher Education Pedagogy*. Practitioner Brief, Washington, DC: National Center for Culturally Responsive Education Systems (NCCRESt).

Kidd, J.K., Sánchez, S.Y. and Thorp, E.K. (2008) Defining moments: Developing culturally responsive dispositions and teaching practices in early childhood preservice teachers. *Teaching and Teacher Education* 24 (2), 316–329.

Klingner, J.K. and Bianco, M. (2006) What is special about special education for culturally and linguistically diverse students with disabilities? In B. Cook and B. Schirmer (eds) *What Is Special about Special Education?* (pp. 37–53). Austin, TX: PRO-ED.

Ladson-Billings, G. (1995) Toward a theory of culturally relevant pedagogy. *American Educational Research Journal* 32 (3), 465–491.

Leatherman, J.M. and Niemeyer, J.A. (2005) Teachers' attitudes toward inclusion: Factors influencing classroom practice. *Journal of Early Childhood Teacher Education* 26 (1), 23–36.

Lerma, L.J. and Stewart, M.L. (2012) Addressing disproportionality in the identification of English Language Learners (ELLs) for special education programs: What

pre-service teachers need to know. *Florida Association of Teacher Educators Journal* 1 (12), 6–24.
Levine, A. (2006) *Educating School Teachers*. Washington, DC: The Education Schools Project.
Lichtman, M. (2011) *Understanding and Evaluating Qualitative Educational Research*. Los Angeles, CA: Sage.
Lidz, C.S. and Peña, E.D. (1996) Dynamic assessment: The model, its relevance as a nonbiased approach, and its application to Latino American preschool children. *Language, Speech, and Hearing Services in Schools* 27 (4), 367–372.
Lim, C-I., Maxwell, K.L., Able-Boone, H. and Zimmer, C.R. (2009) Cultural and linguistic diversity in early childhood teacher preparation: The impact of contextual characteristics on coursework and practical. *Early Childhood Research Quarterly* 24, 64–76.
López-Reyna, N.A., Bay, M., Zazycki, D. and Snowden, P.A. (2011) Advancing culturally responsive personnel preparation in special education: Barriers and supports for change. In E.D. McCray, P. Alvarez McHatton, and C.L. Beverly (eds) *Knowledge, Skills, and Dispositions for Culturally Competent and Interculturally Sensitive Leaders in Education* (pp. 104–121). Gainesville, FL: CreateSpace Independent Publishing Platform.
Lowenstein, K.L. (2009) The work of multicultural teacher education: Reconceptualizing white teacher candidates as learners. *Review of Educational Research* 97 (1), 163–196.
Lucas, T., Villegas, A. and Gonzalez, M. (2008) Linguistically responsive teacher education: Preparing classroom teachers to teach English language learners. *Journal of Teacher Education* 59 (4), 361–373.
McFarland, L. (2008) Anecdotal records: Valuable tools for assessing young children's development. *Dimensions of Early Childhood* 36 (1), 31–36.
McHatton, P.A., Thomas, D. and Lehman, K. (2006) Lessons learned from service-learning: Preparing professionals through community involvement. *Mentoring and Tutoring: Partnership in Learning* 14 (1), 67–79.
Miles, M.B., Huberman, A.M. and Saldaña, D. (2019) *Qualitative Data Analysis: A Sourcebook of New Methods* (4th edition). London: Sage.
Miller, K J. and Fuller, D.P. (2006) Developing cultural competency in early childhood preservice educators through a cultural self-analysis project. *Journal of Early Childhood Teacher Education* 27 (1), 35–45.
Moll, L.C., Amanti, C., Neff, D. and Gonzalez, N. (1992) Funds of knowledge for teaching: Using a qualitative approach to connect homes and classrooms. *Theory into Practice* 31 (2), 132–141.
Morocco, C.C. (2001) Teaching for understanding with students with disabilities: New directions for research on access to the general education curriculum. *Learning Disability Quarterly* 24 (1), 5–13.
Moss, C.M. and Brookhart, S.M. (2019) *Advancing Formative Assessment in Every Classroom: A Guide for Instructional Leaders*. Alexandria, VA: ASCD.
National Association for the Education of Young Children (NAEYC) (2009) *Developmentally Appropriate Practice in Early Childhood Programs Serving Children from Birth through Age 8: A Position Statement of the National Association for the Education of Young Children*. Washington, DC: NAEYC.
National Council for Accreditation of Teacher Education (NCATE) (2010) *Transforming Teacher Education through Clinical Practice: A National Strategy to Prepare Effective Teachers*. Report of the Blue Ribbon Panel on Clinical Preparation and Partnerships for Improved Student Learning. Washington, DC: NCATE. Retrieved from http://caepnet.org/~/media/Files/caep/accreditation-resources/blue-ribbon-panel.pdf.
Nieto, S. and Bode, P. (2011) *Affirming Diversity: The Sociopolitical Context of Multicultural Education* (6th edition). Boston, MA: Allyn & Bacon.
Ntuli, E., Nyarambi, A. and Traore, M. (2014) Assessment in early childhood education: Threats and challenges to effective assessment of immigrant children. *Journal of Research in Special Educational Needs* 14 (4), 221–228.

Pak, J. (2016) Learning stories. *Teaching Young Children* 9 (2), 1–4.
Peisner-Feinberg, E.S., Burchinal, M.R., Clifford, R.M., Culkin, M.L., Howes, C., Kagan, S.L. and Yazejian, N. (2001) The relation of preschool child-care quality to children's cognitive and social developmental trajectories through second grade. *Child Development* 72 (5), 1534–1553.
Pretti-Frontczak, K., Giallourakis, A., Janas, D. and Hayes, A. (2002) Using a family-centered preservice curriculum to prepare early intervention and early childhood special education personnel. *Teacher Education and Special Education* 25 (3), 291–297.
Rhodes, L.K. and Nathenson-Mejia, S. (1992) Anecdotal records: A powerful tool for ongoing literacy assessment. *The Reading Teacher* 45 (7), 502–509.
Saeki, E., Segool, N., Pendergast, L. and von der Embse, N. (2018) The influence of test based accountability policies on early elementary teachers: School climate, environmental stress, and teacher stress. *Psychology in the Schools* 55 (4), 391–403.
Sahlberg, P. (2007) Education policies for raising student learning: The Finnish approach. *Journal of Education Policy* 22 (2), 147–171.
Salvia, J., Ysseldyke, J. and Witmer, S. (2017) *Assessment in Special and Inclusive Education* (13th edition). Belmont, CA: Cengage Learning.
Samson, J.F. and Collins, B.A. (2012) *Preparing All Teachers to Meet the Needs of English Language Learners: Applying Research to Policy and Practice for Teacher Effectiveness*. Washington, DC: Center for American Progress.
Sánchez, S.Y. (1999) Learning from the stories of culturally and linguistically diverse families and communities: A sociohistorical lens. *Remedial and Special Education* 20 (6), 351–359.
Sandall, S., Hemmeter, M.L., Smith, B.J. and McLean, M.E. (eds) (2005) *DEC Recommended Practices: A Comprehensive Guide for Practical Application in Early Intervention/Early Childhood Special Education*. Missoula, MT: Division for Early Childhood of the Council for Exceptional Children.
Schmidt, P.R. (1998) The ABC's of cultural understanding and communication. *Equity & Excellence in Education* 31 (2), 28–38.
Seidl, B. and Pugach, M. (2009) Support and teaching in the vulnerable moments: Preparing special educators for diversity. *Multiple Voices for Ethnically Diverse Exceptional Learners* 11 (2), 57–75.
Shepard, L.A. (2005) Linking formative assessment to scaffolding. *Educational Leadership* 63 (3), 66–70.
Shulman, L.S. (1987) Knowledge and teaching: Foundations of the new reform. *Harvard Educational Review* 57 (1), 1–23.
Stayton, V.D. (2003) Introduction to DEC personnel preparation recommended practices. In V.D. Stayton, P.S. Miller and L.A. Dinnebeil (eds) *DEC Personnel Preparation in Early Childhood Special Education: Implementing the DEC Recommended Practices* (pp. 1–10). Missoula, MT: Division for Early Childhood of the Council for Exceptional Children.
Stayton, V.D., Miller, P.S. and Dinnebeil, L.A. (2003) *DEC Personnel Preparation in Early Childhood Special Education: Implementing the DEC Recommended Practices*. Missoula, MT: Division for Early Childhood of the Council for Exceptional Children.
Tabors, P.O. (2008) *One Child, Two Languages: A Guide for Early Educators of Children Learning English as a Second Language* (2nd edn). Baltimore, MD: Brookes Publishing.
Talbert-Johnson, C. (2006) Preparing highly qualified teacher candidates for urban schools: The importance of dispositions. *Education and Urban Society* 39 (1), 147–160.
Turner, J.D. (2007) Beyond cultural awareness: Prospective teachers' visions of culturally responsive literacy teaching. *Action in Teacher Education* 29 (3), 12–24.
US Department of Education (2018) *The 40th Annual Report to Congress on the Implementation of the Individuals with Disabilities Education Act*. Retrieved from https://www2.ed.gov/about/reports/annual/osep/2018/parts-b-c/40th-arc-for-idea.pdf.

Villegas, A.M. and Lucas, T. (2002) *Educating Culturally Responsive Teachers: A Coherent Approach.* Albany, NY: State University of New York Press.

Villegas, A.M. and Lucas, T. (2007) The culturally responsive teacher. *Educational Leadership* 64 (6), 28–33.

Wager, A.A., Graue, M.E. and Harrigan, K. (2015) Swimming upstream in a torrent of assessment. In B. Perry, A. MacDonald and A. Gervasoni (eds) *Mathematics and Transition to School: International Perspectives* (pp. 15–30). Dordrecht: Springer.

Wells, J.C. and Sheehey, P.H. (2012) Person-centered planning: Strategies to encourage participation and facilitate communication. *Teaching Exceptional Children* 44 (3), 32–39.

Workman, E. (2013) *2013 Legislative Session – P-3 policies.* Denver, CO: Education Commission of the States. Retrieved from https://www.ecs.org/clearinghouse/01/10/04/11004.pdf.

Zehler, A.M. Fleischman, H.L., Hopstock, P.J., Pendzick, M.L., and Stephenson, T.G. (2003) *The Descriptive Study of Services to LEP Students and LEP Students with Disabilities.* US Department of Education, Office of English Language Acquisition, Language Enhancement, and Academic Achievement of LEP Students. Arlington, VA: Development Associates, Inc.

Zeichner, K. (2010) Rethinking the connections between campus courses and field experiences in college- and university-based teacher education. *Journal of Teacher Education* 61 (1-2), 89–99.

Zepeda, M., Castro, D.C. and Cronin, S. (2011) Preparing early childhood teachers to work with young dual language learners. *Child Development Perspectives* 5 (1), 10–14.

9 Language, Learning, and Disability in an Era of Accountability

Marlene Zepeda and Michael J. Orosco

Accountability in the field of education is not a new phenomenon. Its emergence can be traced to the passage of the 1965 Elementary and Secondary Education Act (ESEA), which emphasized equal educational opportunity and established educational standards with a general accountability mandate (Thomas & Brady, 2005). A central intent of this federal legislation was to provide additional resources to at-risk children, particularly low-income children who were viewed as in need of extra support. Since that time, accountability pressures as a means of school improvement have intensified and moved beyond the elementary and secondary school realm to other educational sectors such as college students and young children ages zero to 5 participating in early education programs. For children enrolled in educational programs from birth to age 5, the Quality Rating Improvement System's (QRIS) focus on accountability grew as a result of participation in President Obama's Race-to-the-Top Early Learning Challenge funding initiative requiring early learning standards, assessments tied to learning standards, and kindergarten entrance assessments as barometers of school readiness. Proponents of accountability posit that holding education entities responsible and sanctionable for child achievement will result in improved educational quality that benefits all children, including underserved populations such as ethnic and racial minority children, children whose first language is not English, and children with disabilities. However, both proponents and critics noted problems with the conceptualization and approach of federal accountability in lifting academic achievement for all children as legislated in the redesigned ESEA of 2001, more commonly known as the No Child Left Behind Act (NCLB) (Darling-Hammond, 2007; Hursh, 2007). More recently, the ESEA has been reformulated as the Every Student Succeeds Act (ESSA), minimizing federal intervention and allowing more latitude and flexibility to states in meeting the federal government's framework of goals and objectives (Lam et al., 2016).

As federal and state education mandates and policies have significant repercussions for the life trajectories of children whose first language is not English and who may have learning disabilities, it is important to analyze how the accountability provisions within and related to ESSA and other policy directives operate to assist or hinder educational progress for them. The intersection of language status and disability as a composite feature is not often considered in policy approaches: rather, they are viewed as mutually exclusive characteristics. This reality complicates the implementation of appropriate educational services for dual language and English language learners with disabilities by limiting our understanding of their development and it often results in a misinterpretation of second language acquisition as a disability and/or as a misdiagnosis of an actual disability due to limited English proficiency (Zetlin et al., 2011).

This chapter focuses first on federal legislation with policy relevance for young dual language and English language learners with disabilities (ages birth to 8 years). Our discussion centers on ESSA as a reformulation of NCLB, on the Common Core State Standards, on the Individuals with Disabilities Education Act (IDEA) and, one of its primary strategies, the Response to Intervention (RTI) approach as an educational remedy advanced to address the over-representation of racial and ethnic minority children including dual language and English language learners classified as learning disabled. Finally, because our focus also includes pre-elementary grade children, we include an appraisal of the importance of Quality Rating and Improvement Systems and kindergarten entrance assessments as part of the larger accountability picture. We conclude with a set of recommendations focused on both process and policy factors to improve educational services for learning disabled children whose home language is not English.

From No Child Left Behind to the Every Student Succeeds Act

The Elementary and Secondary Education Act (ESEA) was redesigned in 2001 as the No Child Left Behind Act. A centerpiece of the legislation required that all school districts receiving federal funds develop academic assessments in reading, mathematics, and science, and report yearly progress in reaching state-established targets (Abedi, 2004). The legislation specified that data for individual subgroups, such as economically disadvantaged students, students from major racial and ethnic groups, students with disabilities, and students whose first language was not English, must be disaggregated (No Child Left Behind Act, 2002) to ensure stronger efforts to address their specific needs. However, English language learners with disabilities were not one of the subgroups specifically mentioned by this legislation (Anderson *et al.*, 2003). Fortunately, the separate consideration of English learners from children possessing disabilities does not continue in the ESSA legislation. Under Title III of ESSA, states are required to report the performance of English learners with a disability versus English learners without a disability (Pompa, 2015).

Under ESSA, the educational needs of English learners are addressed in a more systematic fashion. For example, states are required to have a standard procedure for classifying students as English learners and a standard procedure for their exit from specialized services. In addition, for English learners in their second year of instruction, growth measures versus proficiency measures may be employed. Growth measures may provide a better picture of how well a student is progressing in their acquisition of English and a check on the effectiveness of instructional approaches. For students who are reclassified, the law requires states to monitor their progress for four years beyond their reclassification date, and assessments can be given "in the language and form most likely to yield accurate data" (ESSA, p. 56). Further, states should have English language development standards in place that reflect differing proficiency levels across all language domains of listening, speaking, reading, and writing and these, in turn, need to be aligned with a state's overall language arts standards.

For children with disabilities, ESSA continues the requirement, consistent with IDEA, that appropriate test accommodations and supports should be provided reflective of the Individualized Educational Program (IEP). Children with disabilities are to continue to have access to appropriate testing accommodations such as additional time, oral assessment, and simplified test wording; however, ESSA places a 1% cap on reporting students with severe cognitive disabilities. This cap is controversial, as the definition of a severe cognitive disability is not clear and limits the flexibility of a school district relative to the number of children with disabilities it may have (Samuels, 2016). The motivation for this cap was to monitor programs that may be placing too many students in alternative assessment plans. For both English learners and children with disabilities, ESSA offers additional funding streams to support literacy, mental health services, improvement in school climate and safety including efforts to reduce bullying, harassment, and the overuse of discipline. Table 9.1 outlines the salient features of ESSA for dual and English language learners as well as for children with disabilities.

The reformulation of ESEA as ESSA has the potential to bring focused attention to the growing population of not only English learners but also English learners with special needs, who constitute approximately 8.5% of all students with disabilities (Data Accountability Center, 2013). However, an accountability framework that guides school systems in setting measurable goals and objectives beginning in third

Table 9.1 Salient features of ESSA for DLLs and ELLs with disabilities

Dual Language and English Language Learners	Children with Disabilities
Assessment in grades 3 through 8 and one assessment in high school	State accountability plans should address the needs of children with disabilities
States set their own goals and set their own consequences for meeting goals	Must be access to the general curriculum and the curriculum must be aligned with challenging academic content standards
Must have English Language Proficiency standards that are in alignment with academic content standards and reflect the four domains of literacy (listening, speaking, reading, and writing)	Ensure accommodation including the incorporation of Universal Design for Learning in both assessment and instruction
Provide annual assessments of English language proficiency	Caps at 1% the number of children taking alternative assessments
The performance of each subgroup must be measured separately including DLLs and ELLs with disabilities	The performance of each subgroup must be measured separately including DLLs and ELLs with disabilities
Establish statewide entrance and exit procedures for identifying DLLs and ELLs	Report incidents of bullying, harassment, and restrictive discipline policies

grade may not be as beneficial for optimizing children's development compared to intervention during a younger-age period. Given what we know about the development of second language acquisition in the early years (Hoff *et al.*, 2012; Zepeda & Rodriguez, 2015) the monitoring of children's progress should begin prior to third grade, when children are learning both their first language often in conjunction with second language exposure. In addition, there is an extensive literature that points out that early identification and intervention promotes a more salutatory learning trajectory for children with disabilities (Shonkoff & Meisels, 2000), and this should be no different for English learners with disabilities. Early learning is repeatedly mentioned in key provisions of ESSA. Titles I, II, and III reference early learning as a primary focus to better coordinate and align developmental and learning expectations from the 0–5 years of age period to early elementary school, and Title IX incorporates the Preschool Development Grant program targeting low to moderate income children.

Common Core State Standards

The Common Core State Standards (CCSSI) (Common Core State Standards Initiative, 2010) describe standards for student understanding at each grade level in clear and specific language to create coherence across grade levels. In doing so, the CCSSI describes content that students are expected to understand at each grade level, as well as corresponding practices that students are expected to demonstrate (e.g., perseverance in dealing with reading comprehension challenges, construction of arguments, ability to critique the reasoning of others). Because of intense political criticism of the CCSSI as federal overreach into the rights of states to determine desirable educational outcomes for their citizenry (Gewertz, 2015), the ESSA legislation does not require states to use the Common Core State Standards. However, ESSA does require states to have in place high academic standards that should be used as benchmarks in assessing and monitoring educational programming. Presently, 42 states and the District of Columbia have adopted the CCSSI (Education Week, 2015), but it not clear whether states will continue to use CCSSI given ESSA directives.

It should be noted that the CCSSI gives little specific acknowledgment of how to implement standards for dual and English language learners, especially in guiding children with learning disabilities. Also, it does not help to address the concern that many teachers are still facing difficulty in implementing standards-based teaching practices. Many teachers offer little opportunity for discourse, and opportunities for students to explain or justify their thinking rarely occur. Further, few teachers can maintain a high level of cognitive demand throughout the lesson. At this point, it is too early to know whether the CCSSI will have a systematic effect on the educational opportunities provided to dual and English language learners. Not only must schools adequately interpret CCSSI policy, but they also need to decide how to implement this recommended model according to the needs of their student body and the community context.

Individuals with Disabilities Education Act (IDEA)

The Individuals with Disabilities Education Act is our nation's central policy overseeing the education of children with disabilities. IDEA was initially enacted as the Education for All Handicapped Children Act (P.L. 94-142) in 1975 (Yell et al., 1998). IDEA is a federal law guaranteeing free appropriate public education to children with disabilities. IDEA provides regulations and guidance for states and public agencies in the provision of early intervention, special education, and related services. In December of 2004, the Individuals with Disabilities Education Improvement Act was rewritten and signed into law. IDEA 2004 expanded the categories of learning disabilities and introduced the concept of the Response to Intervention (RTI) model. The central purpose of redefining the learning disability category and introducing the RTI model was to reduce the misdiagnosis of students with learning disabilities.

The Individuals with Disabilities Education Act consists of four general parts: A, B, C, and D. Part A refers to the general provisions of the law, Part B directs services for children and youth ages 3–21, Part C focuses on early intervention services for infants and toddlers with disabilities ages birth to age 2, and Part D concentrates on program improvement, personnel preparation, and research and application. What follows is a discussion of Parts B and C as they relate to services for English learners with disabilities.

Part B of IDEA provides free appropriate public education (FAPE) to children ages 3–21 with disabilities who require special education and related services. In the annual report to Congress regarding the implementation of IDEA, the number of Limited English Proficient children reported by states is disaggregated by educational environment such as separate class, separate school, or home services (US Department of Education, Office of Special Education and Rehabilitation Services, 2015). In the Office of Special Education Programs' 2015 annual report to Congress, information about racial and ethnic groups is reported, but these data are not disaggregated by language status. According to this report, American Indian, Alaska Native, Black or African American, Native Hawaiian or Pacific Islanders had higher risk ratios and thus higher likelihood for being served (US Department of Education, Office of Special Education and Rehabilitative Services, 2015). The *Condition of Education Report 2015* from the National Center on Education Statistics (Kena *et al.*, 2015) indicates that 13% of public school children ages 3–21 received special education services under IDEA, representing a decline of 6.4 million children since 2004. Again, language status of the various subgroups is not reported, thus making it difficult to know the circumstances for English learners with disabilities.

Part C of IDEA concentrates on the youngest learners, ages 0–3 years old. The goal of Part C is to offer support services to families with infants and toddlers with developmental delays, with the hope of reducing the costs of intervention at later stages of development (Cole *et al.*, 2011; Council for Exceptional Children, 2011). Within Part C, latitude is given to states to construct an interagency comprehensive, coordinated, multidisciplinary family-centered system of early intervention that establishes eligibility requirements for participation and guides service delivery. Given that funding for Part C is affected by state budgets and legislation, variability exists across the country with respect to implementation (Adams *et al.*, 2013). Although the determination of eligibility is left to the discretion of each state, the 2011 IDEA Part C Final Regulations indicate that service delivery must be "culturally competent," including parental notification in their home language. However, in screening and assessment, regulations have moved away from using the native language of the parents to using "the language normally used by the child, if determined developmentally appropriate for the child by qualified personnel conducting the evaluation or assessment" (American Speech-Language-Hearing Association, 2011). In such cases, where a child's home language must be used but there are no available resources (i.e., interpreters) to assist, then, as per Part C guidelines, programs may not be held accountable.

IDEA contains a Child Find mandate applicable to both Part B and Part C that requires all school districts to identify, locate, and assess all children from birth to age 21 and to provide them with appropriate services that will help them succeed in school. Whether rates of identification and referral are representative of the child population within a state is not clear. In Hawaii, for example, an evaluation of Child Find efforts found conflicting evidence regarding the equitable representation of dual and English language learners depending upon the Census metric used for comparison (Shapiro & Derrington, 2004). As IDEA leaves it up to individual states to define what is meant by disproportionality of ethnic and racial minority with disabilities (NASEM, 2017), there is no consistent national profile for dual and English language learners. Although the Child Find mandate is well intentioned, the determination of eligibility may be compromised by a school district's inability to understand the role of second language acquisition in normal child growth and development, as well as by the sociocultural barriers preventing parental participation. Sociocultural factors include parental beliefs regarding disabilities that do not coincide with educators" perceptions, power differentials between school district personnel and families that can contribute to miscommunication, and basic income-related factors, such as lack of transportation to attend meetings (Family Empowerment and Disability Council, 2012; Harry, 2008).

Accountability within the parameters of IDEA aligns with the objectives of ESSA through the provision of an Individualized Educational Program (IEP) designed to meet a child's specific needs and appropriate assessment, including any needed accommodation such as extra time, use of picture vocabulary cards, or simplified English. However, even though Title III of ESSA requires reporting of dual and English language learners with disabilities, it is not clear how these new ESSA requirements will coordinate with IDEA reporting requirements. Prior to ESSA there had been a general lack of awareness about how ESEA legislation and IDEA legislation apply to the education of dual and English language learners with disabilities. This ambiguity has led to practices that may impinge upon dual and English language learners' right to a free and appropriate education in the least restrictive environment that is provided within the context of a culturally and linguistically valid research-based curriculum delivered by adequately prepared educators (MA2 RTI Working Group, 2010). Only time will tell how the new ESSA reporting requirements will interact with IDEA to provide a clearer focus on dual and English language learners with disabilities.

Response to Intervention (RTI)

The Individuals with Disabilities Education Act of 2004 identified Response to Intervention (RTI) as an alternative method for the identification of children with learning disabilities. Specifically, RTI as an educational approach came about as an alternative to the discrepancy model that was widely used. Among the criticisms of the discrepancy model for young children was the inability of standardized tests to accurately identify children prior to third grade and inform instruction about needed supports to address learning difficulties (Orosco & Klingner, 2010). Research has demonstrated that the discrepancy model contributes to a disproportionate number of ethnic and racial minority children, some of whom are English language learners, being classified as learning disabled (Artiles et al., 2005). Both false negatives and false positives for young children whose home language is not English have been reported (Samson & Lesaux, 2009). In addition, there is the important related issue of inappropriate assessment, conducted in a language that the child does not understand and containing test items developed for children outside their racial and cultural groups.

RTI is an assessment intervention model that allows schools to deliver evidence-based instructional methods that have been shown to be effective for the prevention of school failure. The RTI model is designed as a 3-tiered approach, where educational intervention within each tier becomes more focused through individualized instruction (Brown & Doolittle, 2008). Specifically, Tier 1 consists of high-quality, scientifically based instruction provided to all children in the classroom; Tier 2 is reserved for children not making adequate progress, and targeted instruction is offered in small-group formats; Tier 3 is reserved for those children experiencing the greatest difficulty, requiring one-on-one attention. RTI is viewed as a positive step due to its explicitness of instruction, especially in the elementary and secondary school grades. The use of RTI has provided (1) screening for at-risk students, (2) monitoring of responsiveness to instruction, and (3) problem solving within secondary and tertiary tiers (Vaughn & Fuchs, 2006).

Because RTI is viewed as a successful approach to assisting children with learning difficulties in the K-12 system, the early childhood field has adapted it for use with preschool children. Renamed "Recognition and Response" (R&R), this early childhood intervention uses the general RTI tiered approach and focuses on universal screening of all children to identify those who would benefit from targeted intervention through the use of small groups (Tier 2) and individualized instruction (Tier 3) (Buysse & Peisner-Feinberg, 2013). In addition to formative assessment and tiered instruction, R&R stresses collaboration among teachers, education specialists, and families to plan and assess learning using pertinent information (National Professional Development Center on Inclusion, 2012). In describing the origins of R&R, Buysse and Peinser-Feinberg (2013) point to its connection to applied behavior analysis with its focus on modifying psychosocial behavior. It is not surprising, then, that a number of R&R hybrids have arisen (e.g., the Pyramid Model, the Teaching Pyramid) that concentrate on children's pro-social development such as behavioral regulation and sustaining attention during learning

(Greenwood *et al.*, 2011), which are considered to be key aspects of preschool education.

Although there are efforts to adapt R&R pedagogical strategies for dual and English language learners in preschool (La Forett *et al.*, 2013), there exists little published evidence documenting the efficacy of R&R for this population. Research with early elementary-age English learners, however, suggests that the general RTI approach holds promise for the improvement of reading performance and instruction (Kamps *et al.*, 2007; Linan-Thompson *et al.*, 2006; Vaughn *et al.*, 2006). In addition, special education experts suggest that RTI holds potential to address the specific needs of DLLs/ELLs through its focus on early intervention and ongoing progress monitoring (La Forett *et al.*, 2012). However, experts caution that pedagogy must focus on children's cultural background and linguistic proficiency with appropriately trained educators who are able to distinguish between a language difference and a language disability for children growing up bilingually (Artiles & Kozleski, 2010; Brown & Doolittle, 2008). Table 9.2 outlines the major elements of RTI and the challenges in its implementation as R&R.

It is important to note that R&R differs from RTI in significant ways. There is less consensus regarding what constitutes a "core curriculum" and what is considered effective pedagogical practice for 3-, 4-, and 5-year-old children relative to children in the K-12 system. Because IDEA does not specifically address the use of RTI interventions for young children, R&R as an emerging approach suffers from a lack of clear guidance and confronts significant implementation challenges due to the mixed delivery systems operating in preschool education (Buysse & Peisner-Feinberg, 2013). Professional organizations focused on young children have attempted to fill the void by issuing reports to clarify how an RTI model may operate within the early childhood landscape while acknowledging such associated

Table 9.2 Response to Intervention and Recognition and Response

Elements of Response to Intervention	Challenges in Adapting Recognition and Response in Early Childhood
Systematic assessment of children's level and rate of performance	Educators lack support for understanding and utilizing systematic assessment
Use of evidence-based practice	Less robust research base on effective evidence-based practice for preschool
Conceptualized as 3 tiers of instruction focused on the general curriculum for all to intensive, individualized support	Less consensus on what constitutes the general curriculum for preschool children and lack of resources to institute intensive, individualized support
Integrates behavioral and academic supports	No clear consensus on what constitutes an academic focus in the early years
Collaborative decision making based on data	In many cases staffing patterns and lack of professional development time hinders collaboration

challenges as diverse settings and varying degrees of provider and teacher preparation (Division for Early Childhood et al., 2013).

Children Ages Birth to 5

Race-to-the-Top Early Learning Challenge

The Race-to-the-Top Early Learning Challenge (RTT-ELC) competitive grants' program was developed by the US Department of Education in 2011 to incentivize states to develop comprehensive early learning systems for children age birth to 5. Although funding under Race to the Top finished in 2015, its policy mandates influenced various states to revise their approach to early learning. Included in the grant program were requirements for clearer learning standards, appropriate assessment, a focus on family engagement, and development of the workforce. Because the primary priority of this effort was the closure of the achievement gap, particular categories of children were identified as high-need targets for services, including children with disabilities or developmental delays; migrant, homeless, or foster children; children inhabiting Indian lands; and English learners. Interestingly, the majority of states that applied in 2011 had the highest concentration of dual and English language learners in their child population (Ackerman & Tazi, 2015).

In addition to targeting particular populations of children, RTT-ELC required that states develop a kindergarten readiness measure aligned with a state's early learning standards. Kindergarten entry assessments (KEAs) were to adhere to the recommendations of the National Research Council report on early childhood assessment (National Research Council, 2008) with respect to its psychometric properties and utility and be appropriate for English learners and children with disabilities. This effort would assist states in understanding how best to coordinate instructional practice between preschool and early elementary services. According to the Education Commission of the States, 25 states and the District of Columbia require kindergarten entry assessments, and other states are considering it (Education Commission of the States, 2014).

Within the early childhood community, there is consensus that KEAs not become a high-stakes test, nor should they be used to bar children from kindergarten (Saluja et al., 2013). Rather, KEAs should be designed to measure school readiness, identify children who may need additional educational attention, and engage parents in supporting the early learning of their children. In a policy brief for the Center for Early Care and Education Research – Dual Language Learners, Espinosa and Garcia (2012) assert that a one-time assessment across multiple developmental domains for young children is especially challenging for children whose home language is not English. According to these authors, the psychometric properties of KEAs must address the norming sample upon which the assessment is based, the content equivalence, and the semantic equivalence of the assessment. In addition to the linguistic and cultural appropriateness of an assessment, these authors stress the importance of the purpose of the assessment, the language and cultural capacity of the test administrator, and the value of involving families in the assessment process.

Quality Rating Improvement Systems

President Obama's Race-to-the-Top initiative catapulted Quality Rating Improvement Systems (QRIS) as the primary method of standardizing early childhood education programs across the country (Goffin & Barnett, 2015). Currently, the majority of states have QRIS schemes in place, and the rest are in the planning stages (QRIS National Learning Network, 2015). QRIS has its origins in market strategies to assist parents in their selection of high-quality child care and early education services; however, under Race-to-the-Top, QRIS became focused on assessment and quality improvement. One of the challenges for emerging QRIS efforts is defining what constitutes quality and what role language and cultural differences play in the definition of quality.

In state QRIS matrices, some attention has been given to aspects of inclusion, that is, provisions made to accommodate children with special needs. In an analysis of state QRIS standards, Horowitz and Squires (2014) found that only 29 out of the 42 states with QRIS systems in place referenced inclusive practices; however, many of these references were minimal. According to Horowitz and Squires' analysis, no state has a way to alert parents with special needs children about the appropriateness of particular early childhood education programs. With respect to young dual and English language learners, the BUILD organization, which provides technical assistance to states about QRIS, has launched a number of initiatives to more closely examine and provide technical assistance to states regarding the importance of culture, dual language learning, and equity issues (Espinosa & Calderon, 2015). Given that QRIS as a policy effort is relatively new, the interface of language status and disability has received limited attention.

Although there is evidence that young children with special needs are able to process two languages (Chen & Gutierrez-Clellen, 2013), the field of early childhood education, focusing on children age 0–5 years, experiences many similar difficulties in understanding the unique challenges of learning disabled children growing up with two languages, as does primary education. Among the basic challenges is a better empirical understanding of bilingual language acquisition from infancy to preschool, how bilingual language development interacts with particular disabilities across developing age stages, and how early learning experiences both within the home setting and in substitute care contribute to development in each language.

A central question within the QRIS approach is what constitutes a quality preschool experience and how best to measure it. There are a number of factors that contribute to the widespread notion that what is good for all children should be good for subsets of children such as dual and English language learners. First, child development theory and research posit that there are universal psychological processes that all humans experience (Kitayama & Markus, 1996; Overton, 2013). The major implication of this universalistic perspective for understanding measures of early education quality is the belief that good quality for all children will result in positive outcomes regardless of a child's background characteristics. Second, researchers and evaluators engaged in examining the development of young dual and English language learners are just beginning to appreciate important distinctions that need to be made in understanding the development of children learning two languages at a young age. (See Castro *et al.*, 2013 for a review.) As a result, the research and evaluation expertise that exists has not been well informed about such important elements as how to accurately identify dual and English language learners within the 0-5 age range, and which, if any, assessment tools are relevant and appropriate.

In the Peisner-Feinberg *et al.* (2014) review of classroom quality measures for dual language learners, they conclude that classroom quality measures function equally well for monolingual and dual language learner populations. However, they point out that measures developed specifically for dual language learners may capture different dimensions of quality than general measures. The controversy about the appropriateness of widely used classroom quality measures is a reflection of the broader discussion regarding the understanding and incorporation of diverse children's background qualities for improved pedagogical practice.

Although high-quality classrooms benefit both monolingual and dual and English language learners, it has been argued that practices associated with current definitions of quality may not be sufficient to support analogous levels of academic success for children who begin their lives speaking a language other than English (August & Shanahan, 2006; Goldenberg, 2013). As classroom quality measures provide the content of teacher education and professional development (see the Center for Advanced Study of Teaching and Learning, 2017), the specific needs of dual language learners are overlooked.

Conclusions and Recommendations

The intent of this chapter has been to provide an analysis of federal accountability policies that relate to the identification and instruction of young dual language learners in the early childhood age range of 0–8 years. Because dual language learners/English learners and children with special needs have been treated as separate categories within accountability policies, the intersection of the language and disability classifications is not often addressed. In addition, children with these two characteristics frequently have accompanying sociocultural correlates, such as low-income and racial and/or ethnic status, which are strong predictors of child outcomes. As accountability extends to educational services for children from birth to age 5, the early childhood field is wrestling with ways to bridge conflicting philosophical and pedagogical positions regarding child growth and development. For the birth to age 5 community, there is the fear of a "push down" effect that narrows the curriculum to decontextualized discrete skills that overshadow the importance of a holistic approach to child development (New, 2009).

One of the recurring themes in the discussion of DLLs/ELLs is the misinterpretation of normal bilingual language development as a sign of a learning disability or, alternatively, acceptance of language delay as a normal aspect of bilingual development without an exploration of any underlying neurological substrate, thus foreclosing early intervention. Because policy requirements have not clearly addressed the intersection of language status and disability, teachers often wait until English proficiency is established before referring children for specialized services (Samson & Lesaux, 2009), promoting a "wait to fail" approach.

The lack of appropriate assessment continues to challenge the field at both the early age ranges and the later primary grades. Progress has been made within the last few decades in documenting the language trajectories of bilingual children (Iglesias & Rojas, 2012; Pearson, 2013), demonstrating that vocabulary comprehension and production are distributed across two languages, necessitating the need to assess both languages to achieve a complete picture. More recent policy approaches (i.e., Head Start Program Standards) are sensitive to this research and provide directives to assess children in both the home language and English. The ESSA legislation does state that "assessments in the language and form most likely to yield accurate data" (ESSA, p. 56) may be employed until English language proficiency is achieved. It remains to be seen whether programs utilize this provision to assess children in their home language as evidence of their development and educational progression.

One promising approach for dual and English language learners with learning disabilities is RTI. RTI has the potential to change the ways that schools think about supporting students that past models could not do. In past approaches, students needed to experience years of academic decline, and possibly several years of poor general education instruction, before adequate instruction and intervention were provided, thus increasing the probability of a student being misidentified with a learning disability (LD), and being placed in special education. RTI moves away from this previous approach by (a) emphasizing the focus on making sure that all students receive an evidence-based, high-quality, and meaningful general education; (b) providing ongoing student progress monitoring that identifies at-risk students, and by providing immediate intervention support for these students prior to special education referral; and (c) having a systematic and strategic plan for improving and building upon instructional capacity at all levels, driven by a student data-based decision-making model (e.g., Fuchs *et al.*, 2003; Marston *et al.*, 2003).

Based on our review of educational policy directives, we offer the following recommendations to assist educators and others who are tasked with the responsibility of making important life decisions for dual and English language learners with disabilities:

(1) *Expand access to, and improve the quality of, early childhood education services to increase early identification and prevention supports.* With increased federal and state attention to preschool education, including the Maternal, Infant, and Early Childhood Home Visiting Initiative (MIECHV) funded through the Affordable Care Act, opportunities exist to provide services to more dual and English language learners with disabilities and to equip early childhood personnel in supporting prevention and targeting early intervention.

(2) *Seek funding support via ESSA or other funding streams to coordinate and align educational services for the 0–5 age range with the primary grades.* One of the constant strains in service delivery for children with learning disabilities has been the disconnect in service provision as the child ages out of one categorically funded program and transitions to another. An effort to coordinate across service sectors, with increased attention to the alignment of developmental expectations, is a goal worth pursuing.

(3) *State policymakers must ensure that assessments are multifaceted, developmentally appropriate, and linguistically and culturally valid for children whose home language is not English.* Because instructional decisions and referral to special education services are based on child assessments, it is critical that these assessments provide children with the opportunity to demonstrate their competence. For young children, assessments that do not measure their abilities in their home language and do not take into account the cultural appropriateness of assessment content can lead to misidentification and inaccurate referral (Abedi, 2006).

(4) *State and local programs should utilize RTI and R&R as curricular organizational approaches within early childhood education.* This can address a recurrent criticism within special education: that children suffer from inappropriate instruction prior to referral (Ortiz & Yates, 2001). With appropriate modifications relevant to dual and English language learners, RTI holds promise in helping policymakers, administrators, educators, and researchers shift the education field

from focusing on finding disability or within-child deficits to focusing on providing the best instruction for all students.
(5) State licensing and credentialing requirements must reflect an *integration of both content knowledge and pedagogical practice expertise within preservice and in-service education and training to address the needs of dual and English language learners with disabilities.* Although knowledgeable teachers and administrators could address the needs of dual and English language learners with disabilities, the sad fact is that the preparation of education personnel seldom includes a focus on normal first and second language development, let alone an appreciation of the sociocultural realities of dual and English language learners with learning disabilities. Appropriate and ongoing professional development would assist in reducing the number of children not accurately diagnosed and not given timely referral (Ortiz *et al.*, 2011).
(6) *Support research that is longitudinal to understand the interaction of second language acquisition for particular disabilities categories.* Understanding how dual and English language learners develop and learn over time will help uncover relevant factors, both correlational and predictive, that can inform prevention and intervention strategies.

References

Abedi, J. (2004) The No Child Left Behind Act and English language learners: Assessment and accountability issues. *Educational Researcher* 33 (1), 4–14.

Abedi, J. (2006) Psychometric issues in the ELL assessment and special education eligibility. *Teachers College Record* 108 (11), 2282–2303.

Ackerman, D.J. and Tazi, Z. (2015) Enhancing young dual language learner's achievement: Exploring strategies and addressing challenges. *ETS Research Report Series* (1), 1–39.

Adams, R.C., Tapia, C. and the Council on Children with Disabilities. (2013) Early intervention, IDEA Part C services and the medical home: Collaboration for best practice and best outcomes. *Pediatrics* 132 (4), 1073–1088.

American Speech-Language-Hearing Association (2011) IDEA Part C Issue Brief: Cultural and linguistic diversity. http://www.asha.org/Advocacy/federal/idea/IDEA-Part-C-Issue-Brief-Cultural-and-Linguistic-Diversity/.

Anderson, M.E., Minnema, J.E., Thurlow, M.L. and Hall-Lande, J. (2003) *Confronting the Unique Challenges of Including English Language Learners with Disabilities in Statewide Assessments*. Minneapolis, MN: University of Minnesota, National Center on Educational Outcomes. Accessed June 6, 2017. http://education.umn.edu/NCEO/OnlinePubs/ELLsDisReport9.html.

Artiles, A.J. and Kozleski, E.B. (2010) What counts as response and intervention in RTI? A sociocultural analysis. *Psicothema* 22 (4), 949–954.

Artiles, A.J., Rueda, R., Salazar, J.J. and Higareda, I. (2005) Within-group diversity in minority disproportionate representation: English learners in urban school districts. *Exceptional Children* 71 (3), 283–300.

August, D. and Shanahan, T. (2006) *Developing Literacy in Second Language Learners: Report of the National Literacy Panel on Second Language Minority Children and Youth*. Mahwah, NJ: Lawrence Erlbaum.

Brown, J.E. and Doolittle, J. (2008) A cultural, linguistic and ecological framework for response to intervention with English language learners. *Teaching Exceptional Children* 40 (5), 66–72.

Buysse, V. and Peisner-Feinberg, E.S. (2013) Response to intervention: Conceptual models for the early childhood field. In V. Buysse and E.S. Peisner-Feinberg (eds) *Handbook of Response to Intervention in Early Childhood* (pp. 3–23). Baltimore, MD: Brookes Publishing.

Castro, D.C., Garcia, E.E. and Markos, A. (2013) *Dual Language Learners: Research Informing Policy*. Chapel Hill, NC: Frank Porter Graham Child Development Institute.

Center for Advanced Study of Teaching and Learning (2017) National Center on Quality Teaching and Learning. Charlottesville, VA: CASTL, Curry School of Education and Human Development, University of Virginia. Accessed June 6, 2017. http://curry.virginia.edu/research/centers/castl/project/NCQTL.

Chen, D. and Gutierrez-Clellan, V. (2013) Early intervention and young dual language learners with special needs. *California Best Practices for Dual Language Learners: Research Overview Papers*. Sacramento, CA: California Department of Education. http://www.cde.ca.gov/sp/cd/ce/documents/dllresearchpapers.pdf.

Cole, P., Oser, C. and Walsh, S. (2011) Building on the foundations of Part C legislation. *Zero to Three 3*, 52–59.

Common Core State Standards Initiative (2010) *Common Core State Standards*. Accessed June 6, 2017. http://www.corestandards.org/.

Council for Exceptional Children, Division for Early Childhood and IDEA Infant and Toddler Coordinators Association (2011) *Individuals with Disabilities: Final Regulations. Side by Side Comparison*. Missoula, MT: Division for Early Childhood, Council for Exceptional Children. http://dec-sped.org/About_DEC/Whats_New?id=128.

Darling-Hammond, L. (2007) Race, inequality, and educational accountability: The irony of "No Child Left Behind". *Race, Ethnicity and Education* 10 (3), 245–260.

Data Accountability Center (2013) Individuals with Disabilities Education Act (IDEA) data [data tables for OSEP state reported data]. https://www.ideadata.org/tables33rd/ar_1-9.pdf.

Division for Early Childhood of the Council for Exceptional Children (DEC), the National Association for the Education of Young Children (NAEYC) and the National Head Start Association (NHSA) (2013) *Framework for Response to Intervention in Early Childhood: Description and Implications*. Missoula, MT: DEC; Washington, DC: NAYEC; Alexandria, VA: NHSA. http://www.naeyc.org/files/naeyc/RTI%20in%20Early%20Childhood.pdf.

Education Commission of the States (2014) *50 States Analysis*. Denver, CO: Education Commission of the States.

Education Week (2015) Common core or something else? A map of state academic standards. June 29, 2015. Accessed June 6, 2017. l.

Espinosa, L.M. and Garcia, E. (2012) Developmental assessment of young dual language learners with a focus on kindergarten entry assessments: Implications for state policies. Working Paper #1. Center for Early Care and Education Research – Dual Language Learners (CERCER-DLL). Chapel Hill, NC: University of North Carolina, Frank Porter Graham Child Development Institute.

Espinosa, L.M. and Calderon, M. (2015) *State Early Learning and Development Standards/Guidelines and Related Practices: How Responsive Are They to the Needs of Young Dual Language Learners?* Boston, MA: BUILD Initiative. http://buildinitiative.org/Portals/0/Uploads/Documents/BuildDLLReport2015.pdf.

Family Empowerment and Disability Council (2012) The Individuals with Disability Act and parent participation. FEDC Issue Brief, May 2012. Accessed June 6, 2017. http://www.efrconline.org/myadmin/files/fedc_Parent_Participation.pdf.

Fuchs, D., Mock, D., Morgan, P.L. and Young, C.L. (2003) Responsiveness-to-intervention: Definitions, evidence, and implications for the learning disabilities construct. *Learning Disabilities Research & Practice* 18 (3), 157–171.

Gewertz, C. (2015) The common core explained. *Education Week*, September 28, 2015. Accessed June 6, 2017. http://www.edweek.org/ew/issues/common-core-state-standards/.

Goffin, S.G. and Barnett, W.S. (2015) Assessing QRIS as a change agent. *Early Childhood Research Quarterly* 30, 179–182.

Goldenberg, C. (2013) Unlocking research on English Learners: What we know – and don't yet know – about effective instruction. *American Educator* Summer, 4–38.

Greenwood, C.R., Bradfield, R., Kaminski, R., Linas, M., Carta, J.J. and Nylander, D. (2011) The response to intervention (RTI) approach in early childhood. *Focus on Exceptional Children* 43 (9), 1–22.

Harry, B. (2008) Collaboration with culturally and linguistically diverse families: Ideal versus reality. *Exceptional Children* 74, 372–388.

Hoff, E., Core, C., Place, S., Rumiche, R., Senor, M. and Parra, M. (2012) Dual language exposure and early bilingual development. *Journal of Child Language* 39 (1), 1–27.

Horowitz, M. and Squires, J. (2014) *QRIS and Inclusion: Do State QRIS Standards Support the Learning Needs of All Children?* (CEELO FastFact). New Brunswick, NJ: Center on Enhancing Early Learning Outcomes. http://ceelo.org/wp-content/uploads/2014/11/ceelo_fast_fact_qris_inclusion.pdf.

Hursh, D. (2007) Exacerbating inequality: The failed promise of the No Child Left Behind Act. *Race, Ethnicity and Education* 10 (3), 295–308.

Iglesias, A. and Rojas, R. (2012) Bilingual language development of ELLs: Modeling the growth of two languages. In B. Goldstein (ed.) *Bilingual Language Development and Disorders: Past, Present, and Future* (pp. 1–30). Baltimore, MD: Brookes Publishing.

Kamps, D., Abbott, M., Greenwood, C., Arreaga-Mayer, C., Wills, H., Longstaff, J. and Walton, C. (2007) Use of evidence-based, small group reading instruction for English language learners in elementary grades: Secondary-tier intervention. *Learning Disability Quarterly* 30, 153–168.

Kena, G., Musu-Gillette, L., Robinson, J., Wang, X., Rathbun, A., Zhang, J., Wilkinson-Flicker, S., Barmer, A. and Dunlop Velez, E. (2015) *The Condition of Education 2015 (NCES 2015–144)*. Washington, DC: US Department of Education, National Center for Education Statistics. http://nces.ed.gov/pubsearch.

Kitayama, S. and Markus, H.R. (1996) Construal of self as cultural frame: Implications for internationalizing psychology. In N.R. Goldberger and J.B. Veroff (eds) *The Culture and Psychology Reader* (pp. 366–383). New York, NY: New York University Press.

LaForett, D.R., Peisner-Feinberg, E. and Buysse, V. (2013) Recognition and response for dual language learners. In V. Buysse and E. Peisner-Feinberg (eds) *Handbook of Response to Intervention in Early Childhood* (pp. 355–369). Baltimore, MD: Brookes Publishing.

LaForett, D.R., Fettig, A., Peisner-Feinberg, E. and Buysse, V. (2012) Recognition and response for dual language learners: Instructional adaptations for young dual language learners. *Young Exceptional Children Monograph Series* 14, 115–132.

Lam, L., Mercer, C., Podolsky, A. and Darling-Hammond, L. (2016) *Evidence-based Interventions: A Guide for States* (Policy Brief, March 31, 2016). Palo Alto, CA: Learning Policy Institute. Accessed June 6, 2017. https://learningpolicyinstitute.org/our-work/publications-resources/evidence-based-interventions-a-guide-for-states/.

Linan-Thompson, S., Vaughn, S., Prater, K. and Cirino, P.T. (2006) The response to intervention of English language learners at risk for reading problems. *Journal of Learning Disabilities* 39 (5), 390–398.

MA 2RTI Working Group (2010) *A Focus on English Language Learners (ELLS) and their Academic Achievement: A Position Statement*. Massachusetts 2RTI Working Group, March 30, 2010. https://bilingualspecialeddotcom.files.wordpress.com/2015/03/2rti-final-5_5_10v2.pdf.

Marston, D., Muyskens, P., Lau, M. and Canter, A. (2003) Problem-solving model for decision making with high-incidence disabilities: The Minneapolis experience. *Learning Disabilities Research & Practice* 18 (3), 187–200.

NASEM (2017) *Promoting the Educational Success of Children and Youth Learning English: Promising Futures*. Washington, DC: National Academies of Science, Engineering and Medicine.

National Professional Development Center on Inclusion (2012) *Response to Intervention (RTI) in Early Childhood: Building Consensus on the Defining Features*. Chapel Hill, NC: University of North Carolina, Frank Porter Graham Child Development Institute.

National Research Council (2008) *Early Childhood Assessment: Why, What and How?* Washington, DC: National Academies Press.

New, R.S. (2009) Early childhood policies (and policy debate) as a sociocultural mirror. *Contemporary Issues in Early Childhood* 10 (3), 309–311.

No Child Left Behind Act of 2001, Pub. L. NCLB No. 107–110, §115, Stat. 1425. (2002)

Orosco, M.J. and Klingner, J. (2010) One school's implementation of RTI with English Learners: "Referring into RTI". *Journal of Learning Disabilities* 43 (3), 269–288.

Ortiz, A.A. and Yates, J.R. (2001) A framework for serving English learners with disabilities. *Journal of Special Education Leadership* 14 (2), 72–80.

Ortiz, A.A., Robertson, P.M., Wilkinson, C.Y., Liu, Y., McGhee, B.D. and Kushner, M.I. (2011) The role of bilingual teachers in preventing inappropriate referrals of ELLs to special education: Implications for response to intervention. *Bilingual Research Journal* 34 (3), 316–333.

Overton, W.F. (2013) Development across the lifespan. In I.B. Weiner and D.K. Freedheim (eds) *Handbook of Psychology: Developmental Psychology* (pp. 13–42). Hoboken, NJ: Wiley.

Pearson, B.Z. (2013) Distinguishing the bilingual as a late talker from the later talker who is bilingual. In L. Rescorla and P. Dale (eds) *Late Talkers: Language Development, Interventions, and Outcomes* (pp. 67–87). Baltimore MD: Brookes Publishing.

Peisner-Feinberg, E., Buysse, V., Fuligni, A., Burchinal, M., Espinosa, L., Halle, T. and Castro, D. (2014) Using early care and education quality measures with dual language learners: A review of the research. *Early Childhood Research Quarterly* 29 (4), 786–803.

Pompa, D. (2015) New education legislation includes important policies for English learners, potential pitfalls for their advocates. Migration Policy Institute commentary, December 2015. Accessed June 6, 2017. http://www.migrationpolicy.org/news/new-education-legislation-includes-important-policies-english-learners-potential-pitfalls-their.

QRIS National Learning Network (2015) Current status of QRIS in the states. February 20, 2015. f.

Saluja, G., Scott-Little, C. and Clifford, R.M. (2000, Fall) Readiness for school: A survey of state policies and definitions. *Early Childhood Research & Practice* 2 (2). http://ecrp.uiuc.edu/v2n2/saluja.html.

Samson, J.E. and Lesaux, N.K. (2009) Language minority learners in special education: Rates and predictors of identification for services. *Journal of Learning Disabilities* 42 (2), 148–162.

Samuels, C. (2016) ESSA panel weighs rules for testing for those with severe cognitive disabilities. Education Week, March 25, 2016. Accessed June 6, 2017. http://blogs.edweek.org/edweek/speced/2016/03/essa_testing_severe_disabilities.html.

Shapiro, B.J. and Derrington, T.M. (2004) Equity and disparity in access to services: An outcome-based evaluation of Child Find in Hawaii. *TECSE* 24 (4), 199–2004.

Shonkoff, J.P. and Meisels, S.J. (eds) (2000) *Handbook of Early Childhood Intervention* (2nd edition). Cambridge: Cambridge University Press.

Thomas, J.Y. and Brady, K.P. (2005) The elementary and secondary education act at 40: Equity, accountability, and the evolving federal role in public education. In L. Parker (ed.) *The Elementary and Secondary Education Act at 40: Reviews of Research, Policy Implementation, Critical Perspectives and Reflections* (pp. 51–67). Thousand Oaks, CA: Sage.

US Department of Education (2015) *37th Annual Report to Congress on the Implementation of the Individuals with Disabilities Act*. Washington, DC: Office of Special Education and Rehabilitative Services. https://www.edpubs.gov/document/ed005611p.pdf?ck=66.

Vaughn, S. and Fuchs, L.S. (2006) A response to "Competing views: A dialogue on response to intervention." Why response to intervention is necessary but not sufficient for identifying students with learning disabilities. *Assessment for Effective Intervention* 32 (1), 58–61.

Vaughn, S., Cirino, P.T., Linan-Thompson, S., Mathes, P.G., Carlson, C.D., Hagan, E.C. and Francis, D.J. (2006) Effectiveness of a Spanish intervention and an English intervention for English language learners at risk for reading problems. *American Educational Research Journal* 43 (3), 449–487.

Yell, M.L., Rogers, D. and Rogers, E.L. (1998) The legal history of special education: What a long, strange trip it's been! *Remedial and Special Education* 19 (4), 219–228.

Zepeda, M. and Rodriguez, J.L. (2015) Bilingual language development in early childhood: Research and policy implications. In Y.M. Caldera and E. Lindsey (eds) *Mexican American Children and Families: Multidisciplinary Perspectives* (pp. 122–130). New York, NY: Routledge.

Zetlin, A., Beltran, D., Salcido, P., Gonzalez, T. and Reyes, T. (2011) Building pathways of optimal support for English language learners in special education. *Teacher Education and Special Education* 34 (1), 59–70.

10 Young Bilingual Children with Disabilities: Challenges and Opportunities for Future Education Policies and Research

Alba A. Ortiz

How do you distinguish cultural and linguistic diversity (CLD) from disabilities? Why is it so difficult to do so? What are best practices in serving children who are dually identified as dual language learners (DLLs) or English learners (ELs) and as children with disabilities? Answering these questions is one of the most important responsibilities of the education communities, because CLD children who come from homes where a language other than English is spoken are the country's fastest-growing segment of the young child population under the age of 8. The contributors to this volume summarize the state of practice in early childhood education for young DLLs with and without disabilities and identify promising, research-based practices – the opportunities – for meeting the needs of these children and ensuring their social and academic success. They also identify challenges in meeting these children's needs, including gaps between research, policy, and practice and a critical shortage of education personnel with expertise in early childhood education for DLLs in general, and for those with disabilities specifically. This chapter discusses key topics, concepts, and themes identified by contributing authors as essential elements of a comprehensive service delivery framework for young DLLs.

The Changing Demography of America's Young Children

The United States is undergoing dramatic demographic changes. In 2017, approximately 51% of our nation's children were from culturally and linguistically diverse backgrounds (Kids Count Data Center, 2018). Hispanics comprised 26% and Black children, 14% of the 28,700,000 children birth to age 11. Dual language learners (DLLs) – young children from homes where a language other than English is spoken and who are learning two (or more languages) at the same time or learning a second language while continuing to develop their first (US Department of Health & Human Services and US Department of Education, 2016) – are the fastest-growing segment of the young child population. DLLs under the age of 8 already make up 33% of the young child population (Child Trends, 2016). Many DLLs are also children of immigrants. Between 1994 and 2017, the number of immigrant children with at least one foreign-born parent grew to 19.6 million, or one-quarter of all US children (Child Trends, 2018). Contrary to popular opinion, the majority of these children were born in the United States.

The changing demographics are reflected in early childhood education programs in public school enrollments. Twenty-six percent of children served by Early Head Start come from homes where a language other than English is spoken at home (Administration for Children and Families (ACF), 2013: Chapter 3), and 29% of those in Head Start are classified as DLLs (US Department of Health & Human Services and US Department of Education, 2016). In 2016, non-Hispanic Whites represented 49% of all public school students, Hispanics comprised 26%, Blacks 15%, Asian/Pacific Islanders 5%, American Indian/Alaskan Native 1%, and students of two or more races 3% (National Center for Education Statistics, 2019). The population of elementary and secondary school students is now a "majority minority." These data have significant implications for the education community: educators have no choice but to increase their understanding of the DLLs and educational policies and practices that advance their social, academic, and economic success. The country's welfare depends on it.

English learners

A specific subset of DLLs is English learners (ELs), children whose primary home language is other than English and who, because of their limited proficiency in English, need language assistance to succeed in school (ESSA, 2015). Students classified as English learners, pre-K through grade 12, are provided a Language Instruction Educational Program (LIEP) to ensure that they acquire English proficiency, meet challenging academic standards, and are able to participate fully in society (US Department of Education, Office of Planning Evaluation and Policy Development, 2012).

The number of ELs has increased by 60% in the last decade, compared to a 7% growth in the general student population (Chao *et al.*, 2013). In terms of public school enrollments, ELs comprise 4.8 million students, or 9.6% of students in grades K-12 (US Department of Education, Office of English Language Acquisition, 2020). Although all share "limited English proficient" status, there are significant within- and across-group differences among ELs in terms of sociocultural background, levels of native language and English proficiency, previous schooling histories, and the type and quality of LIEPs by which they are served. For example, ELs represent 400 language groups, from high-incidence languages like Spanish and Vietnamese to less common ones such as Ukrainian and Bengali, and more than 150 different native North American languages (McFarland, 2016; US Census Bureau, 2015). The largest proportion, 91%, comes from homes where Spanish is spoken (Administration for Children and Families, 2013: Chapter 3).

ELs with disabilities

It is estimated that 10–20% of young children will experience developmental delays, with rates being higher for children from low-income backgrounds. Approximately 14% of ELs are identified as having disabilities and are served under the Individuals with Disabilities Education Improvement Act (McFarland *et al.*, 2019). However, special education representation patterns vary considerably across states (Blanchett *et al.*, 2009) and by racial/ethnic group membership, socioeconomic status, and/or language status (e.g., Artiles *et al.*, 2005; Coutinho *et al.*, 2002; Skiba *et al.*, 2015). Latinos, the largest segment of the young EL and bilingual populations, proportionately are underrepresented in special education programs (Donovan & Cross, 2002). However, those who are also English learners are overrepresented in the upper grades and more likely to be identified as having disabilities than are English-proficient Latinos (Artiles *et al.*, 2005).

The identification of ELs and other bilingual children with disabilities is challenging for a variety of reasons, including (a) great variability in the language and cultural backgrounds of this population, (b) confounding variables such as low socioeconomic status and low parental education, and (c) limited availability of assessments that are valid for this population. The identification process is further complicated by the shortage of educators who are bilingual and who have deep expertise on English language and bilingual language development, and by a limited research base to guide the identification process. Too often, educators succumb to stereotypes, positive or negative, of the students they serve and ignore factors such as social class, education, nationality, language, and academic difficulties, thus increasing the risk that students will be overrepresented in special education programs or that those with special needs will be overlooked and may not receive services to which they are entitled (García & Ortiz, 2004). For example, Asian Americans have historically been typecast as intelligent, hardworking, well educated, and prosperous (Li & Wang, 2008) and under-identified as students with disabilities. In contrast, English learners are over-identified, because their limited English proficiency is inaccurately interpreted as indicating speech and language disorders.

Factors Influencing the Achievement of DLLs

Research documents significant benefits associated with bilingualism, including cognitive flexibility, divergent thinking, creativity, and greater earning power in a global economy (Gándara, 2018). Bilingual individuals are more likely to understand diverse points of view and, thus, to be better able to function effectively in cross-cultural settings. Unfortunately, however, DLLs do not always reap the benefits associated with their bilingualism. Despite decades of legal mandates and school reform initiatives aimed specifically at closing achievement gaps between student subgroups, DLLs continue to experience widespread underachievement; low rates of social promotion, retention, and school attrition; and disproportionate representation in remedial and special education programs (Ortiz et al., 2018). For example, of all racial/ethnic groups, Latinos, who comprise the majority of the DLL population, have the highest dropout rates; those who are immigrants leave school at rates nearly double those of native-born peers (43% versus 15%, respectively; National Center for Education Statistics, 2004). On the 2017 National Assessment of Educational Progress, 68% of ELs scored at or below the basic reading proficiency level, compared to 28% of non-EL peers (US Department of Education, Office of English Language Acquisition, 2018). These results are essentially the same as those reported for the 2007 NAEP assessment (i.e., 70% of ELs performed at or below the basic level). These data are concerning, because low academic achievement is the most common reason for referring students to special education (Hibel et al., 2010), and reading disabilities are the most frequently identified problem (Wagner et al., 2005). Moreover, these trends persist despite a robust body of literature identifying the characteristics of effective schools for DLLs (e.g., Collier & Thomas, 2004; Goldenberg, 2008; Scanlan & Lopez, 2015).

Myriad factors influence the achievement of DLLs, among the most salient of which are language, culture, and socioeconomic status.

Language

As indicated earlier, DLLs are children whose language skills are influenced by exposure to two languages. Some are simultaneous bilinguals and acquire two (or more) languages simultaneously, while others are sequential bilinguals and acquire a second language after the age of 3 or begin learning English when they enter school settings. The second language acquisition process assumes knowledge in a first language and encompasses predictable stages of acquisition (Krashen & Terrell, 1983). In the "silent period" or pre-production stage, children focus on understanding how the new language works and then move to the early production stage, communicating using single words, phrases, and simple sentences. In the speech emergence stage, children demonstrate greater vocabulary knowledge and produce longer sentences, but rely on context clues to understand messages and make frequent errors in their own language use. Children with beginning fluency are able to interact comfortably in social situations but still struggle with vocabulary and academic language (language of teachers and texts and related instructional materials), while those with intermediate fluency are able to interact more easily in social and academic contexts and are able to use language for higher-level purposes (e.g., offering opinions). When children reach the advanced fluency stage, they can communicate effectively across contexts with minimal support. Children with intermediate fluency are able to converse easily in social and academic contexts, although there may be gaps in vocabulary and grammar knowledge, while those with advanced fluency are comfortable communicating across contexts, and their language use approximates that of native English speakers. Although there are significant individual differences, the general consensus is that it takes between four and seven years for children with strong first language skills to achieve advanced fluency in English (Cummins, 1981; Goldenberg, 2008; Thomas & Collier, 2002).

As they develop English proficiency, DLLs call upon all their native language and English resources, separately and together, to meet their communication goals and to ensure that their language fits the needs of the person(s) with whom they are interacting, as well as the specific topic, task, or context (García & Li Wei, 2014). This phenomenon, referred to as "translanguaging," goes beyond linguistic features such as codeswitching (i.e., shifting from one language to another) to include the strategic use of two (or more) languages for efficiency of communication, to support learning, and to enhance meaning, in real time. As they become fully bilingual and biliterate, ELs develop the ability to suppress dual language use to perform tasks when asked to do so in a specific language (Otheguy *et al.*, 2015).

Culture

Sociocultural theory, developed from the work of Vygotsky (1978), posits that learning is a social process embedded in the cultural context of children's everyday lives and their interactions with others. Given that, children's functioning is best understood by observing their participation in family routines and the practices of their communities, because these reflect the group's values and beliefs, communication styles, norms and expectations for behaviors, and traditions and customs. These socialization practices determine how children interpret the meanings of symbols, artifacts, and behaviors; how they define themselves; and how they view and make sense of the world and events around them (Banks & McGhee, 1989).

Culture is at work in each and every encounter between educators and culturally and linguistically diverse children and their families. Each participant is working from his or her cultural reference (Samovar & Porter, 1995). All too often, the cultural values, curricular standards, and teaching practices that characterize childcare and educational organizations are grounded in dominant cultural values (see Chapter 6). Children whose families share cultural values similar to those of the educational settings and of the educators are more likely to succeed; those from different cultural backgrounds will not because of dissonance between the organizational and home cultures. It is critical that educators understand the integral relationship between language and culture and that they interpret student behaviors within a cultural context (Cartledge & Kourea, 2008). Otherwise, it is impossible to provide care and education that is linguistically and culturally responsive.

To develop cultural responsiveness, teachers need to understand their own culture and develop a "sociocultural consciousness" or awareness that culture is the lens through which individuals see the world (Ladson-Billings, 1995). This helps them understand that just as their behavior reflects their personal cultural background, so does that of the children and families with whom they work. Culturally competent educators feel comfortable, and effective, in working with children and families whose cultures and life experiences differ from their own (Lynch & Hanson, 2011). They establish linkages with families and communities and empower them as true partners in their children's education. Learning from, rather than about, a family assumes that the family is the expert about their children and their lives, and the teacher is the learner (see Chapter 6). This facilitates equalization of power dynamics between families and educators.

To implement a strength-based, family-centered approach when working with DLLs, educators must understand the child's sociocultural context, including the historical, sociopolitical, and economic forces that impact diverse families' lives and, ultimately, the decisions they make as family members of young bilingual learners and young bilingual children with disabilities. In culturally responsive programs for DLLs, linguistic and cultural differences are viewed as assets, and children's "funds of knowledge" (Moll *et al.*, 1992), the knowledge and skills they acquire in their homes and communities and that help define their cultural identities, are celebrated and incorporated in the process of teaching and learning (US Department of Education, Office of Planning Evaluation and Policy Development, 2012). DLLs are provided with multiple opportunities to develop their personal identities and positive attitudes about themselves and to develop an understanding of the culture of others (US Department of Education, Office of Planning Evaluation and Policy Development, 2012). The culture of schools is made visible, and the basis and rationale for norms and expectations are explicitly communicated. Children are taught that different people, in different settings, have different norms and expectations for behavior and that they may have to adapt their behavior to that context. Teachers help them understand that the process of acculturation or cross-cultural competence does not make their own culturally based behavior wrong or less valuable.

Not surprisingly, incorporating funds of knowledge in the teaching-learning process has positive effects on student achievement. Moreover, in-depth knowledge of students' background and home contexts helps teachers to challenge the notion that marginalized groups lack social and cultural capital.

Socioeconomic status

Bilingualism is often associated with culturally and linguistically diverse children who live in poverty. For example, Hispanic children are twice more likely to live in poverty than non-Hispanic children (Gamboa, 2015). In addition, children from recent immigrant families are typically from low SES families and are more likely to use a language other than English at home (Bohman *et al.*, 2010). When the risks associated with poverty occur during preschool years, they have longlasting consequences (Engle & Black, 2008). The gap between educational outcome for students significantly behind their peers on measures of school readiness (e.g., physical health, socio-emotional development, cognitive abilities, language development) is predictive of almost all educational benchmarks, including truancy, behavior problems, achievement test scores, grade retention, special education placement, and school attrition. For example, children from low SES backgrounds tend to receive reduced language input in comparison to children from higher SES levels, which affects their vocabulary development (Hart & Risley, 1995). This makes it difficult to determine whether low performance is the result of economic disadvantage or the presence of disabilities. According to Engle and Black (2008), access to high-quality child care and early education programs, characterized by access to educators with expertise specific to working with children from low-income homes, small teacher-to-child ratios, implementation of an evidence-based curriculum, and interventions of sufficient intensity and duration to ensure that children achieve learning goals, minimizes the negative effects of poverty. These are the hallmark of Recognition and Response (R&R), a multi-tiered system of support framework in early childhood education (discussed in a later section).

Research-based Practice in the Education of English Learners

Child development is the result of complex interactions between, and among, the child, family, community, environmental factors, and societal forces (Bronfenbrenner, 1979). Therefore, when large numbers of children from an identifiable group (e.g., racial/ethnic, language background) fail, the focus has to shift away from locating the problem within students to examining the characteristics of schools, programs, and personnel that may produce "pedagogically-induced" learning disabilities (Cummins, 1986). Cummins' (1986, 1989) framework for empowering language minority students is grounded in the premise that the educational system, and the societal values it reflects, are instrumental variables in the success (empowerment) or failure (disabling) of students of color and students from low-income communities. As Cummins so clearly articulates, culturally and linguistically diverse children fail when (a) educators assume subtractive, rather than additive, orientations toward students' native languages and cultures; (b) family and community members are excluded from their children's schooling because they are perceived as having little to offer in support of their children's education; (c) assessment approaches locate the sources of achievement problems in students themselves, ignoring the influence of factors such as the cultures of schools and educators; and (d) instruction is teacher-led rather than student directed. Improving the achievement of DLLs and ELs requires that educators challenge unequal power relationships and, instead, promote linguistic and cultural diversity and communicate an unwavering confidence that English learners can, and will, succeed.

Children with disabilities and their families from diverse language communities often face challenges that are intersected by issues of poverty, language, race, gender, culture, immigration status, and ethnicity. Adelman's (1992) typology of the causes of learning problems helps educators distinguish among root causes of learning problems, including those resulting from inadequacies of the instructional environment (Type I), from the interaction between individual and environmental characteristics (Type II), or from the presence of disabilities (Type III). Multi-layered analyses of the intersections of individual, environmental, and organizational factors help ensure that interventions address the actual problem, not just the symptoms associated with student failure (García & Ortiz, 2013). Unless prevention and early intervention strategies are in place to address the needs of Type I and Type II learning problems, educators will inaccurately conclude that learning problems are an artifact of the presence of disabilities (Type III); this, in turn, will maintain persistent patterns of disproportionate representation of multicultural populations in special education.

The success of programs and services for young DLLs requires a shift of focus away from locating problems only within students to also examining environmental and organizational factors that influence educational outcomes. Accountability requirements of the Every Student Succeeds Act of 2015, and its precursor, the No Child Left Behind Act of 2001, require that schools and districts disaggregate achievement data by race/ethnicity, socioeconomic status, language proficiency, and disability. Interventions are then designed to improve performance of subgroups that do not meet achievement standards, ignoring that many students are members of two or more, and sometimes all, of these accountability subgroups (e.g., a Latino student from a low-income home who is an English learner and has been identified as a student with disabilities). Theoretical frameworks such as Cummins' (1986, 1989) empowerment framework and typologies such as those proposed by Adelman (1992) underscore that programs and services for DLLs and ELs cannot be improved when educational organizations adopt a systems model of service delivery that integrates the medical model (disability in the context of pathology and impairment), the social model (disability as a social construction reflecting social class, racial/ethnic, and cultural influences), and the transactional model (disability in the context of child and family interactions with institutions such as schools and social service agencies) (García & Ortiz, 2008). The intersection of language status and disability is not often considered in policy approaches but, rather, they areviewed as mutually exclusive characteristics. This hinders implementation of appropriate educational services for dual language and English language learners with disabilities and often results in misdiagnosis of language differences as disabilities.

Effective programs for DLLs and ELs

Children from birth to age 5 who are from families with incomes below the poverty guidelines are eligible for Head Start and Early Head Start services. Early Head Start serves pregnant women or families who have an infant from 0 to 12 months of age or an infant from 0 to 18 months of age with a certified disability. The goal of Early Head Start is to provide early, continuous, intensive, and comprehensive child development and family support services ((US Department of Health & Human Services and Administration for Children & Families, 2019).

Services are provided both through home- and center-based services (for eligible children ages 6 weeks to 30 months) that focus on early childhood development as well as health and nutrition and parenting skills. Children from birth to age 3 who are at risk or have documented delays or disabilities are served under Part C of the Individuals with Disabilities Education Act (IDEA). Head Start also has a mandate to ensure that 10% of children enrolled are identified with a disability. There is, therefore, some overlap between the populations served through Part C and Early Head Start.

Language Instruction Educational Programs (LIEPs) for ELs typically follow one of two approaches (US Department of Education, Office of Planning Evaluation and Policy Development, 2012). In English as a second language (ESL) programs, language and content/subject matter are taught in English, almost exclusively, although the native language can be used as a scaffold (e.g., translating vocabulary words into the native language to communicate a concept that students are having difficulty understanding). At the elementary level, ESL is provided on a pull-out or push-in basis; at the secondary level, students enroll in ESL classes and/or receive sheltered English instruction in content classes. Across grades, the majority of ELs, almost 85%, are served in ESL programs (National Center for Education Statistics, 2004). In contrast, bilingual education programs (e.g., one-way and two-way dual language programs, transitional and maintenance bilingual education) provide both native language and English as a second language instruction. These programs are based on an increasing body of research indicating that ELs who receive L1 instruction achieve better than those who do not and that L1 skills contribute positively to students' acquisition of a second language (August & Shanahan, 2006; Collier & Thomas, 2004; Genesee *et al.*, 2005; Goldenberg, 2008). DLLs who do not meet the criteria for classification as ELs are typically taught in English-only general education classrooms. This is also the case for ELs whose parents refuse placement in an LIEP. Whether DLLs in mainstream classes receive any native language support depends on their teachers' own language skills and their familiarity with best practices in educating children from homes where a language other than English is present.

Multi-tiered systems of support for DLLs

Multi-tiered systems of support (MTSS) that include Response to Intervention (RTI) approaches represent systemic approaches to the improvement of the education of young children because of their emphasis on providing equitable access to core instruction to all students and their emphasis on differentiation of instruction to meet the needs of individual students and groups of students. This is also the case for Recognition and Response (R&R) frameworks, the early childhood education equivalent of RTI (Buysse & Peisner-Feinberg, 2013). Both R&R and RTI for DLLs and ELs include a focus on prevention of behavioral and achievement difficulties through an effective core curriculum, early intervention for children performing below expected levels, and special education processes that are valid for second language learners. Results of classroom-based universal screening and progress monitoring tools are used to plan and redirect instruction and to identify students who may need supplemental interventions to master learning objectives. Teachers use intentional teaching strategies to deliver a high-quality, developmentally appropriate core curriculum (Tier 1) and provide supplemental, small-group intervention for students performing below expected levels (Tier 2). Targeted intervention in identified areas of need is typically provided in groups of three to six students, 15 to 30 minutes a day, for a time of sufficient duration to meet learning goals (e.g., three to six months). Students who continue to experience difficulty receive even more intensive, individualized supports to address skills gaps (Tier 3). R&R models do not specifically address the needs of DLLs, but research on elementary-age English learners suggests that the focus on early intervention and ongoing progress monitoring is beneficial for all DLLs, particularly in terms of building foundational skills for language and literacy development.

Essential components of R&R and RTI frameworks

For RTI and R&R models to benefit DLLs, they must be implemented by educators with expertise specific to DLLs and must accommodate children's cultural background and linguistic proficiency across the curriculum (Artiles & Kozleski, 2010; Brown & Doolittle, 2008). The essential elements of R&R and RTI frameworks are a systematic assessment program, including universal screening, progress monitoring, and benchmarking, effective core instruction for all students, and increasingly intensive supplemental intervention for children performing below expected levels.

Effective assessment

Assessment programs for DLLs typically involve eligibility assessments, e.g., language proficiency tests to determine initial and continuing eligibility for enrollment in bilingual education and ESL programs, screening and curriculum-based assessments to monitor progress in relation to the actual instruction and to identify struggling learners, and accountability assessments to determine whether students have met grade-level content and district or state-mandated achievement standards (Ortiz *et al.*, 2018). As indicated previously, teachers use these data to plan and deliver instruction, pinpoint specific areas of difficulty for students performing below expected levels, and evaluate the effectiveness of instruction and intervention. In early childhood education programs, teachers use the Assessment Cycle to gather information about children and plan instruction (Dichtelmiller, 2011). The cycle involves observing and collecting information about children's knowledge, skills, and behaviors in the context of daily routines at home and at school. These data are then used to establish learning objectives and determine how much scaffolding a child will need to achieve those objectives. Teachers continuously evaluate ongoing observation and portfolio data to determine progress toward mastery of the objectives and to communicate this information to parents and fellow educators.

Assessments are only as good as the measures used to obtain them. Therefore, to limit bias and increase the likelihood of accurate assessment results, educators must (a) use instruments and procedures designed for DLLs and/or ELs, or that included representative samples of these students in instrument development; (b) ensure that assessment tools are valid and reliable; (c) use equivalent assessments in the native language and in English; (d) correlate results of formal assessments with informal, curriculum-based measures; and (e) interpret results in relationship to students' levels of native language and English proficiency (Ortiz *et al.*, 2018; Ortiz & Yates, 2002). Unfortunately, even though linguistic diversity is a defining characteristic of DLLs and limited English proficiency is a defining characteristic of ELs, oral language assessment data are not routinely available for educational planning purposes, in all likelihood because of the limited availability of oral language screening, assessment, and progress monitoring tools specifically for these students (Ortiz *et al.*, 2018). Available formal assessment instruments and informal oral language measures should routinely be used to describe students' receptive and expressive language skills in social and academic contexts, in the native language and in English. In assessing performance in language and other domains, dynamic assessment procedures can reduce bias and possibly reduce overrepresentation of DLLs in special education (Kapantzoglou *et al.*, 2012; Peña *et al.*, 2014). If it is not feasible to assess native language skills, then progress toward achieving age-appropriate English proficiency should continuously be monitored. By examining language proficiency and achievement data, in combination, teachers can more easily see what they need to teach, in which language, and with what supports. They are then able to evaluate the results of language instruction and intervention and are in a better position to distinguish language differences from language disorder.

Effective instruction

Response to Intervention models suggest that, with effective core instruction, 75–80% of students, including DLLs, should meet grade-level expectations (Klingner *et al.*, 2008; Shapiro, 2014). For example, the majority of students in bilingual education classes are expected to make progress, in both languages, across all domains, consistent with the language(s) of core instruction. The majority of ELs in ESL programs are expected to meet language and content standards consistent with their level of English proficiency and the ESL supports provided. If there are patterns of limited performance for identifiable groups of DLLs (e.g., those from low-income homes), the focus should shift to improving core instruction and ensuring that the curriculum is responsive to the needs of these students. This may require changing or adapting the instructional programs, verifying fidelity of implementation of curriculum and instruction, and/or identifying practices that are most effective for individuals and groups of students (Ortiz *et al.*, 2018). Increasing the effectiveness of core instruction may also necessitate differentiating instruction to accommodate varying levels of L1 and L2 proficiency, different ages and grades, and diverse educational coaching to ensure that teachers have the requisite knowledge and skills to foster student success.

Effective instruction for ELLs includes explicit skill instruction in the context of higher-order skills. For example, literacy instruction focuses on both skills and meaning and incorporates the components that have been shown to be determinants of literacy achievement for both monolingual students and ELLs: phonemic awareness, phonics, fluency, vocabulary, and comprehension, as well as study strategies (Goldenberg, 2008; Snow *et al.*, 1998). Teachers draw on students' prior experiences, linking their funds of knowledge (Moll *et al.*, 1992) to what they need to learn. Curriculum and instruction provide opportunities for students to develop the conversational and academic language proficiency needed to understand classroom language use (e.g., teacher talk and the language of texts and related materials) across the content areas (Gersten *et al.*, 2007).

Once language and literacy performance levels have been established through universal screenings, it is important to examine whether core instruction (i.e., Tier 1) has been implemented with fidelity, is consistent with students' proficiency in each language, has been differentiated to address L1 and/or L2 needs of individual students, and has utilized culturally responsive strategies known to be effective for ELs (Hoover & Erickson, 2015; Ortiz *et al.*, 2011; Wilkinson *et al.*, 2006). Culturally responsive strategies ensure that students have access to curriculum and instruction and such strategies empower them intellectually, socially, emotionally, and politically by using cultural referents and their background experiences to impart knowledge, skills, and attitudes (Ladson-Billings, 1994). Among high-leverage strategies for English learners are student-centered learning, peer interaction and collaboration, experiential learning, and personalized, differentiated support. Strategies for ensuring high levels of language proficiency(ies) include consistent exposure to the language(s) of instruction, flexible language use, native language instruction and/or strategic use of the native language when instruction is in English, the use of scaffolds (e.g., visuals, advance organizers, repetition and review), explicit vocabulary instruction, and a focus on developing metalinguistic awareness and transfer of skills across languages.

Effective intervention

In addition to core instruction, some students will require supplemental interventions to ensure that they master social and academic goals and objectives. These interventions are provided in addition to, they do not replace, core instruction. Explicit skill instruction must incorporate a focus on language development in the native language and/or in English, depending on the language(s) of instruction, with emphasis given to developing vocabulary knowledge (Cavazos & Ortiz, 2014). If instruction is in English only, ESL strategies, including native language supports (e.g., native language previews, interpretation, bilingual dictionaries, native language books or videos) should be used to ensure that children understand the language and content of the lessons. As interventions are planned and implemented, it is important to incorporate strategies and procedures that allow for frequent and continuous monitoring of student progress. Progress monitoring data gathered during intervention can be used to group and regroup students, to further adapt instruction, and to determine whether intervention goals have been met (Klingner *et al.*, 2008). Documentation of the specific nature of supplemental interventions and the results of progress measures provides evidence that students have had appropriate instruction and helps identify what interventions have, and have not, been successful (Ortiz *et al.*, 2018). When student difficulties persist, even after high-quality interventions have been provided over time, the student should be referred to the school's campus-based problem-solving team (e.g., grade-level team) and/or to an R&R or RTI team. A special education referral may be considered when the evidence indicates that the student has not made sufficient progress, despite supplemental interventions that are specifically aligned with identified needs, are sufficiently intense, and adequately assessed.

Identifying and Serving ELs with Disabilities

ELs often have complex histories that can make it difficult to provide appropriate instruction or to know what constitutes adequate progress. Struggling learners may not receive appropriate core instruction that addresses both their language learning and academic needs, may not receive high-quality supplemental interventions in a timely manner, and the results of interventions may not be given enough consideration before a special education referral is initiated (Ortiz *et al.*, 2018; Wilkinson *et al.*, 2006).

Special education referral

To make a referral decision, educators must consider data about multiple factors that have an impact on student performance, including students' native language and English proficiency, the instructional programs in which students have been enrolled, the language(s) of instruction, significant life events, the validity of assessments used to establish performance levels, and the timeliness and quality of interventions provided to students experiencing learning difficulties.

Full and individual evaluations

The Full and Individual Evaluation (FIE) must be provided and administered in the language and form that is most likely to yield accurate information on what the child knows and can do academically, developmentally, and functionally, unless it is not feasible to do so (Individuals with Disabilities Education Improvement Act, 2004).

There are times when bilingual personnel are not available, and monolingual clinicians must conduct assessments in bilingual populations. Monolingual assessors must have deep understanding of bilingual children, bilingual language development, and cultural differences and be trained in techniques to limit bias in the assessment process, including the use of interpreters. When children are referred to special education, eligibility determinations must be based on culturally and linguistically responsive assessment practices.

Assessment personnel should select formal assessment tools that have been validated for DLLs and/or ELs and informal instruments and procedures that address the specific concerns articulated by the teacher, problem-solving teams, referral committees, and parents (Wilkinson et al., 2006). Unless they are being used for the express purpose of assessing proficiency in a particular language, ELs should receive credit for what they know and can do, regardless of the language(s) in which they demonstrate knowledge and skills. That is, students should receive credit for correct answers in Spanish, even though the test prompt was in English. Likewise, correct answers that incorporate translanguaging strategies should be given full credit. Not to do so ignores research that shows that ELs call on all their linguistic resources to understand and make meaning and that assessing each language independently underestimates their true abilities (Grosjean, 1989).

Parent/family input is an important element of the assessment process because it provides valuable information about children's language acquisition, communication effectiveness, and behavior in the context of the home and the community. Information collected from parents regarding possible developmental delays has been shown to be valid and reliable and offer a rich and accurate surveillance method and enable providers to monitor development and to decide which students should be referred and when (Glascoe, 2000). These data will help educators interpret similarities and differences in performance between home and school and identify potential sources of communication, behavior, or achievement difficulties (Ortiz et al., 2018; Wilkinson et al., 2006).

To mitigate against inappropriate identification of disabilities, the Individuals with Disabilities Education Improvement Act (Individuals with Disabilities Education Improvement Act, 2004) requires that educators address what is popularly referred to as the "exclusionary clause." That is, they must provide assurances that students' learning problems are not primarily the result of limited English proficiency, cultural factors, environmental or economic disadvantage, or lack of access to appropriate instruction [CFR § 300.306(b)(1)(i)(iii)]. For example, children from low SES backgrounds typically perform below expected levels on standardized tests because these measures are experience-dependent and require that students respond using standard English. Therefore, during the assessment process, it is difficult to determine whether low language skills are the result of lack of access to, or differences in, the quantity and quality of the input or are due to language learning difficulties. In the case of DLLs and ELs, ruling out these factors requires evidence and documentation that students have not made the expected progress despite having high-quality native language and/or ESL support specifically targeted to improve language skills critical to school success. Similar evidence must be presented for the supplemental interventions provided to children experiencing language- or literacy-related difficulties.

Reporting and interpreting results

The assessment report should describe the nature of evaluations (e.g., they were conducted by a bilingual professional, assessments were administered only in English, or the assessor used an interpreter) and any adaptations of instruments or procedures (e.g., use of translated instruments). Assessors should correlate results with the results of other data, such as that obtained from informal assessments and with outcomes of early intervention efforts. Most importantly, they should correlate results with the referral reasons, the student's schooling history (e.g., language proficiency characteristics and how these have changed over time; academic progress within and across grades), and with the questions posed by the referral agent(s). The basis for a recommendation that the student qualifies for special education should go beyond simply documenting test results. This is particularly important when assessment results do not corroborate the original reasons for referral. If they are recommending special education services, assessors should make recommendations for instruction, including accommodations and adaptations that will increase the likelihood of student success.

Determining eligibility

Special education eligibility determinations should be made by multidisciplinary teams (MDT) that include representatives with expertise in the education of DLLs and ELs (Ortiz & Yates, 2002). The teams should include personnel who have been key players in the student's instructional program and those who participated in early intervention activities designed to resolve student difficulties. For example, if the student has been in an ESL program, both the general education and the ESL teachers should serve on the MDT. Instructional specialists who provided supplemental instruction should also be invited to participate. If assessment personnel have not been trained to assess ELLs, someone who can interpret assessment data from the perspective of cultural and linguistic diversity would be an important addition to the team. Parents should also be invited to attend, and an interpreter should be provided, if needed, to allow family members to participate meaningfully in team meetings (Ortiz et al., 2018; Ortiz & Yates, 2001).

Full and Individual Evaluation (FIE) data (which provide a detailed assessment of the student's various domains of development), along with documentation of the results of general education instruction and early intervention efforts, should be the basis of special education eligibility determinations. MDTs must assure that the FIE represents best practices in the assessment of ELLs and that they have the data needed to rule out limited English proficiency, cultural or other background characteristics, or lack of appropriate instruction as the cause of student difficulties (Ortiz et al., 2011; Ortiz et al., 2018; Wilkinson et al., 2006). If the student is eligible, an IEP will be developed and the least restrictive environment for serving the student will be selected.

Individualized Education Programs (IEPs)

IEPs should (a) identify students' levels of language proficiency in the native language and in English; (b) specify the language(s) of instruction; (c) provide for language intervention to support native language development and/or English acquisition; (d) include a language use plan indicating who will be responsible for which goals and objectives and in which language; and (e) outline instructional recommendations consistent with the principles of culturally and linguistically responsive curriculum and instruction (Ortiz et al., 2018; Ortiz & Yates, 2008).

DLLs and ELs identified as students with disabilities are held to the same high standards as their native English-speaking peers, although it is recognized that they may not make progress toward meeting those standards at the same rate or pace as nondisabled peers (ESSA, 2015; IDEA, 2004). For most students with special needs, goals and standards remain the same but the sequence of objectives is modified, and specialized teaching strategies and materials are developed to meet their specific educational needs (Christensen et al., 2009; Seppanen et al., 1995). For students with severe disabilities, additional standards may have to be developed to meet the needs of these students. For example, standards may be extended to include goals related to independent living, community integration, and school-to-work transition. In all cases, indicators that students have met expected standards will likely vary according to the students' ages, grades, developmental levels, and disabilities. Instructional programs for DLLs and ELs with disabilities must additionally consider how to implement performance standards while simultaneously addressing students' cultural characteristics and language needs, as well as their identified disabilities (Cloud, 2002). In addition to content standards, these students will also be assessed on progress toward meeting English-as-a-second-language standards. These include learning to use English for social and academic purposes and in culturally appropriate ways (Short, 2000).

Educators should not assume that ELs should be taught in English. ELs who are eligible for special education services do not lose their right to bilingual education. They have the right to pedagogically sound programs that not only meet needs associated with their disabilities but that also accommodate their language status. If students have not acquired the language of their parents or caretakers through the normal process of language acquisition, it is unlikely that they will be able to acquire English skills more easily. Students need to develop their native language foundation as a basis for skill development in English. Thus, ELLs with disabilities should receive instruction in their native language with ESL instruction, as appropriate. The language of instruction decision is, of course, driven by current data about the student's native language dominance and proficiency and previous schooling history. Even when the decision is to provide English-only instruction, educators should provide native language support whenever possible and should reinforce to parents that continuing to use their native language at home is critical to building the foundation for English acquisition (Coelho, 2004). IEPs should incorporate recommendations that parents can use in the home context to support their child's education, including, for example, native language stimulation through activities like talking, telling stories, and reading or looking at books.

Preparing Educators to Work Effectively with these Students

Educator preparation programs have not responded adequately to demographic changes in the US student population or to the increasing number of ELs enrolled in today's schools. For example, in 2008, just over 20 states explicitly required teachers to have certification specific to teaching ELs (Ballantyne et al., 2008). Another 19 states allude to requiring specialized training for teachers of ELs, but their certification requirements were unclear. Highly qualified teachers are key to the success of ELs. Of candidates who earned a bachelor's degree in elementary education in 2016, only 2% majored in multilingual or multicultural education and only 4% in English-as-a-second-language instruction (King, 2018). Moreover, a survey conducted by the National

Council on Teacher Quality found that only 24% of teacher preparation programs included strategies for teaching English learners in key areas, such as reading or support for struggling readers (Greenberg *et al.*, 2013).

Because ELs are the fastest growing subgroup of public school students (Education Commission of the States, 2013), all educators will likely serve ELs and ELs with disabilities over the course of their professional careers. Ortiz and Robertson (2018) identify foundational knowledge and skills needed by educators who provide language and literacy instruction for ELs and ELs with disabilities (pp. 181–183). These skills also apply to those working with the general population of DLLs.

Language and linguistics

Educators understand native language development, including its role in second language acquisition; the stages of second language acquisition; language variation; and the relationship between language and literacy acquisition (Fillmore & Snow, 2000). They understand the basic structures of language (e.g., phonology, morphology, syntax, semantics, pragmatics) and how the similarities and differences between languages influence one another (e.g., dialectal variations, the transfer of linguistic features across languages). In addition, they recognize the advantages of, and promote, bilingualism and biliteracy.

Cultural variability

Culturally competent teachers are aware of their own cultural identity and how it influences their values, beliefs, and worldviews (Pratt-Johnson, 2006). They work to understand students' cultural backgrounds and strive to integrate culturally based norms, experiences, and funds of knowledge (Gonzáles *et al.*, 2005) in instruction and intervention (Orosco & O'Connor, 2014).

Educational contexts

Educators are familiar with theories, philosophies, approaches, policy, and law related to the education of ELs. They are also able to apply principles of universal design in creating linguistically and culturally responsive learning environments that accommodate individual differences (National Center on Universal Design for Learning, 2017).

Literacy foundations

Teachers understand essential components of literacy instruction for ELs, as well as the interrelationships among listening, speaking, reading, and writing development and select and design developmentally appropriate, research-based language and literacy instruction for ELs.

Language and literacy assessment

Teachers of ELs are equipped to assess oral language skills in the native language and in English, and literacy skills in English, and in the native language if the student has had native language literacy instruction (Robertson et al., 2017). In interpreting performance, educators understand the importance of comparing performance of ELs experiencing difficulties to peers who have similar language proficiency, cultural and experiential background, and learning characteristics (i.e., "true peers"; Brown & Doolittle, 2008).

Instruction/intervention

Educators provide opportunities for students to develop full and productive proficiencies in the native language and/or English, consistent with high expectations for all students (August & Hakuta, 1997; Goldenberg, 2008). They provide challenging curriculum and instruction that nest basic skill development in the context of higher-order thinking and problem solving. Because it provides the foundation for achieving high levels of English, native language instruction or support is a key instructional strategy in schools where ELLs experience academic success (Cummins, 1981, 1986; Krashen, 1991; Snow et al., 1998). Whether students are in a bilingual education or an ESL program, teachers provide a structured program of English language development. General education teachers also support ELLs in their classroom by using similar strategies.

Collaboration

Educators share knowledge and expertise across programs and accept joint responsibility for planning and implementing instruction to address the complex needs of ELs, including those who require more intensive intervention (García & Ortiz, 2008; Ortiz et al., 2011).

Professional and ethical practice

Teachers continuously assess their own strengths and needs in serving ELs, including those with language- and/or literacy-related difficulties and disabilities (Cartledge & Kourea, 2008). They participate in ongoing professional development and communities of practice (Mak & Pun, 2015) and seek mechanisms for increasing knowledge and skills to enhance their teaching practices. They also advocate for students and their families and for linguistically and culturally responsive policies and practices at the local, state, and national levels to help ensure equity and access of educational opportunity for ELs. Comprehensive and asset-based perspectives capitalize on students' social and cultural capital and build on students' strengths and needs (National Academies of Sciences, Engineering, and Medicine, 2017).

In addition to the competencies listed above, working with families is a critical competency for educators who work with young DLLs and their families.

Working with families

An authentic and reciprocated relationship-building approach to working with families is not only more beneficial for the overall development of young children with disabilities, but it is also more likely to forge a strong link between families, communities, and schools that can help families develop the strong lifelong skills needed to advocate for the services needed by their children. Educators must work to eliminate barriers to family involvement, including racial and cultural stereotypes and power imbalances resulting from racial/ethnic, cultural, and class differences (Gay, 2013). For example, they make sure that parents and families understand their children's rights to appropriate, fair, and equitable educational opportunities that are responsive to their children's linguistic, cultural, and academic needs. They help parents understand their right to participate in decisions affecting their children's education and to receive timely information about academic progress. Advocates stress the importance of allowing different forms of parent engagement (or non-engagement) and recognize the benefits of grassroots efforts in which parents and community members work together to advocate for programs and services that reflect their personal concerns and needs. Parent engagement is more likely to be sustained when it reflects family and community priorities and mutually respectful, supportive relationships among families, community members, and educators.

In summary, teacher education programs should assess the strengths of their programs and areas where improvement is needed and should develop plans to prepare prospective teachers to meet the needs of students acquiring English as a second language and being served in LIEPs. In the light of demographic data that show that public school student enrollment is now "majority-minority" and that ELs are the fastest growing subgroup (McFarland *et al.*, 2017), teacher education programs that prepare teachers to serve ELs should be the norm rather than the exception.

Ongoing professional development

Teachers must have a repertoire of effective instructional practices for working with English learners. If they do not, they must have professional development that familiarizes them with these practices, which models and demonstrates their implementation, and provides access to coaches who can help teachers use these practices in their own classes and provide feedback to facilitate effective use of these practices (Ortiz & Robertson, 2018). A comprehensive, customized approach to professional development includes follow-up supports, through embedded participation and increased learning and implementation of newly learned instructional practices.

In effective schools for ELLs, professional development activities ensure that teachers share a common knowledge base concerning the education of diverse learners (García et al., 1995; Ortiz, 2002). All educators, including related services personnel and instructional coaches and specialists, regularly participate in professional development that focuses on second language acquisition; the relationship of the native language to the development of English proficiency; assessment of native language and English as a second language proficiency; sociocultural influences on learning; native language and English as a second language teaching methodology; assessment strategies for determining students' first and/or second language proficiency and for monitoring progress, particularly in relation to language and literacy development; and strategies for working with culturally and linguistically diverse families and communities (Ortiz, 2002). Fully credentialed, highly qualified bilingual and ESL teachers continuously acquire new knowledge regarding best practices in the education of ELLs, and fully credentialed, highly qualified general and special education teachers develop a repertoire of skills and knowledge to ensure the success of ELLs (Montecel & Cortez, 2002).

Next Steps: Research Available and Needed

Although more is needed, there does exist a knowledge base associated with the education of these students and the ways to enhance early childhood, general education, and special education policies and practices to better serve these learners. Researchers have documented cultural influences on teaching and learning, the processes involved in second language acquisition, the important advantage of using the native language(s) in instruction, and effective techniques for native and English-as-a-second-language instruction (Cummins, 2007). Ignoring available research leaves educators with few options but to generalize the outcomes of studies conducted with native English speakers. This may explain why legislation, policy, and laws, aimed at closing the achievement gap and resolving disproportionate representation, have failed to do so.

The education of CLD students cannot be improved until research more closely represents the demography of the nation's public schools and of students with special education needs. Culturally and linguistically diverse researchers who can lend an "insider" perspective must work with fellow researchers and educators to ensure that research and recommendations for service delivery based on findings are culturally and linguistically responsive. Research is needed to refine the existing body of knowledge associated with such topics as the disproportionate representation of DLL students in special education, distinguishing second language and dialectal differences from language and learning disabilities, and cultural differences in perceptions of disabilities. However, it is also important to focus on topics that have had little or no coverage in the research literature: DLLs with gifts and talents, those with severe cognitive or sensory disabilities, positive behavioral supports, Recognition and Response and Response to Intervention approaches provided in the native language or English as a second language, effective instructional arrangements for DLL and EL students with disabilities, and students with disabilities who speak languages other than Spanish.

The contributors to this volume have identified gaps in the research literature specific to dual language learners with, or at risk of having, developmental delays or disabilities. Among the topics covered are the following.

Language and linguistics

Research is needed on language development of English learners who are simultaneous and sequential bilinguals, including the roles of translanguaging and cross-linguistic transfer in second language acquisition. Such data are important in identifying children who may have developmental delays or disabilities and in ensuring that children have access to early intervention.

Sociocultural factors

Additional research is needed on the effects of sociocultural factors such as social class, racism, prejudice, discrimination, oppression, and deficit thinking on child development. Studies should include a focus on understanding family and community funds of knowledge and the contributions of these to child development. Research on cultural influences on communication emphasizes that the native language is the foundation for second language learning and that parents play a critical role in ensuring that their children develop effective communication skills and secure cultural identities. Research on sociocultural factors is crucial to ensuring that early care and early childhood personnel support native language and second language acquisition and provide culturally responsive learning environments. Researchers should continue to explore how organizational and educator cultures influence the teaching-learning process.

Learner development and individual differences

Development of appropriate programs and services for dual language learners and English learners is a complex task because of the heterogeneity of the population. Rather than focusing on single identity markers, like ethnicity or language proficiency, researchers must simultaneously examine the intersection of these and other sociocultural factors that influence child development. While research on dual language learners and English learners with mild/moderate disabilities is limited, research on children with severe disabilities is non-existent.

Literacy foundations

Understanding the interrelationships between oral language and literacy development in young children goes hand in hand with understanding the developmental stages of native language and English as a second language literacy and biliteracy development. Research in this domain should include a focus on literacy practices in the homes of dual language learners and English learners and explore how parents and families can support literacy development under varying conditions (e.g., diversity of language(s) spoken in the home, parent literacy). Research should also examine how oral traditions (e.g., storytelling) support literacy acquisition. Debunking deficit orientations – that parents lack the social and cultural capital or that they do not value education – should be a central goal of this research.

Educational contexts

Educators need information about the characteristics of schools and learning environments, including Culturally and Linguistically responsive (CLR) Recognition and Response, Multi-tiered Systems of Support, and Response to Intervention frameworks that support dual language learners and English learners. They also need access to inclusive education models and practices for dual language learners and English learners with, or at risk of having, developmental delays or disabilities. Research on effective educational contexts and practices can advance state and federal laws, regulations, and policies to ensure that students achieve their maximum social, academic, and economic potential.

Assessment

School, classroom, and child-level instructional planning depends on valid and reliable assessments for dual language learners and English learners in early care and early childhood programs. In particular, research is needed on valid and reliable tools for several purposes, including screening and progress monitoring in the areas of oral language and literacy development and special education eligibility assessments for young children. Evaluation research on the outcomes of early childhood education for dual language learners and English learners, with or at risk of having developmental delays or disabilities, is crucial to program design. An important aspect of this work is the design of culturally and linguistically responsive accountability systems and instruments for this population.

Instruction/intervention

Educators are required to use evidence-based practices in instruction but find it difficult to do so because of the dearth of research on instruction and intervention for dual language learners and English learners, including those with, or at risk of having, developmental delays or disabilities. Research can provide guidance for the development of curricula, instructional materials, technology, and strategies that respond to the diversity of students' cultural backgrounds, range of language and literacy levels, and types and severity of disabilities. Research on multi-tiered systems of support, response to intervention, and recognition and response is essential to the development of criteria for distinguishing linguistic and cultural differences from disabilities. Intervention research could also lead to the development of effective programs and instructional strategies for young children with disabilities.

Collaboration

Models and strategies for consultation and collaboration to meet the needs of dual language learners and English learners with disabilities are essential to advancing the philosophy that educators and families have joint responsibility for the success of these students. Key to collaboration is building professional learning communities or communities of practice that bring together personnel across programs to capture the multidisciplinary expertise needed to address these students' complex needs.

Parents, families, communities

Understanding the linguistic and cultural environments in which children are reared is central to supporting child development and program planning and instruction. By examining how children's identity is formed and how their culture(s) is reflected in communication and behavior, teachers can implement strategies that ensure student success. Research is needed on family perceptions of abilities/disabilities and the resources that families have, or may need, to support their children with disabilities. Researchers should explore effective ways to ensure that parents have the knowledge, skills, and power to advocate for their rights and those of their children with developmental delays or disabilities.

Educator preparation

Finally, dual language learners and English learners have the right to an education provided by highly qualified early childhood education professionals. To that end, researchers should identify the essential characteristics and dispositions of prospective educators who will serve this student population. They must identify approaches to preservice and in-service preparation that will produce culturally and linguistically responsive educators with expertise specific to dual language learners and English learners with, or at risk of having, developmental delays or disabilities. Preparing a culturally competent educator workforce cannot be accomplished without culturally competent teacher educators.

Conclusion

In conclusion, researchers and practitioners must acknowledge the tremendous racial/ethnic, linguistic, and cultural diversity of this country and be prepared to meet the needs of dual language learners and English learners with, or at risk of having, developmental delays or disabilities. Working together, they can identify best practices in the education of these diverse populations and forge answers to one of the most important questions in education today: What works, for which learners, under what conditions, in what contexts, and in which language(s)?

References

Adelman, H.S. (1992) LD: The next 25 years. *Journal of Learning Disabilities* 25 (1), 17–22.
Administration for Children and Families (ACF) (2013) *Report to Congress on Dual Language Learners in Head Start and Early Head Start Programs*. Washington, DC: US Department of Health and Human Services.
Artiles, A.J. and Kozleski, E.B. (2010) What counts as response and intervention in RTI? A sociocultural analysis. *Psicothema* 22 (4), 949–954. Retrieved from https://www.redalyc.org/pdf/727/72715515062.pdf.
Artiles, A.J., Rueda, R., Salazar, J.J. and Higareda, I. (2005) Within-group diversity in minority disproportionate representation: English language learners in urban school districts. *Exceptional Children* 71, 283–300.
August, D. and Hakuta, K. (eds) (1997) *Educating Language-minority Children: A Research Agenda*. Washington, DC: National Academies Press.
August, D. and Shanahan, T. (2006) *Developing Literacy in Second Language Learners: Report of the National Literacy Panel for Language-Minority Children and Youth*. Mahwah, NJ: Lawrence Erlbaum.
Ballantyne, K.G., Sanderman, A.R. and Levy, J. (2008) *Educating English Language Learners: Building Teacher Capacity*. Washington, DC: National Clearinghouse for English Language Acquisition.

Banks, J.A. and McGhee, C.A. (1989) *Multicultural Education.* Needham Heights, MA: Allyn & Bacon.

Blanchett, W.J., Klingner, J.K. and Harry, B. (2009) The intersection of race, cultue, language, and disability: Implications for urban education. *Urban Education* 44 (4), 389–409.

Bohman, T.M., Bedore, L.M., Peña, E.D., Mendez-Perez, A. and Gillam, R.B. (2010) What you hear and what you say: Language performance in Spanish–English bilinguals. *International Journal of Bilingual Education and Bilingualism* 13 (3), 325–344.

Bronfenbrenner, U. (1979) *The Ecology of Human Development.* Cambridge, MA: Harvard University Press.

Brown, J.E. and Doolittle, J. (2008) A cultural, linguistic, and ecological framework for response to intervention with English language learners. *Teaching Exceptional Children* 40 (5), 66–72.

Buysse, V. and Peisner-Feinberg, E. (2013) Response to intervention: Conceptual foundations for the early childhood field. In V. Buysse and E.S. Peisner-Feinberg (eds) *Handbook of Response to Intervention in Early Childhood* (pp. 3–23). Baltimore, MD: Brookes Publishing.

Cartledge, G. and Kourea, L. (2008) Culturally responsive classrooms for culturally diverse students with and at risk for disabilities. *Exceptional Children* 74 (3), 351–371.

Cavazos, L. and Ortiz, A.A. (2014) Response to Intervention for English language learners with reading difficulties. Paper presented at the annual meeting of the National Association for Bilingual Education, San Diego, California.

Cavazos, L., Linán-Thompson, S. and Ortiz, A. (2018) Job-embedded professional development for teachers of English Learners: Preventing literacy difficulties through effective core instruction. *Teacher Education and Special Education* 41 (3), 203–214.

Chao, J., Schenkel, J. and Olsen, L. (2013) *Educating English Language Learners: Grantmaking Strategies for Closing America's Other Achievement Gap.* Portland, OR: Grantmakers for Education. Available from https://edfunders.org/sites/default/files/Educating%20English%20Language%20Learners_April%202013.pdf.

Child Trends (2016) *Dual Language Learners.* Bethesda, MD: Child Trends. Retrieved from. https://www.childtrends.org/indicators/dual-language-learners.

Child Trends (2018) *Trends in Immigrant Children.* Bethesda, MD: Child Trends. Retrieved from https://www.childtrends.org/indicators/immigrant-children.

Christensen, L.L., Thurlow, M.L. and Wang, T. (2009) *Improving Accommodations Outcomes: Monitoring Instructional and Assessment Accommodations for Students with Disabilities.* Minneapolis, MN: University of Minnesota, National Center on Educational Outcomes.

Cloud, N. (2002) Culturally and linguistically responsive instructional planning. In A.J. Artiles and A.A. Ortiz (eds) *English Language Learners with Special Education Needs: Identification, Assessment, and Instruction* (pp. 107–131). McHenry, IL: Center for Applied Linguistics and Delta Systems.

Coelho, E. (2004) *Adding English. A Guide to Teaching in Multilingual Classrooms.* Toronto: Pippin.

Collier, V.P. and Thomas, W.P. (2004) The astounding effectiveness of dual-language education for all. *NABE Journal of Research and Practice* 2 (1), 1–20.

Coutinho, M.J., Oswald, D.P. and Best, A.M. (2002) The influence of sociodemographic and gender identification on identification of minority students as having learning disabilities. *Journal of Special Education* 23 (1), 49–51.

Cummins, J. (1981) Age on arrival and immigrant second language learning in Canada. A reassessment. *Applied Linguistics* 2 (2), 132–149.

Cummins, J. (1986) Empowering minority students: A framework for intervention. *Harvard Educational Review* 56 (1), 18–37.

Cummins, J. (1989) A theoretical framework for bilingual special education. *Exceptional Children* 56 (2), 111–119.

Cummins, J. (2007) Rethinking monolingual instructional strategies in multilingual classrooms. *Canadian Journal of Applied Linguistics* 10 (2), 221–240.

Dichtelmiller, M.L. (2011) *The Power of Assessment: Transforming Teaching and Learning*. Washington, DC: Teaching Strategies.

Donovan, S.M.M. and Cross, C.T. (eds) (2002) *Minority Students in Special and Gifted Education*. Washington, DC: National Academies Press and the National Research Council Committee on Minority Representation in Special Education.

Education Commission of the States (2013) English language learners: A growing-yet underserved-student population. *Progress of Education Reform* 14 (6), 1–7.

Engle, P.L. and Black, M.M. (2008) The effect of poverty on child development and educational outcomes. *Annals of the New York Academy of Sciences* vol. 1136, pp. 243–256. Retrieved from https://nyaspubs.onlinelibrary.wiley.com/doi/full/10.1196/annals.1425.023.

ESSA (2015) Every Student Succeeds Act of 2015, Pub. L. No. 114-95 § 114 Stat.1177 (2015–2016).

Fillmore, L.W. and Snow, C.E. (2000) *What Teachers Need to Know about Language*. Washington, DC: Center for Applied Linguistics. Retrieved from http://www.ventrislearning.com/wp-content/uploads/2017/02/Wong_Fillmore-2000.pdf.

Gamboa, S. (2015) More Latino kids in low-income but more financially stable households. NBC Latino News. By Susan Gamboa, December 8, 2015. Retrieved from https://www.nbcnews.com/news/latino/more-latino-kids-financially-stable-low-income-households-n476146.

Gándara, P. (2018) The economic value of bilingualism in the United States. *Bilingual Research Journal* 41 (4), 334–343.

García, O. and Li Wei (2014) *Translanguaging: Language, Bilingualism, and Education*. London: Palgrave MacMillan.

García, S.B. and Ortiz, A.A. (2004) *Preventing Disproportionate Representation: Culturally and Linguistically Responsive Prereferral Intervention*. Denver, CO: National Center for Culturally Responsive Educational Systems (NCCRESt). Available from http://www.nccrest.org.

García, S.B. and Ortiz, A.A. (2008) A framework for culturally and linguistically responsive design of response-to-intervention models. *Multiple Voices* 11 (1), 24–41.

García, S.B. and Ortiz, A. (2013) Intersectionality as a framework for transformative research in special education. *Multiple Voices for Ethnically Diverse Exceptional Learners* 13 (2), 32–47.

García, S.B., Wilkinson, C.Y. and Ortiz, A.A. (1995) Enhancing achievement for language minority students: Classroom, school, and family contexts. *Education and Urban Society* 27 (4), 441–462.

Gay, G. (2013) Teaching to and through cultural diversity. *Curriculum Inquiry* 43 (1), 48–70.

Genesee, F., Lindholm-Leary, K., Saunders, W. and Christian, D. (2005) English language learners in US schools: An overview of research findings. *Journal of Education for Students Placed at Risk* 10 (4), 363–385.

Gersten, R., Baker, S.K., Shanahan, T., Linan-Thompson, S., Chiappe, P. and Scarcella, R. (2007) *Effective Literacy and English Language Instruction for English Learners in the Elementary Grades: A Practice Guide (NCEE 2007–4011)*. Washington, DC: National Center for Education Evaluation and Regional Assistance, Institute of Education Sciences, US. Department of Education.

Glascoe, F.P. (2000) Evidence-based approach to developmental and behavioural surveillance using parents' concerns. *Child: Care, Health and Development* 26 (2), 137–149.

Goldenberg, C. (2008) Teaching English language learners: What the research does - and does not - say. *American Educator* 32 (2), 8–44.

González, N., Moll, L.C. and Amanti, C. (eds) (2005) *Funds of Knowledge: Theorizing Practices in Households, Communities, and Classrooms*. Mahwah, NJ: Lawrence Erlbaum.

Greenberg, J., McKee, A. and Walsh, K. (2013) *Teacher Prep Review. A Review of the Nation's Teacher Preparation Programs*. Washington, DC: National Council on Teacher Quality. Retrieved from https://papers.ssrn.com/sol3/papers.cfm?abstract_id=2354106.

Grosjean, F. (1989) Neurolinguists, beware! The bilingual is not two monolinguals in one person. *Brain and Language* 36 (1), 3–15.

Hart, B. and Risley, T.R. (1995) *Meaningful Differences in the Everyday Experience of Young American Children*. Baltimore, MD: Brookes Publishing.

Hibel, J., Farkas, G. and Morgan, P.L. (2010) Who is placed into special education? *Sociology of Education* 83, 312–332.

Hoover, J.J. and Erickson, J. (2015) Culturally responsive special education referrals of English Learners in one rural county school district: Pilot project. *Rural Special Education Quarterly* 34 (4), 18–28.

IDEA (2004) Individuals with Disabilities Education Improvement Act, 20 U.S.C. 1400 (2004).

Kapantzoglou, M., Restrepo, M.A. and Thompson, M.S. (2012) Dynamic assessment of word learning skills: Identifying language impairment in bilingual children. *Language, Speech, and Hearing Services in Schools* 43 (1), 81–96.

Kids Count Data Center (2018) Child population by race and age group in the United States. Baltimore, MD: Annie E. Casey Foundation. Retrieved from https://datacenter.kidscount.org/data/tables/8446-child-population-by-race-and-age-group?loc=1&loct=1#detailed/1/any/false/871,870,573,869,36,868,867,133/68,69,67,12,70,66,71,13|62/17077,17078.

King, J.E. (2018) *Education Students and Diversity: A Review of New Evidence*. Washington, DC: American Association for Colleges of Teacher Education. Retrieved from https://aacte.org/colleges-of-education-a-national-portrait.

Klingner, J.K., Mendez Barletta, L. and Hoover, J.J. (2008) Response to intervention and English language learners. In J.K. Klinger, J.J. Hoover and L. Baca (eds) *Why Do English Language Learners Struggle with Reading? Distinguishing Language Acquisition from Learning Disabilities* (pp. 37–56). Thousand Oaks, CA: Corwin Press.

Krashen, S.D. (1991) *Bilingual Education: A Focus on Current Research*. Washington, DC: National Clearinghouse for Bilingual Education.

Krashen, S.D. and Terrell, T.D. (1983) *The Natural Approach: Language Acquisition in the Classroom*. Hayward, CA: Alemany Press.

Ladson-Billings, G. (1994) *The Dreamkeepers: Successful Teachers of African American Children*. San Francisco, CA: Josssey-Bass.

Ladson-Billings, G. (1995) Toward a theory of culturally relevant pedagogy. *American Educational Research Journal* 32 (3), 465–491.

Li, G. and Wang, L. (2008) *Model Minority Myth Revisited: An Interdisciplinary Approach to Demystifying Asian American Educational Experiences*. Charlotte, NC: Information Age Publishing.

Lynch, E.W. and Hanson, M.J. (2011) *Developing Cross-cultural Competence: A Guide for Working with Children and their Families* (4th edition). Baltimore, MD: Brookes Publishing.

Mak, B. and Pun, S. (2015) Cultivating a teacher community of practice for sustainable professional development: Beyond planned efforts. *Theory & Practice* 21 (1), 4–21.

McFarland, J. (2016) Diversity in home languages: Examining English learners in US public schools. NCES Blog, February 18, 2016. Retrieved from https://nces.ed.gov/blogs/nces/post/diversity-in-homelanguages-examining-english-learners-in-u-spublic-schools.

McFarland, J., Hussar, B., Zhang, J., Wang, X., Wang, K., Hein, S., Diliberti, M., Forrest Cataldi, E., Bullock Mann, F. and Barmer, A. (2019) *The Condition of Education 2019* (NCES 2019-144). US Department of Education. Washington, DC: National Center for Education Statistics. Retrieved from https://nces.ed.gov/pubs2019/2019144.pdf.

McFarland, J., Hussar, B., de Brey, C., Snyder, T., Wang, X., Wilkinson-Flicker, S., Gebrekristos, S., Zhang, J., Rathbun, A., Barmer, A., Bullock Mann, F. and Hinz, S. (2017) *The Condition of Education 2017* (NCES 2017–144). US Department of Education. Washington, DC: National Center for Education Statistics. Retrieved from https://nces.ed.gov/pubsearch/pubsinfo.asp?pubid=2017144.

Moll, L.C., Amanti, C., Neff, D. and González, N. (1992) Funds of knowledge for teaching: Using a qualitative approach to connect homes and classrooms. *Theory into Practice* 31, 132–141.

Montecel, M.R. and Cortez, J.D. (2002) Successful bilingual education programs: Development and dissemination of criteria to identify promising and exemplary practices in bilingual education at the national level. *Bilingual Research Journal* 26 (1), 1–21.

National Academies of Sciences, Engineering, and Medicine (NASEM) (2017) *Promoting the Educational Success of Children and Youth Learning English: Promising Futures*. Washington, DC: National Academies Press.

National Center for Education Statistics (2004) *Schools and Staffing Survey*. Table 6: Of schools that had limited-English-proficient (LEP) students, types of LEP programs, by school type and selected school characteristics: 2003-2004. Washington, DC: National Center for Education Statistics. Retrieved from https://nces.ed.gov/surveys/sass/tables/sass_2004_06.asp.

National Center for Education Statistics (2019) *Status and Trends in the Education of Racial and Ethnic Groups: Indicator 6: Elementary and Secondary Enrollment*. US Department of Education, Institute for Educational Sciences. Washington, DC: National Center for Education Statistics. Retrieved from https://nces.ed.gov/programs/raceindicators/indicator_RBB.asp.

National Center on Universal Design for Learning (2017) Universal design for learning guidelines. Retrieved from www.udlcenter.org/aboutudl/udlguidelinestheorypractice.

No Child Left Behind Act of 2001, PL 107–110, 115 Stat. 1425, 20 U. S. C. §§ 6301 et seq.

Orosco, M.J. and O'Connor, R. (2014) Culturally responsive instruction for English language learners with disabilities. *Journal of Learning Disabilities* 47 (6), 515–531.

Ortiz, A.A. (2002) Prevention of school failure and early intervention for English Language Learners. In A.J. Artiles and A.A. Ortiz (eds) *English Language Learners with Special Education Needs: Identification, Assessment, and Instruction* (pp. 31–48). Washington, DC: Center for Applied Linguistics and Delta Systems.

Ortiz, A.A. and Yates, J.R. (2001) A framework for serving English learners with disabilities. *Journal of Special Education Leadership* 14 (2), 72–80.

Ortiz, A.A. and Yates, J.R. (2002) Considerations in the assessment of English language learners referred to special education. In A.J. Artiles and A.A. Ortiz (eds) *English Language Learners with Special Education Needs: Identification, Assessment, and Instruction* (pp. 65–85). Washington, DC: Center for Applied Linguistics and Delta Systems.

Ortiz, A.A. and Yates, J.R. (2008) Enhancing scientifically based research for culturally and linguistically diverse exceptional learners. *Multiple Voices for Ethnically Diverse Learners* 11 (1), 13–23.

Ortiz, A.A. and Robertson, P.M. (2018) Preparing teachers to serve English learners with language-and/or literacy-related difficulties and disabilities. *Teacher Education and Special Education* 41 (3), 176–187.

Ortiz, A.A., Robertson, P.M and Wilkinson, C.Y. (2018) Language and iteracy assessment record for English learners in bilingual education: A framework for instructional planning and decision-making. *Preventing School Failure: Alternative Education for Children and Youth* 62 (4), 250–265.

Ortiz, A.A., Robertson, P.M., Wilkinson, C.Y, Liu, J. and McGhee, B.D. and Kushner, M. (2011) The role of bilingual education teachers in preventing inappropriate referrals of ELLs to special education: Implications for response to intervention. *Bilingual Research Journal: Journal of the Association for Bilingual Education* 34 (3), 316–333.

Otheguy, R., García, O. and Reid, W. (2015) Clarifying translanguaging and deconstructing named languages: A perspective from linguistics. *Applied Linguistics Review* 6 (3), 281–307.

Peña, E.D., Gillam, R.B. and Bedore, L.M. (2014) Dynamic assessment of narrative ability in English accurately identifies language impairment in English language learners. *Journal of Speech, Language, and Hearing Research* 57 (6), 2208–2220.

Pratt-Johnson, Y. (2006) Communicating cross-culturally: What teachers should know. *Internet TESL Journal for Teachers of English as a Second Language*, 12 (2). Retrieved from http://iteslj.org/Articles/Pratt-Johnson-CrossCultural.html.

Robertson, P.M, McFarland, L.A., Sciuchetti, M.B. and García, S.B. (2017) Connecting the dots: An exploration of how pre-service special education teachers make sense of disability and diversity. *Teaching and Teacher Education* 65 (1), 34–47.

Samovar, L.A. and Porter, R.E. (1995) *Communication between Cultures* (2nd edn). Belmont, CA: Wadsworth.

Scanlan, M.K. and López, F.A. (2015) *Leadership for Culturally and Linguistically Responsive Schools*. New York, NY: Routledge.

Seppanen, P., Schaeffer, R. and Julian, N.R. (1995) *Matching State Goals to a Model of Outcomes and Indicators for Age 3* (Technical Report 13). Minneapolis, MN: University of Minnesota, National Center on Educational Outcomes.

Shapiro, E.S. (2014) Tiered instruction and intervention in a response to-intervention-model. RTI Action Network. New York, NY: National Center for Learning Disabilities. Retrieved from http://www.rtinetwork.org/essential/tieredinstruction/tiered-instruction-and-intervention-rti-model.

Short, D. (2000) *The ESL Standards: Bridging the Academic Gap for English Language Learners*. Washington, DC: Center for Applied Linguistics. Retrieved from https://www.ericdigests.org/2001-3/esl.htm.

Short, D. (2002) Language learning in sheltered social studies classrooms. *TESOL Journal* 11 (1), 18–24.

Skiba, R.J., Artiles, A.J., Kozleski, E.B., Losen, D.J. and Harry, E.G. (2015) Risks and consequences of oversimplifying educational inequities: A response to Morgan *et al*. *Educational Researcher* 45 (3), 221–225.

Snow, C.E., Burns, M.S. and Griffin, P. (1998) *Preventing Reading Difficulties in Young Children*. Washington, DC: National Academy Press.

Thomas, W. and Collier, V. (2002) *A National Study of School Effectiveness for Language Minority Students' Long-term Academic Achievement*. Santa Cruz, CA: Center for Research on Education, Diversity & Excellence.

US Census Bureau (2015) Census Bureau reports at least 350 languages spoken in US homes: Most comprehensive language data ever released from the Census Bureau. Retrieved from https://census.gov/newsroom/press-releases/2015/cb15-185.html.

US Department of Education, Office of English Language Acquisition (2017) *Fast Facts: Profiles of English Learners (ELs)*. Retrieved from https://ncela.ed.gov/files/fast_facts/OELAFastFactsProfilesOfELs.pdf.

US Department of Education, Office of English Language Acquisition (2018) *Fast Facts: English Learner (EL) Trends from the Nation's Report Card*. Washington, DC: OELA. Retrieved from https://ncela.ed.gov/files/fast_facts/ELs-NAEP_Card.pdf.

US Department of Education, Office of English Language Acquisition (2020) *English Learners: Demographic Trends*. Washington, DC: OELA. Retrieved from https://ncela.ed.gov/files/fast_facts/19-0193_Del4.4_ELDemographicTrends_021220_508.pdf.

US Department of Education, Office of Planning Evaluation and Policy Development (2012) *Language Instruction Educational Programs (LIEPs): A Review of the Foundational Literature*. Washington, DC: Office of Planning Evaluation and Policy Development, Policy and Program Studies Service.

US Department of Health and Human Services (2019) *Poverty Guidelines and Determining Eligibility for Participation in Head Start Programs*. Washington, DC: Office of Head Start. Retrieved from https://eclkc.ohs.acf.hhs.gov/eligibility-ersea/article/poverty-guidelines-determining-eligibility-participation-head-start.

US Department of Health & Human Services and Administration for Children & Families (2019) *Poverty Guidelines and Determining Eligibility for Participation in Head Start Programs*. Washington, DC: Office of Head Start. Retrieved from https://eclkc.ohs.acf.hhs.gov/eligibility-ersea/article/poverty-guidelines-determining-eligibility-participation-head-start.

US Department of Health & Human Services and US Department of Education (2016) *Policy Statement on Supporting the Development of Children Who Are Dual Language Learners in Early Childhood Programs*. Washington, DC. Retrieved from: https://eclkc.ohs.acf.hhs.gov/sites/default/files/pdf/dll-policy-statement-final.pdf.

Vygotsky, L.S. (1978) *Mind in Society: The Development of Higher Psychological Processes*. Cambridge, MA: Harvard University Press.

Wagner, R.K., Francis, D.J. and Morris, R.D. (2005) Identifying English learners with learning disabilities. Key challenges and possible approaches. *Learning Disabilities Research and Practice* 20 (1), 6–15.

Wilkinson, C.Y., Ortiz, A.A., Robertson, P. and Kushner, M.I. (2006) English language learners with reading-related LD: Linking data from multiple sources to make eligibility determinations. *Journal of Learning Disabilities* 39 (2), 129–141.

Index

Page numbers in **bold** refer to information in figures or tables.

ABCs of Cultural Understanding and Communication Model 141
academic skills 103, 185
    assessment 98
    language 186, 194
    performance 137–8
access 13
    to bilingual education 15
    to special education services 53
accountability 21, 163–6, 174, 206
accreditation 139, 149, 154
acculturation 56, 69, 188
adult ESL classes 56
African Americans, gestures 113–14
Alberta Language and Development Questionnaire (ALDeQ) 104
Alliance for a Better Community 49
Arizona 71
Asian families 7, 53, 185
assessments 58, **82–3**, **166**, 176, 189
    Bilingual English Spanish Assessment (BESA) 102–3
    Clinical Evaluation of Language Fundamentals (CELF) 92, 96–8, 103
    dynamic assessments 148
    formative assessments 140, 145–8, 156
    language 9, 93, 99–100, 102–3, **105**, 175
    large scale 72
    norming 28–9, 172
    parental involvement 104, 196–7
    process 50, 80, 192–3, 196–7
    Response to Intervention (RTI) 170
    tools 174, 193, 205–6
asset-based perspective 10, 65–6, 69, 132, 142
at-risk students 49, 101–2, 163, 170, 176
autism spectrum disorders (ASD) 9, 118, 119
    bilingual children 35–6
    sociocultural contexts 12, 14

behavior 120, 131
benchmarks 80, 167, 188, 192
bias 124–5
BID (briefing, interaction and debriefing) process 105–6
bilingual education 19, 66–7, 184, 193, 201
    and disabled children 15, 21, 69, 118
    eligibility 192, 199
    federal legislation 27–8
    focus on acquisition of English 13, 20, 201–2
    teacher preparation 138
    see also inclusion
Bilingual Education Act (Title VII) (1968) 27–8
Bilingual English Spanish Assessment (BESA) 102–3
bilingual population 6–7, 27, 46, 137–8, 183, 184
bilingual speech-language pathologists 98–9, 100, 118, 196
bilingualism, benefits of 10, 59, 101, 185
Bronfenbrenner's ecological system model 113
BUILD organization 173

CAEP (Council of the Accreditation of Educator Preparation) (formerly NCATE) 139, 150
child development 174
    conceptual framework 10–12
    developmental competencies 16–18
    growth trajectories 58–9
    sociocultural context 10–11, 12–13
Child Find program 54, 168–9
child rearing practices 116, 119–20
Chinese families 7, 118

Chinese languages 34, 94, 130
   bilingual speech-language pathologists 118
classroom practice 71, 129–32, 144, 174, 194
Clinical Evaluation of Language Fundamentals (CELF) 96–8
   CELF-4 92, 97, 103
code switching 33, 67, 92, 186
cognitive disabilities 165
cognitive skills 29, 34, 93
collaboration **83**
   with families 68–70, **84**, 127, 140, 142, 147, 150
   between professionals 68, 170, 197–8, 201, 206
collectivism 77
Common Core State Standards (CCSSI) 164, 166–7
communication skills 67, 71
communication with parents 67, 69–70, 127–8, 168
communities **19**
   cultural practices 112–13, 130–1, 187
   funds of knowledge 141–2, 204
   working with 54, 56, 202
   see also sociocultural contexts
comprehensible input 78–9
conceptual vocabulary 30, 33
constructivism 145
continuity 130
converging evidence 58, 103, 104, 107, 193, 197
core instruction 191, 192, 193–5
Council for Exceptional Children (CEC) 139, 140
Council of the Accreditation of Educator Preparation (CAEP) (formerly NCATE) 139, 150
critical praxis 68, 72, 77, 81, 142
cross-cultural competence 188
cross-linguistic effects 33–4, 204
cultural awareness 28, **82**, 143, 200
cultural capital 188, 201, 205
cultural context 9, 122, 186–8
   beliefs about special needs 119–20
   child development 10–11
   cultural diversity 8, **82**
cultural hybridity 123
cultural reference 187
culturally and linguistically responsive teaching 187, 200, 205
   approaches 72–3
   literacy 73–4
   peer-assisted learning 76–7
   reading comprehension 75–6
   responsive tiered interventions **84**
   scaffolding 77–9
   strategies 56–7, 66, 194
   teacher training 142–5, 150, 152–3, 155–6
   vocabulary 74–5
culturally sustaining pedagogy (CSP) 72, 114–15, 127–32
Cummins' empowerment framework 189, 190

daily communication journals 69–70
deficit perspective 8–9, 15, 113, 121, 142, 205
developmental competencies 16–18
developmental delays 49–50
developmental disorders 18, 35–6
diagnosis *see* identification
dialect 71
differentiation 73, 194
disabilities 8–9, **19**, 66
   conceptualization 120
   models of 190
   over-identification 99–100, 101, 170, 175, 182, 185, 190, 197
   under-identification 53, 101
discrepancy model 169–70
discrimination 20, 115, 120
diversity 8
   cultural and linguistic (CLD) 182, 203
   of early childcare personnel 48, 53
   linguistic diversity 71, 121, 142, 189, 193, 207
dominant language 29, 33
Dominican families, gestures 113–14
Down syndrome (DS) 35–6, 118
dual language learners (DLL) *see* young bilingual children
dual language programs 59, 70–1
dynamic assessments 148

Early Childhood Longitudinal Study 17, 53
Early Head Start 49, 51–2, 183, 190–1
   Early Head Start and Child Experiences Study (Baby FACES) 52
early identification 57, 58, 166, 169
early intervention professionals 48–9, 50
   multicultural workforce 53
   professional development 48, 54, 56, 57, 58

early intervention programs 3, 48, 49, **84**
    benefits of 166
    and federal law 49–52, 99–100
    improvement of 52–9
    settings 130
    see also Early Head Start; Individuals with Disabilities Education Act (IDEA) (2004); interventions
early learning 14–15, 19, 47
    see also preschool children
Early Learning and Development Standards 13
ecological system model 113
Education Commission of States 149
Education for All Handicapped Children Act (1975) 167
    see also Individuals with Disabilities Education Act (IDEA) (2004)
educator preparation *see* preservice teacher training
Elementary and Secondary Education Act (ESEA) (1965) 163, 164
eligibility
    assessments 192–3
    Individuals with Disabilities Education Act (IDEA) (2004) 49–50, 168, 169
    special education 197–8
emergent bilinguals *see* young bilingual children
emotional bonds 128, 129
English as a second language (ESL) 56, 191, 193, 201, 203, 205
English language 34
    English-only schools 13, 28, 91–2, 95, 97, 100, 128
    focus on acquisition of 8, 13, 20, 66, 165
    language development standards 165
    see also L2 acquisition
English language learners *see* young bilingual children
errors 31–2, 35
ethnicity 8, 121, 168
European Union 102
evaluation *see* assessments
Every Student Succeeds Act (ESSA) (2015) 163–4, 165–6, 167, 169, 176, 190
exposure to language
    age of 27, 94, 95
    effect on skill development 32, 91, 185–6
    in the family 36–8, 46
expressive language skills 30, 34–5, 90, 113–14, 193

families **19**, 21
    emotional bonds 128, 129
    environment 14, 17–18, 38–9, 40–1, 112–13, 206–7
    family-centered approach 56, 132, 142, 150, 152, 156, 187–8, 189
    funds of knowledge 204
    involvement in assessment process 142, 196
    language use 18, 36–8, 40–1, 46, 94–5, 117
    learning from 120–2, 125–7
    and preservice teachers 140–2
    relationship building 41, 121–9, 202
    working with 48, 51–2, 54, 68–70, **84**, 115, 147, 202, 205
    see also home language; parents; sociocultural contexts
family story projects 131–2, 140–1
fathers, language choice 37, 38, 94
federal programs 71, **82**, 101, 149, 174–7, 190–1
    Common Core State Standards (CCSSI) 164, 166–7
    early intervention 49–52, 99–100
    No Child Left Behind 163–6
    overreach of 166–7
    Quality Rating Improvement System (QRIS) 163, 164, 173–4
    see also Individuals with Disabilities Education Act (IDEA) (2004); Response to Intervention (RTI); state regulations
flexible grouping 77
fluency 74, 76, 186
formative assessments 140, 145–8, 156
Full and Individual Evaluation (FIE) 196–7, 198
funding 54, 172
    Every Student Succeeds Act (ESSA) (2015) 165–6
    teacher training 149, 154–5
funds of knowledge 130, 141, 187–8, 194, 204

gestures 32, 113–14
grammar
    assessment 97, 102
    development of 29, 31–2, 33, 34, 93–4
group learning 74, 76–7, 79–80
growth measures 165
growth trajectories 58–9

Harry, Beth 122–3
Hawaii 169

Head Start 30–1, 53, 55, 57, 91, 190–1
heritage language *see* home language
Hispanic communities *see* Spanish speakers
home language
    assessment 201
    communication with parents 168
    foundation for L2 18, 65–7, **82**, 186, 191
    loss of 13, 18, 40, 57, 92, 95, 100
    parental support 69, 94, 116–17, 125, 128–9
    use in the classroom 37–8, 70–1, 191, 194, 199, 201
    see also families
home visits 51–2, 124, 126, 142

identification 169, 174, 184
    early identification 57, 58, 166
    effect of anti-immigrant policies 12
    English language learners 195–9
    Response to Intervention (RTI) 169–70
identity 91–3, 206
immigrants 6, 183
    anti-immigrant policies 12
    compromised status 54, 56
    generational status 38–9, 46, 47–8, 53, 101, 116–17, 188
    host communities 14, 114
    immigration history 141
    refugees 106–7
    stereotypes 124–5
inclusion
    inclusive practice 21, 148–9, 173
    practicum settings 153–4, 155
    programs 15–16, 67–8, 79
    see also bilingual education
individual characteristics 16, **19**, 205
Individualized Education Programs (IEP) 67, 72, 140, 142, 165, 169, 198–9
Individuals with Disabilities Education Act (IDEA) (2004) 127, 164, 167–9
    exclusionary clause 197
    family-centered approach 115
    implementation of 53–4
    Part B 168
    Part C 49–51, 55–6, 57, 168, 191
    reporting requirements 168, 169
    see also Individualized Education Programs (IEP); Response to Intervention (RTI)
integrative framework 2, 11–12, 19–20
international comparisons 15–16
interpreters, use of 58, 105–7, 127, 198

interventions 28, 52–4
    design of 15, **84**, 188–9, 190
    inclusive classrooms 66, 79–80
    lack of research 206
    supplemental 94, 192, 195, 197
    see also early intervention programs; Federal programs

kindergarten 91, 163
    entry assessments (KEAs) 8, 164, 172–3
    kindergarten readiness 17, 47
    Part C programs 51

L1 *see* home language
L2 acquisition 16, 78, 128
    building on L1 18, 40, 65–7, 67–8, 191, 200
    exposure 94, 95
    and learning disorders 80, 107
    progress monitoring 165–6
    teacher core competencies **82**, 144–5, 203
    see also English language; language acquisition
labelling objects 96
language acquisition **82**, 117
    bilingual children 173, 175, 177, 186
    language experiences 36–8, 40–1, 103
    see also L2 acquisition
language assessments 9, 93, 99–100, 102–3, 175
language characteristics 99, 200
language development 93, 144–5
    bilingual children 28–34, 40–1, 66, 204
    grammar 31–2
    identification of delays 8–9
    phonology 29
    pragmatic development 32–3
    vocabulary 29–31
language differences 91, 93, 98, 107–8, 171, 193
language disorders 171
    assessment 99, 102–3, **105**
    in bilingual children 31–2, 35, 95, 97, 103
    with developmental disorders 35–6
    English language model of 97–8
    and language differences 91, 93, 98, 107–8, 171, 193
    language learning disabilities 90–3
    specific language impairment 34–5, 118

Language Instruction Educational
    Programs (LIEPs) 183–4, 191, 202
Language Interdependence theory 33–4
language processing 34–5, 103
language proficiency **105**, 165, 176, 185,
    193, 198
language status 190
language use 6–7, 14, 46–7, 184
language variation 93–5
large scale assessment 72
Latino community 54–5, 98, 184, 185
    autism spectrum disorder (ASD) 9,
        119–20
    language use 7, 96, 117
learning disabilities 189
    diagnosis 47
    and English proficiency 9
learning stories 147
learning styles 143–4
least-to-most strategy 148
limited English proficient *see* young
    bilingual children
linguistic diversity 71, 121, 142, 189, 193, 207
literacy
    assessment 201
    community practices 39, 130–1, 205
    instruction 73–9, 194, 200
    multiple literacies 73
local variations 99–100

Making Action Plans (MAPs) 147
Mandarin *see* Chinese languages
marginalization 20, 115, 123, 188
Massachusetts 71
Maternal, Infant and Early Childhood
    Home Visiting Initiative (MIECHV)
    176
mathematics instruction 74, 79
Mexican families 7, 113–14, 119
migrants *see* immigrants
minoritized groups 8, 9, 15, 20
minority languages 91, 94
missed identity 91
mistaken identity 91, 92–3
Monarch Center 149–52, 156
monolingual children 3, 8, 27–8
    comparison with bilingual children
        17, 28–9, 30–1, 40, 90
    specific language impairment 35
morphology 31, 35, 94
mothers
    background 17, 38–9
    gestures 113–14
    language choice 36–7, 38, 39, 93–4,
        94–5

motivation 16, **19**
multi-layered analysis 189
multi-sensory activities 74
multi-tiered support systems 79–81, **84**,
    170, 191–2, 205, 206
    see also Response to Intervention (RTI)

National Council of La Raza 49
National Early Intervention Longitudinal
    Study (NEILS) 50–1
National Institute of Health 102
Native Americans 7, 53, 95–6, 97, 116
native language *see* home language
Navajo 95–6, 97
NCATE 150
    see also Council of the Accreditation
        of Educator Preparation
        (CAEP) (formerly NCATE)
No Child Left Behind Act (NCLB) (2002)
    163–6, 190
    see also Every Student Succeeds Act
        (ESSA) (2015)
non-verbal cues 32–3
normed assessments 96–8, 102–3, 172

Obama, Barack 163, 173
Office of Special Education Programs
    (OSEP) 50
one-parent-one-language approach 94
ongoing assessments *see* formative
    assessments
oral language skills 16, 90, 91, 193, 201,
    205, 206

parents 116–17, 205
    beliefs 113, 117–20, 169
    communication with 67, 69–70,
        127–8, 168
    education 93, 184
    input from 104, 106
    parenting practices 14, 56–7
    role in education 68, 100, 128–9
    see also families; sociocultural
        contexts
Part C programs *see* Individuals with
    Disabilities Education Act (IDEA)
    (2004)
peer-assisted learning 74, 76–7, 194
personality 16, **19**
Person-centered planning 147
phonology 29, 33, 34
physical disabilities 126
poverty 47, 56
    association with bilingualism 36,
        100–1, 188

deficit perspective 121, 123
federal programs 51
Native Americans 116
see also socioeconomic status
pragmatic development 32–3, 40
preschool children 13, 58
    Quality Rating Improvement System (QRIS) 174
    Recognition & Response (R&R) 170–1
    see also early childhood care
Preschool Development Grant program 166
Preschool Language Scale 3 98
preservice teacher training
    blended programs 148–56
    candidate assessment 150
    cultural awareness 28
    culturally and linguistically responsive learning (CRL) 142–5, 155–6, 199–202, 207
    dual certification 151
    family focus 131–2, 140–2
    field experience 139, 144, 148–9, 150, 152–3, 154, 155
    formative assessments 145–8
    program reform 148–56
    state regulations 177
    syllabus improvement 152–4
    see also teacher training
production errors 31–2, 35
proficiency measures 165, 176, 185, 193, 198
progress monitoring 80, 90, 171, 176, 192–3, 195
psychometric tests 172
Puerto Rican families 7, 119, 122
Pyramid model 170

Quality Rating Improvement System (QRIS) 163, 164, 173–4
questionnaires 104, 142

Race-to-the-Top Early Learning Challenge (RTT-ELC) 163, 172–3
reading comprehension 75–6, 166, 185
reading disabilities 185
receptive language skills 34–5, 90–1, 113, 193
reciprocity 122–3, 126, 127, 132
    educator-family relationship 121
    reciprocal teaching 75
Recognition & Response (R&R) 170–1, 176, 189, 191–2, 204, 205
referral 169, 195–6

reflection *see* critical praxis
refugees 106–7
religious perspective 119
research based practice 70
    English language learners 189–95
    multi-tiered support systems 191–2
    program development 190–1
resilience 10, 21, 129
Response to Intervention (RTI) 79, 169–72, 193
    and Individuals with Disabilities Education Act (IDEA) (2004) 164, 167
    and young bilingual children 175, 176–7, 191, 192, 204, 205
    see also multi-tiered support systems; Recognition & Response (R&R)
responsive teaching *see* culturally and linguistically responsive teaching
rewards, community achievement 77
Rogoff, B. 10, 17, 112–13, 114

scaffolding 147–8
    culturally and linguistically responsive learning (CRL) 74, 77–9, 191, 194
    and formative assessment 146, 193
    for preservice teachers 145
school readiness 8, 172–3, 188
schools
    classroom environment 71, 144, 194
    classroom quality measures 174
    language assessment policies 99–100
    teacher's language choice 37–8
semantic representations 30, 33, 35
sentence repetition 103
sequential language learners 27, 35, 36, 47, 67, 186, 204
siblings, language choice 37, 94
simultaneous language learners 27, 35, 47, 185, 204
situated nature of learning 65, 81
skilled dialogue framework 123
social capital 188, 201, 205
social emotional competencies 17
social organization of learning 65, 81
socialization 95–6, 99
sociocultural contexts 140, 169, 186–8
    and child development 10–11, 12–13, 17, 112–15, 204–5
    dual language programs 70–1
    gestures 113–14
    integrative approach 2, 12, **19**, 175, 189
    responsiveness to 80, 121, 126, 144

working with families 65–6, 122–9
   see also communities; families; parents
socioeconomic status
   child development 47, 100–2, 188–9, 197
   language assessment 93, 97, 103, 184
   and language development 30–1
   see also poverty
Spanish language 34, 35, 102
Spanish speakers 7, 101, 188
   assessment tools 28, 92, 97–8, 103
   home language 31, 37, 51–2, 53, 94–5, 117, 125
   in special education programs 91
special education 19, 20, 127
   and Individuals with Disabilities Education Act (IDEA) (2004) 168
   programs 13, 91, 139
   referral 15, 101, 195–6
   teachers 138
   see also disabilities
Special Education Early Childhood Speciality Sets 139
special needs, beliefs about 118–20
specific language impairment 34–5, 118
standardized tests 99–100
   validity 105, 107–8
state data collection 50–1
state regulations 99–100, 149, 156, 164, 173, 176–7, 192
   Individuals with Disabilities Education Act (IDEA) (2004) 167, 168
   teacher training approval 154–6
   see also federal programs
stereotypes 124–5, 126, 142, 185, 202
story structures 95–6
strength-based approach *see* asset-based perspective
summative assessments 145–6

Tagalog 7
teacher training 4–5, 21, 205
   cultural awareness 28, 139–40
   professional development 54, 56–7, 58, 79, **83**, 114–15, 150–1, 177, 201, 202–3
   see also preservice teacher training

teachers
   bilingual 184, 196
   capacity 71, 98–9
   competencies 48–9, 53, 71, **82–3**, 138–40
   diversity of 138
   language choice 37–8, 93–4
   relationship with students 144
   sociocultural awareness 187
teaching practices **83**
   culturally sustaining 124–31
   dual language 49
   literacy **82**
   responsive 115, 138
   see also culturally and linguistically responsive teaching
Teaching Pyramid 170
third space 123, 145
tiered support systems *see* multi-tiered support systems
translanguaging 186, 196, 204
two-way immersion 70–1

universal design for learning (UDL) 72–3
universal screening 170, 192, 194
US Department of Education 102, 172

Vietnamese speakers 7
vocabulary
   across two languages 17, 29–31, 33, 36–7, 93–4, 175
   culturally and linguistically responsive learning (CRL) 74–5
   development of 35, 96, 103, 186, 188, 195
   gestures 113–14

written language skills 16, 90, 91

young bilingual children 2–3, 46, 59, 167
   with disabilities (DLLsWD) 3–4, 18, 64–5, 69–70, 164–6, 168, 175, 182, 184–5, 190
   emergent bilinguals 59
   English language learners 183–4

For Product Safety Concerns and Information please contact our EU Authorised Representative:

Easy Access System Europe

Mustamäe tee 50

10621 Tallinn

Estonia

gpsr.requests@easproject.com

www.ingramcontent.com/pod-product-compliance
Ingram Content Group UK Ltd.
Pitfield, Milton Keynes, MK11 3LW, UK
UKHW021913200326